CANADA, A
WORKING
HISTORY

CANADA, A
WORKING
HISTORY

JASON RUSSELL

DUNDURN
TORONTO

Publisher and acquiring editor: Scott Fraser | Editor: Michael Carroll
Cover designer: Laura Boyle
Cover image: Punch clock: shutterstock.com/Somphop Krittayaworagul | timecard: shutterstock.com/Martin Janecek
Printer: Marquis Book Printing Inc.

Library and Archives Canada Cataloguing in Publication

Title: Canada, a working history / Jason Russell.
Names: Russell, Jason, 1968- author.
Description: Includes bibliographical references and index.
Identifiers: Canadiana (print) 20200391534 | Canadiana (ebook) 20200391631 | ISBN
  9781459746022 (softcover) | ISBN 9781459746039 (PDF) | ISBN 9781459746046 (EPUB)
Subjects: LCSH: Work—Social aspects—Canada—History. | LCSH: Labor—Canada—History.
Classification: LCC HD6957.C3 R87 2021 | DDC 306.3/60971—dc23

We acknowledge the support of the Canada Council for the Arts and the Ontario Arts Council for our publishing program. We also acknowledge the financial support of the Government of Ontario, through the Ontario Book Publishing Tax Credit and Ontario Creates, and the Government of Canada.

VISIT US AT

 dundurn.com | @dundurnpress | 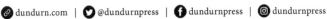 dundurnpress | dundurnpress

Dundurn Press
1382 Queen Street East
Toronto, Ontario, Canada
M4L 1C9

For my son, Thomas Liepins Russell

CONTENTS

INTRODUCTION

This book is about how work in Canada changed from the period of European colonization to 2020. It is intended to provide a broad overview of major developments and trends in Canada and show how work was shaped by wider influences in Canadian society. Work is a central human activity that has innate value whether or not it involves receiving compensation. The historical development of work in Canada parallels the nation's progress. Workers in their many times, places, and occupations made Canada, and their work is ongoing.

The narrative is divided into six parts, which cover time periods of varying scope. Part I describes European colonization to the years before Confederation in 1867. Canada was initially a collection of disparate colonies and long-established Indigenous nations that was formed into a country, with the different political actors involved showing varied levels of enthusiasm for the new nation. Canada's ties with Britain remained strong during the long period from colonization to Confederation, and the nation was gradually formed within the context of an occasionally fraught relationship with the United States.

Part II details a shorter period from Confederation to the 1930s. Canada experienced profound change between 1867 and 1939. Canadian workers most importantly left their civilian jobs in droves in 1914 to enlist in the army to fight in Europe. Many of them did not return to resume their civilian lives. Canadians built a railway from coast to coast, welcomed scores of immigrants, built new cities and factories, and experienced industrialization. They also formed workers' organizations, created new business structures, and combined themselves into professions.

Part III covers the critical period from 1945 to 1969. Canada was much different at the end of the Second World War than when the conflict started. The Great Depression drove unemployment to record heights in the 1930s, and the war eliminated it in short order. Canada became a major contributor to the war effort. Women streamed into industrial jobs in large numbers for the first time. Unions were inspired by the struggles waged by their American comrades, and they gained the right to engage in legal collective bargaining.

The 1950s and 1960s were prosperous decades for many but not all Canadians. Wages often met or exceeded the cost of living. Working-class people were able to own their homes rather than rent. A vibrant consumer culture shaped people's identities and also furnished a wide array of new goods and services. This was part of the era of the Cold War ideological struggle, and work and employment were touched by it. Women demanded social change in the 1960s, and the structure of families was transformed. Important social programs were introduced that immeasurably improved the lives of working people.

Part IV examines work in Canada in the 1970s and 1980s. The 1970s were a sort of socio-economic interregnum between the 1960s and 1980s, but they still brought substantial change to work and labour. Women became an ever-larger percentage of unionized workers, especially in the public sector. A crucial legislative change in the late 1960s gave federal public sector workers the right to formally unionize and engage in collective bargaining, and that right spread across the provinces, as well.

The 1970s were an important economic turning point for workers of all types. Wage increases gradually stopped providing expanded standards of living. The postwar baby-boom generation graduated from high school and post-secondary education and entered the paid workforce. Media culture continued to include representations of working life.

Part V encompasses the 1990s and 2000s. The pace of change in working life markedly accelerated during those decades. There were major labour struggles, and governments made deliberate policy decisions that did things like deregulate areas of the economy that harmed workers. Canada experienced early globalization, and its economy became even more oriented toward services and away from manufacturing. The Cold War ended during this period, but its demise did not bring significant benefits to working Canadians.

Part VI discusses the period from the turn of the millennium to 2020 and beyond. Canadians approached the end of the 20th century with mixed feelings of anticipation and trepidation. The new century brought enormous opportunity for workers who were well educated and possessed marketable skills but also came with uncertainty and upheaval for other workers. It almost came to seem as if Canada were going back to the pre–Second World War period, with the growing prevalence of non-standard work arrangements.

Work continued to bifurcate along gender, racial, and ethnic lines into the new century. Women did not earn as much as men for doing equal work, and immigrants and people of colour were often relegated to low-wage jobs. Technology permeated virtually every workplace, but it was used for control and surveillance as much as to enhance profitability.

The history of work in Canada has often been tumultuous, sometimes violent, and shaped by technological change. It has shaped society while being reciprocally moulded by it. Work in Canada altered over time and space. It is the product of many different influences, including race, gender, class, ethnicity, and place and is fundamentally about the individual and collective experiences of people who toil at paid and unpaid tasks. As we will see, work in Canada has ultimately never been dull.

NAME	PART I European Arrival to Confederation	
DAY	TIME IN	TIME OUT
1	7 48	16 17
2	7 45	16 15
	7 42	

1 BEFORE AND AFTER EUROPEAN COLONIZATION

The history of work in Canada begins with the land. North America, which also includes the United States of America and Mexico, began to be created 175 million years ago when the supercontinent Pangaea was gradually broken into new continents. Containing widely varying topography, North America possessed a range of climates, from tropical temperatures in the far south to sub-zero cold and ice in the distant north. Three oceans — Atlantic, Pacific, and Arctic — surrounded North America along with the Caribbean Sea. These were names that did not exist prior to the arrival of European settlers, and the many Indigenous Peoples and communities who lived in what would become Canada — a word derived from the Haudenosaunee word for *village* — thought of the land in terms far different from those who came from the other side of the Atlantic. Indigenous Peoples lived on the land and considered themselves part of it. For many Europeans, land was something to be transformed and put to use.

The early impact of geography, the arrival of Indigenous Peoples, and the eventual appearance and proliferation of European colonists in North America were part of a long stretch of years leading toward Canada's ultimate independence from Britain. What happened in the 16th century when Europeans arrived in what would become Canada may seem remote and inconsequential compared to what would happen in more recent decades, but crucial patterns of working and living were established in pre-Confederation Canada that would endure and shape the country and its workers far into the 20th century. The pre-Confederation period involved colonization, the introduction of European work methods and property ownership, slavery and indentured servitude, a system of law that favoured employers over workers, and the grievous death and displacement of Indigenous Peoples for whom the European idea of work was entirely unknown.

There was a long-standing consensus among historians, anthropologists, archaeologists, and other academics that deemed that North, Central, and South America were first populated by people from Asia who made their way across an ice bridge spanning what became known as the Bering Strait. That view is now being contested, since Indigenous Peoples may have come from different places at different times, but it is clear they were living in North America 20,000 years ago. Some Indigenous groups were more technologically advanced than others, with several like the Maya and Aztecs leaving wondrous cities erected in jungles and clear evidence of sophisticated if somewhat violent societies.

The Indigenous Peoples of Mexico, Central America, and South America left more clues about how they lived than their counterparts farther north. There is often a public assumption that Indigenous Peoples everywhere leave oral records of their history if they did not have technology to hand down written accounts. The way Indigenous Peoples lived in what is now Canada is revealed through archaeology, what was observed about them when Europeans came across the ocean, and the traditions they have preserved. Their lives are often misrepresented in contemporary portrayals and descriptions of them. There is considerable variation in the estimates of how many people lived in the Americas prior to European contact, with the numbers ranging from 8 to 112 million. They were not always nomadic, as often portrayed in media, with many living in established communities and engaged in agriculture.

There is peril in generalizing what it meant to be Indigenous in pre-colonial North America. There were clear social hierarchies in some Indigenous nations such as those on the coast of what is now British Columbia. The leadership of some nations was chosen by women rather than men. Indeed, hundreds of languages were spoken across North and South America before European arrival. The land and interaction with it was key to their survival. Nations living on the plains were dependent on the buffalo for food, shelter, and clothing. In comparison, nations in coastal areas, like the Mi'kmaq, were closely tied to fishing. Indigenous Peoples engaged in trade, and some used basic forms of currency such as beads, but the idea of accumulating surplus wealth through exploiting labour was not part of daily life.

The nations that lived across North America did share some cultural similarities with Europeans. They lived in a world shaped by their own ideas of spirituality and the afterlife, but their gods were linked to nature. Europeans had also once been organized on tribal lines, although their nation-states were forms of large groups with competing interests. Indigenous nations did not use religion as a lever to compel people to work, while the Christian deity was routinely employed by wealthy property owners and aristocrats to rain down fire and brimstone on the workers of Europe. People worked during the pre-colonial period, but it was the work of everyday life: hunting, fishing, making clothes, farming, building as part of a community. That all changed when Europeans began arriving.

The first Europeans to come to North America were Vikings who, while hardy seafarers and fierce warriors, were not capable of bringing immigrants across the Atlantic in large numbers and changing the continent. Archaeological evidence shows that a Viking settlement existed at L'Anse aux Meadows in northern Newfoundland in the late 10th century, with the likely purpose of obtaining timber. Vikings had a history of engaging in commercial trade and knew about making a profit. The Newfoundland settlement founded by Leif Erikson did not endure, but settlements in Greenland lasted for several hundred years. Vikings, or Norsemen, also kept a record of their travels through their sagas, so they left an account of the Vinland settlement that could be substantiated through archaeology. They did not fundamentally alter Newfoundland or any other areas of the continent, but their successors had a profound and lasting influence.

European colonization that began in the 15th century is undergoing new and necessary reconsideration in the 21st century. The reasons people braved the long and uncertain crossing across the Atlantic were often not well conveyed in older histories of colonization. Wealth and political influence were the principal motivations behind colonization. The United Kingdom had yet to be formed in the 15th century, and Spain was the pre-eminent European power at that time, followed by France. Europeans had long traded with Asia and Africa, and the routes to those regions — both water and land — were long and easily disrupted. Countries understandably wanted a shorter route to Asia. The first forays across the Atlantic from Western Europe were led by people interested in trade and accumulating wealth, and they were not always inspired by anything more noble. The "discovery" of the New World is popularly associated with the voyage of Christopher Columbus, an Italian explorer financed by the monarchs of Castile and Aragon. In 1492, he landed on an island the Indigenous Lucayan people called Guanahani and Columbus renamed San Salvador (part of the Bahamian archipelago). Thus began a process of Europeans — French, Spanish, English, Portuguese, and Dutch — steadily crossing the Atlantic to exploit the physical resources of North, South, and Central America and the people living there. Indeed, the term *Americas* was derived from the Latin base of the name Amerigo Vespucci, another Italian explorer, who sailed for Spain and Portugal and proved that the coasts of the newly found lands across the ocean were not part of Asia.

Colonization patterns were not uniform across the Americas. The first Europeans to head to the East Coast of Canada came to fish on the Grand Banks, then returned home with the holds of their ships full of salted cod. Interaction with Indigenous Peoples happened to the extent required to finish fishing and sail home. The land that became occupied by Canada and the United States was not known in the 15th and 16th centuries to hold vast deposits of gold and silver, but both metals were found in abundance in Mexico and in territories farther south. Indeed, it was so ubiquitous that the Aztecs quickly realized that the Spanish coveted gold more than anything else and consequently gave them a quantity of it with the understanding they would get back on their ships and leave.

The land that became Canada and the United States was still a veritable treasure trove of other natural resources such as fish, timber, furs, and herbs. Most people living in Europe in the 15th and 16th centuries were poor, cold, and hungry for the entirety of their lives, which helps explain the interest England, Spain, France, and Portugal had in fishing in waters off North America's Atlantic coast.

Europeans might have been hungry in those centuries and routinely ravaged by diseases such as bubonic plague, but they did not smoke. That situation changed when they observed Indigenous nations harvesting and smoking tobacco, a plant that holds sacred properties for many Indigenous Peoples, including the Huron. It is one of four sacred herbs, along with sweetgrass, cedar, and sage.

Recognizing the role that tobacco played in the lives of Indigenous people, Europeans quickly noted that the plant held great commercial potential, and it became a crop to be grown and exported back across the ocean. The recreational use of tobacco quickly became common in Europe. The process of bringing plants and animals back and forth across the Atlantic was not confined to tobacco. The tomato, which is usually associated with Italian and other Mediterranean cuisines, came from Peru. Coffee was first grown in Ethiopia and was deliberately introduced to Central and South America for commercial reasons. Tea was grown in China but became a staple of the British colonial diet and would eventually play a key role in starting the American Revolution.

Indigenous communities responded in varying ways to European arrival. The Aztecs fought the Spanish and were defeated despite their superior numbers. The Beothuk in Newfoundland avoided English settlers and fought them when the two groups came into contact. Most Indigenous people found Europeans to be entirely alien both in appearance and in social and cultural practices. Indigenous societies were numerous and vibrant prior to the end of the 15th century, but they were not prepared for the influx of disease the Europeans brought with them. Europeans were so frequently exposed to perils such as smallpox, influenza, measles, and tuberculosis that, while many still died from exposure, they had at least some immunity against such diseases. Indigenous people had no defences and up to 90 percent of them died as a result of exposure to foreign illnesses.

The death of so many Indigenous people across the Americas due to European contact, whether through disease or warfare, made the colonization process different from what occurred in other parts of the world. Later, Europeans colonized most of Africa, while Britain made India into a colony, but the populations of Africa and the Indian subcontinent were not wiped out as a result of that. North America was virtually emptied of the people who had been living there for millennia before European arrival, which meant that resistance proved difficult while making the process of bringing immigrants from Europe much easier.

The European nations that came to North America staked out different settlement areas, some of which were near one another. They also brought conflicts with them. An English settlement was founded in Jamestown in what is now Virginia in 1607. Spain eventually claimed most of Central and South America and a wide swath of North America. France's principal colonies were Quebec, Louisiana, and islands in the Caribbean. The Portuguese colony in South America eventually became Brazil. The Dutch had smaller colonies in what is now the northeastern United States and in the Caribbean. Settlers in the Americas came from a Europe that included great diversity in terms of language, culture, and geography, but less so when it came to government and politics. Monarchs still had great power in Europe, and the Catholic Church was even more influential than many kings. England had a parliament, but few people had voting rights. Most average Europeans had little political power and lived lives that were bounded by rigid social parameters. Europe in the 15th and 16th centuries was a place where God was invoked to justify the burning of supposed witches, the waging of war, and the preservation of a feudal economic system that kept aristocrats wealthy and in power. This was the system that was introduced in the Americas.

2 SLAVERY

As so many people sailed west in hope of gaining fame and fortune, a key problem arose: Who would do the work necessary to generate wealth? Controlling workers in countries like England posed challenges for aristocrats and merchants with money, but the social order was still occasionally upset by popular dissent. The Reformation, which brought the rise of Protestant faiths and weakened the hold of the Catholic Church on European society, produced social changes, but the class structure of Europe did not immediately change as a result of it. The challenge with settling North America was that spending weeks travelling across the ocean while risking exposure to disease and possible death cost money. Peasants did not have the resources to cross an ocean. Initial European communities in North America consequently failed to closely reflect the demographics of their home nations. They were disproportionately comprised of soldiers, clergy, and traders, virtually all of whom were overwhelmingly male. Efforts to enslave Indigenous people were made, particularly by the Spanish, but they were not successful in colder climates. A seemingly easy and lasting solution was seized upon: enslave Africans.

The consequences of forcibly bringing people from Africa to toil across the Americas did not occur to slave traders or the people who paid them. Slavery was entirely related to labour shortages, and slaves worked harder and lived far harsher lives than anyone else who came across the Atlantic. The first slave ship to land in British North America was called the *White Lion*, and it arrived at Jamestown in late summer 1619 carrying 20 enslaved Africans. The problem of alleviating the colonial labour shortage had been found but at enormous human cost. The 20 Africans who were taken against their will to Jamestown eventually became part of 12 million seized from their home territories and transported to the western hemisphere, with approximately two million dying along the way.[1]

African slavery was important to North America for several reasons. Slavery had not been a common practice in Europe since the Roman Empire spread across that continent. There were countries where peasants lived as vassals of the aristocracy, especially in Russia, but putting people into bondage in Europe because of skin colour was uncommon when it was introduced in the Americas. Using enslaved labour required the deliberate process of dehumanizing someone based on race. Enslaved workers were brutally treated, and this became a pattern for future relations with workers of colour as well as people from different ethnic backgrounds. Slaves also suffered immeasurably because they came as individuals and not in families. They were never able to form lasting family bonds because they lived under the continual threat of seeing their parents, siblings, spouses, and children sold to another master.

Slavery had a profound impact on global commerce from the late 1600s to the mid-1800s. Several European countries became dependent on it for economic growth. It made the production and sale of crops such as tobacco, molasses, cotton, sugar, and coffee possible. Slavery also fostered the formation of a rigid class structure in the various American colonies. Landowners and merchants were at the top of colonial society, followed by white tradespeople and farmers, with slaves and Indigenous people at the bottom. African-American historian W.E.B. Du Bois theorized in the early 20th century that poor whites were compensated with a psychological wage, which meant they could take comfort that they were not at the bottom of social hierarchies because their race always put them above poor African Americans. This process really had its genesis in the 17th century, and it applied in Canada as much as it did in the United States.

Canadians might note with satisfaction that slavery was widespread in the United States up until the end of that country's Civil War in 1865, and that the British Empire began outlawing slavery in its colonies in 1834. Slavery was common enough that slave owners had runaway slave notices printed in newspapers. For example, a man named John Rock published a notice in the *Nova Scotia Gazette and Weekly Chronicle* in 1772 in which he promised a $2 reward to whoever could locate an enslaved girl named Thursday.

There were 3,000 enslaved Black people in Canada in the 1790s, with the highest percentage found in the Maritime colonies. Canada had a population of more than 161,000 in 1790. In contrast, there were over 595,000 enslaved people in the United States in 1781, which had a population of 3.5 million. There were proportionally far more enslaved Black people in the United States than in Canada, which shows the key role that enslaved labour played in the U.S. economy.[2]

Canadian historian H. Clare Pentland explained that the reason slavery was not as prevalent in Canada as it was in the United States can be attributed to climate rather than any possible moral reason. Slave owners needed to force slaves to work year-round to maximize their horrid investment in human bondage, and the cold climate in Canada mitigated against having anyone work intensely throughout the year. There was another solution that was instead introduced in North America starting in the colonial period: indentured servitude.[3]

3 EARLY WORK REGULATION

The Black Death, an epidemic of bubonic plague, ravaged Europe in the middle part of the 14th century, and in the process eliminated between 30 and 60 percent of the continent's population. It also had a profound impact on work and labour. The plague originated in Asia and spread westward, cutting a swath through the global population. It was the first plague pandemic experienced in Europe and was caused by infection brought by flea-bearing rodents. There was scant medical knowledge in the 14th century — religious faith was the main defence — and the plague's rapid spread illustrated the nature of public hygiene at that time. Cities and towns were dangerous environments. There was considerable lawlessness, human waste and sewage ran through streets, bathing was rare if it happened at all, water was often undrinkable, and life expectancy was short. It was inevitable that plague would thrive in such conditions. One consequence of the disease was to build resistance to it among those Europeans who survived it.

A significant labour shortage was one of the main side effects of the plague. Skilled craftsmen, noting there was now a dearth of people like them, attempted to raise their wage rates. The aristocracy's response was immediate and punitive: the Statute of Labourers, the first major labour law in England, was enacted in 1351. It forbade craftsmen from raising wage rates and enabled aristocrats to compel someone who was not engaged in work to labour for them, thus providing the basis for later regulation of work and labour. It also showed that labour shortages would be met with punitive measures rather than better wages to attract workers. The 1351 statute was followed in 1563 by the Statute of Artificers, or Statute of Apprentices, which regulated agricultural labour and entry to craft guilds. The 1563 law mandated that anyone trained in a craft could not refuse to work. All men between the ages of 12 and 60 could be compelled to labour in agriculture, as were unmarried women between the ages of 12 and 40. Hardly anyone in 16th-century England lived beyond their mid-forties, so they faced the prospect of spending their entire lives working regardless of their interest in doing so.

Those early laws all informed later regulation of work in Britain and Canada. There were key reasons that the ruling classes in Britain and other European countries used punitive measures to control workers. There were no organized police forces before the latter 19th century, so punishments had to be brutal and public to dissuade people from breaking laws. There also had to be no question in people's minds that the aristocracy and church should not be challenged. The fact that coercion rather than persuasion was employed to motivate workers is also fundamental. Employers in England did not actively compete for workers by offering higher wages. The solution in the 17th and 18th centuries was coercion and violence.

4 EUROPEAN EMPLOYERS AND NORTH AMERICAN WORKERS

When Canadians are taught about European colonization in elementary and secondary school, they gain some insights into what life was like for settlers in what is now Canada, and talk inevitably turns to farming and trapping. In reality, the state, meaning government, was often the largest employer and was behind most economic activity. The British and French governments were major employers because of the military garrisons they maintained in their respective colonies. The upkeep of military facilities and provisioning troops was a major source of employment and revenue for merchants and craftsmen.

As much as the colonization process was enormously detrimental for Indigenous Peoples, it was also terribly hazardous for people who took to sea in wooden sailing ships to cross the world's oceans. Navigation was not a more exact science until the late 17th century and the invention of the first chronometers. Using the stars for navigation was possible provided a skilled navigator was on board a ship, but storms, wind, and currents easily upset long sea voyages. Stepping onto the deck of a sailing ship was an act of faith that could as easily lead to an early death as it did an uncertain future in a strange land.

Colonies posed enormous perils for the countries that founded them. Sending ships across oceans was costly, and there was always great risk that ships and their crews would be lost. There was also the fundamental reality that some countries were wealthier than others. Spain had greater resources than England in the 15th century, but fortunes change and England was becoming stronger by the 17th century. However, parliaments and monarchs were loath to assume too much liability while hoping to reap the bounty of the new lands far away. Having someone else assume risk on behalf of the Crown was a seemingly simple solution to the problems of founding colonies and engaging in trade. In England's case, the East India Company was the first example of an organization established for overseas expansion, and it would be followed by other such enterprises.[4]

Joint-stock corporations comprised of shareholders were first created in China in the seventh century, and they later appeared in other parts of the world. For instance, the Virginia Company came into existence in 1606 and the Hudson's Bay Company was founded in 1670. A joint-stock corporation is made up of different owners who can jointly enjoy a firm's profits while also sharing any risks. Pooling investment resources makes it easier to quickly expand a company's operations. In the case of colonial firms such as the Hudson's Bay Company and the Virginia Company, using such entities was supposed to shield the British government from financial liability. If a firm went under, it was theoretically a problem for its shareholders and not for the British Treasury.

The establishment of early corporations also reflected the expansion of capitalism as an economic system. The term *capitalism* refers to the formation of social relations that permit production of goods and services to be organized so that surplus value, meaning profit, is created. Bartering and commercial trade existed for centuries before Europeans began colonizing other continents, but capitalism was different from preceding practices. Industrialization is often associated with the emergence of capitalism, but as Ellen Meiksins Wood has forcefully argued, the genesis of capitalism was in 16th-century England. This means that capitalism was indeed part of the motivation for the colonization of North America.[5]

It is important to note that the emergence of capitalism was not universally welcomed in Britain and other countries. The 17th century was a period of social upheaval in Britain, principally because of the English Civil Wars (1642–51). Groups such as the Levellers and Diggers demanded political reform and great economic equality. Indeed, Digger leader Gerrard Winstanley and his followers advocated for allowing people to farm and use land as they needed. However, private property rights ultimately prevailed.

The East India Company eventually became a state within a state, with its own army and vast financial resources. In modern terms, it became too big to fail. The Hudson's Bay Company did not possess similar military resources but proved more enduring than its counterpart on the Indian subcontinent. European explorers quickly noted the abundance of wildlife in the Americas, and interest in trading furs quickly developed. Animal skins were a necessity for Indigenous Peoples in the Americas and a luxury for Europeans. Hats that were made using fur and assembled with mercury nitrate, which caused neurological illness — hence the expression "mad as a hatter" was associated with the milliners who made them — were fashionable in England and Continental Europe by the 17th century, and the Hudson's Bay Company was created to develop the fur trade. It was granted control over a vast territory called Rupert's Land, so named for Prince Rupert, a nephew of King Charles I and cousin of Charles II, and it developed a network of trading posts known as factories.

The Hudson's Bay Company became Canada's most enduring corporation. Its shareholders, like those of the East India Company, were based far away in London and its fortunes were dependent on a cast of explorers, trappers, Indigenous hunters, and indentured servants. The company reshaped the meaning of work for Indigenous Peoples across British North America as they moved from trapping for subsistence to trapping for profits. The methods used for hunting and trapping were changed by European technology as steel and gunpowder found their way into Indigenous hands. The people who ran the company's interests in the colonies were committed to seeing Britain expand and acquire power but were principally concerned with enriching themselves and the firm. The people who performed menial work for the Hudson's Bay Company had more basic goals such as gaining freedom in a new land.

Slavery made European colonization possible, and so, too, did indentured servitude. An indenture was a simple but insidious agreement. Poor people were offered the chance to come to British North America and have their passage paid by an employer but were legally bound to that employer until they had worked long enough to pay off the cost of the transatlantic trip. Indentured servants lived better lives than enslaved workers but still faced the prospect of having their periods of indenture extended for capricious reasons. An employer could appeal to a magistrate to impose additional time if a worker was found to have violated any terms of the indenture, and indentured servants were treated abysmally. The popularity of indentured servitude was such that it is estimated that up to 48 percent of the Europeans who came to the Thirteen Colonies before 1775 were indentured servants. Workers could not easily resist instructions given by employers, who were universally called masters during the colonial period, and the weight of law and the state was on the side of those masters.[6]

The Hudson's Bay Company made extensive use of indentured servants because it also faced labour shortages despite reaping enormous profits. Retaining workers once they arrived in the colonies was as difficult as inducing them to voluntarily make the journey. The company seized on the idea of choosing workers who were thought to be easily controlled and unlikely to violate the terms of their indentures. Workers from the Orkney Islands, off the northeastern coast of Scotland, were thought to be so sufficiently pliable that they would make good indentured servants. However, the company's leaders were mistaken, since Orcadians, as they were called at the time, attempted to escape in the 18th century once they experienced life under the company's control. They were not the only indentured servants who responded to their conditions by trying to break the terms of their bondage to their employers, and their efforts showed both defiance and desperation. The weight of the state was entirely behind employers, while workers had negligible rights in the employment contract, yet still pushed back in the face of overwhelming odds against them. The idea of running away, which Hudson's Bay Company indentured servants tried to do, raises the question of where they thought they would go. There was no easy route back to Britain or Ireland, so the alternative was to simply run into the wilderness, which shows how desperate people could become in the colonial environment.[7]

5 EUROPEAN CONFLICTS AND NORTH AMERICAN CONSEQUENCES

The European colonies in North America were always influenced by events and policies on the other side of the Atlantic. For instance, the 17th-century English colonies felt the effects of the English Civil Wars. The dictates of the Catholic Church had a profound impact on how European colonists interacted with Indigenous Peoples. A conflict that occurred in Europe in the mid-18th century had a particularly lasting impact on the future of the colonies in Canada. Canadians are taught as schoolchildren about the fall of the French colony at Quebec in 1759 as a result of the Battle of the Plains of Abraham, but the fact that the defeat of the French was part of a wider conflict called the Seven Years' War is often not sufficiently understood. That was really the first European conflict that happened on close to a global scale. The war included Britain, France, Spain, Portugal, Prussia and other German principalities, Russia, the Mughal Empire in India, and Sweden.

The Seven Years' War had several consequences for the Americas. Britain emerged stronger from it, acquiring Florida from Spain, taking possession of valuable islands in the Caribbean, and essentially pushing

France out of India. France ceded half of its Louisiana colony, the area west of the Mississippi River, to Spain, and lost Quebec. The Battle of the Plains of Abraham and the events that it triggered were consequently just one of many incidents that transpired while the war was fought between 1756 and 1763.

Britain and France fought each other in North America through their alliances with Indigenous Peoples and also through their colonists. The British North American colonies were far more populous than those controlled by France. Attracting or forcing settlers to the Americas proved more difficult for France than for Britain. The famed Filles du Roi, a group of approximately 800 women who came to New France (Quebec) at the behest of the French government to marry and help alleviate the huge gender imbalance in the colony, are also often discussed in the history taught in Canadian schools. The Filles du Roi story became a cherished part of Quebec history, but the women who came to New France in that capacity endured harsh conditions. Married almost immediately after arriving, they were able to choose their husbands and were given some domestic supplies by the French government, but New France was a markedly different environment compared to what they had known in France. The Filles du Roi certainly helped increase the size of the colonial population. Nevertheless, at the end of the Seven Years' War, there were close to two million people living in the British colonies in the Americas and around 50,000 in those controlled by France.[8]

The soldiers who battled for Britain and France were also workers, even if soldiers are not often viewed in those terms. They were employed in armies rife with class differences. The British Army and Royal Navy were led by men who came from privileged backgrounds and who could purchase their officer commissions. The ranks of the army and crews of the navy were overwhelmingly made up of men who were often forced into service. The Royal Navy operated press gangs that essentially rounded up indigent men to force them into service. British Army recruiting sergeants offered to buy pints of beer for men in English pubs, and once the beer was consumed, the drinkers found a coin at the bottom of their empty mugs and learned they had just unwittingly joined the army by taking the king's shilling.

British military discipline was extremely harsh. Men who were flogged on board ships were required to knot the lashes used on them. Armies marched into battle in opposing lines, partly to concentrate musket fire but also to keep men regimented and stop them from fleeing. Going into land or naval battle brought a high risk of death, and diseases arising from injury often sent men to graves in fields and burial at sea. The treatment of soldiers and sailors was part of a wider system of employing violence, implied and actual, to dominate people regardless of their vocations.

Working life was also hard because of the nature of everyday existence in the 18th century. The settlers who came to North American colonies still rarely bathed, if ever. King Louis XIV, the French monarch who ruled from 1643 to 1715, was known to have only bathed twice in his life and he was at the top of France's social hierarchy. Frequent changes of clothes were instead Louis's method of staying clean. His subjects, like people living in other European countries, were usually infested with lice and preferred to drink beer and other alcoholic drinks because they were safer than water. Their lives were, in the words of 17th-century philosopher Thomas Hobbes, often nasty, brutish, and short.[9]

The soldiers who met one another in the Battle of the Plains of Abraham were far from home and often lived harsh, desperate lives. The battle itself became part of Canadian legend and lore, but officers in European armies viewed the colonies as backwaters and preferred to be close to the main action back home. The British, led by General James Wolfe, scaled the heights above the St. Lawrence River and met the French, led by the Marquis de Montcalm, on the plains. The fight was brief compared to other engagements of that period and both commanding officers died as a result of it, with Wolfe falling on the battlefield from a musket shot and Montcalm dying after the engagement, also as a result of musket fire. It marked the beginning of the end of a significant French presence in the Americas.

The French loss at Quebec and eventual withdrawal from the continent shaped Québécois identity, with the defeat becoming known as La Conquête (The Conquest). It concluded with the Treaty of Paris, though Britain offered to return Quebec to France in return for Guadeloupe in the Caribbean. Islands in the Caribbean like Guadeloupe with their huge sugar cane plantations were much more lucrative colonies for Britain and France than vast tracts of cold, forested land farther north. The French declined, which was a commentary on the little value they placed on New

France. They also made a strategic decision, since the Comte de Vergennes, France's foreign minister a few years after the Treaty of Paris, speculated that the lack of a French threat close to the British North American colonies would put those colonies into revolt against Britain. His prediction was correct: the American colonies rebelled in less than 15 years.

In the meantime, the economies of the British colonies in Canada were significantly altered following 1763. French-speaking settlers in Acadia in what is now Nova Scotia were forcibly removed from their communities, with many going to Louisiana where they became Cajuns. The British initially tried to suppress the Catholic Church and French language in Quebec after the departure of France, but that effort was abandoned in a few years. Events farther south also informed British policy after the start of the American colonies' rebellion in 1776. The British military became the biggest economic influence in the Canadian colonies by the end of the 18th century, since it bought provisions for troops and raw materials to send home. The merchant class prospered under the British, but workers did not acquire more rights as the colonies slowly expanded.[10]

There was still overwhelming reliance on staples such as timber and fish for economic prosperity as the colonies became further entwined in the British imperial economy. Britain practised a system known as mercantilism. That economic policy, largely governed through Navigation Acts, mandated how goods could move by ship around the British Empire. Timber, cotton, sugar, and other commodities were exported to Britain where they were turned into finished goods then re-exported. The Royal Navy became dominant by the end of the 18th century, which made it possible for Britain to bring home raw materials from its colonies and then export finished goods. Other countries that sought to trade with Britain faced the prospect of having tariffs imposed on their goods. The Canadian loggers who cut down trees that were eventually made into masts and planks for Royal Navy ships were part of an economic regime that included enslaved workers on Jamaican plantations, early industrial workers in cities like Glasgow and Manchester, and Indians toiling on East India Company projects. The workers themselves may not have realized they were small cogs helping to drive a much larger economic system.

6 THE WAR OF 1812 AND THE UNITED STATES

The American Revolution had a profound impact on all British North American colonies. It was a long struggle that has been mythologized in the United States. The revolution was rooted in grievances against control by faraway Britain. The colonies had elected assemblies but wanted more power over their affairs and economic policy. It also started in urban rather than rural settings. The famed Boston Tea Party, in which rebels disguised as Indigenous warriors stormed a merchant ship and threw several tons of tea into Boston's harbour, was a protest against British mercantilism. The tea trade was dominated by the East India Company, and the British wanted the colonists to automatically accept the shipment and pay an excise tax. The problem was that the colonists did not have the money to pay the tax. The colonies, having contributed men to the French and Indian Wars that were part of the wider Seven Years' War, lacked industrial strength like Britain's but were fully capable of fielding an army.

The initial revolutionary years did not go well for the Americans, but the tide turned with French help. Britain was desperate to hold on to its North American possessions and poured resources into the struggle. The final result was a close American victory and British withdrawal from the Thirteen Colonies. The revolution led to a migration north to Canada. American supporters of Britain were derisively called Tories in the United States, but they eventually became hailed as Loyalists in the remaining North American colonies. The British government need not have worried over the loss of the Thirteen Colonies, since Britain's position in India, which became known as the Jewel in the Crown, was strengthened in the years after 1776 and the American Declaration of Independence.

Britain's North American colonies shared common traits with the colonies founded in the South Pacific. They became settler societies that were part of a wider British diaspora. The movement of British settlers had profound impacts. Indigenous populations were either coerced or forced off their lands, British common law formed the basis for colonial legal systems, and the English language eventually proliferated around the world. Britain later acquired other colonies and territories, yet widespread settlement by colonists was limited in many of them while the United States, Canada, Australia, and New Zealand were shaped by settlers.[11]

The British learned much from the American Revolution. They were careful about sending large numbers of immigrants to colonies unless they could be certain those colonists would not start fomenting dissent against the government in London. The Canadian colonies, Australia, and New Zealand were all recipients of British immigrants, with Australia initially serving as a penal colony. While the Americans wanted representative government, Britain still retained power over assemblies in its colonies. The voting franchise was limited in Britain, since voters had to be property owners, and it was similarly curtailed in the colonies.

The Revolutionary War provided Americans with myths and legends that endure to the present day, and the turn of the 19th century brought an event — the War of 1812 — that would do the same for Canadians. The United States was a comparatively weak country focused on agriculture in 1800. The revolution and American Constitution influenced events in Europe and coincided with them. The French Revolution began in 1789, the same year the U.S. Constitution became law, and it seemed as if old social structures and institutions were being fundamentally challenged. The British aristocracy were aghast at what happened in France, and the idea of slow social change and maintenance of existing social order was exemplified by the pamphlets of Irish politician and philosopher Edmund Burke, whose polemics later shaped conservative political ideology. The writings of economist Adam Smith also shaped British policy in the late 18th and early 19th centuries.

People living in the colonies were not necessarily aware of Burke or Smith, but they knew what had happened in the United States and France. By 1812, they were also conscious of growing tension with America. There was no real defined border between the United States and Britain's Canadian colonies in the early 1800s. Quebec was Lower Canada and the territory that eventually became Ontario was Upper Canada. Those seemingly odd choices of names for the two colonies were based on their positions in relation to the St. Lawrence River. Lower Canada was at the opening, or mouth, of the river as it met the Atlantic Ocean, while Upper Canada was farther west up the river's length. Skirmishing between Americans living near the colonies, such as along the Niagara River, occurred prior to 1812, but the real trouble between Britain and the United States revolved around trade and British efforts to harass American ships. Britain was ascendant in 1812, having just led a coalition to defeat France and Napoleon Bonaparte, and the United States was in no position to challenge the Royal Navy. Invading Canada was instead the easiest way for the United States to battle Britain, and it ostensibly seemed as if the Americans would prevail.

The War of 1812 created some common beliefs among Canadians, including the story that Laura Secord took a treacherous journey to warn British troops of an impending American attack, the Canadian militia formed the heart of the fight against the United States, and Major-General Isaac Brock became a military hero after falling at the Battle of Queenston Heights. What actually happened was different from what Canadians came to believe. Secord did warn British commanders, British Army regular troops were the core of Canada's defence, Brock much preferred to be in Britain preparing for a final confrontation with

Napoleon, and the war would not have been won without the help of Indigenous warriors. The struggle was viewed as a victory in Canada, while the Americans, too, believed they had triumphed. The fact that the United States did not force Britain off the continent and annex Canada suggests the Canadian interpretation is correct.

The War of 1812, like all major conflicts, had consequences beyond combat. The reference to "the rocket's red glare" in the "The Star-Spangled Banner," the American national anthem, was about the British Army burning Washington in 1813 and the subsequent American defence of Fort McHenry in Baltimore. It impacted how Canadians would live and work into the 19th century. Most of the immigrants who settled in Canada prior to 1812 were Americans, but that pattern stopped during the war and did not resume after it ended in December 1814 with the signing of the Treaty of Ghent.

Britain rewarded military veterans with plots of land in the Canadian colonies even if they did not know how to farm, and veterans consequently became a source of immigration. Some of them also unfortunately became indigent, since they never mastered farming proficiently. Workers who previously passed back and forth between New York State and Upper Canada now came more often from Britain and Ireland. Canadians remained divided by ethnicity, language, religion, and class, but the country became a place to live and work that was separate from the United States even if the larger nation to the south continued to pose a threat as the 19th century progressed.

7 THE 1837 REBELLIONS, RESPONSIBLE GOVERNMENT, AND WORKER CONTROL

From 1815 to 1837, the populations of Upper and Lower Canada and the Maritimes increased but also witnessed social division that exploded into rebellion. There was a nascent middle class in the Canadian colonies prior to 1867, and there were wealthy property owners, merchants, craftsmen, and unskilled labourers of different types who lived in a defined class hierarchy.

Efforts to replicate the English class system in Canada were actively championed by wealthy citizens. There were two principal controlling groups in Upper and Lower Canada: the Family Compact in the former and the Château Clique in the latter. The two groups were comprised of the leading families and government figures in the two colonies. Irish, English, and Scottish immigration shaped the nature of the colonial workforce in Upper and Lower Canada and the Maritimes. This was a period when the early Canadian working class was formed and that group entered into conflict with the property-owning class.

Discontent with a lack of representative government and resentment over the colonial socio-economic structure led to the rebellions in Upper and Lower Canada in 1837. The rebellion in Upper Canada was led by William Lyon Mackenzie, a journalist and firebrand who railed against the Family Compact from his home in Toronto. Mackenzie failed following an abortive confrontation with the local militia at Montgomery's Tavern, fled to New York State beyond Britain's reach, then occupied Navy Island in the Niagara River, declaring it a sovereign republic, only to be chased back into the United States by British troops. The Lower Canada Rebellion was principally led by Louis-Joseph Papineau. That part of the 1837 rebellion involved the deployment of more militia than in Upper Canada, and many deaths. The immediate result was the imprisonment of the leading rebels in both colonies. Mackenzie may have been radical when it involved power structures in Upper Canada, but not when it came to worker rights: he also led an effort by other newspaper publishers to break an 1836 strike by printers and apprentices.[12]

The 1837 rebellions were driven by class interests and did motivate Britain to take steps to address the colonists' concerns. There was certainly nobody in London who wanted to see another successful rebellion in Canada and the possible absorption of the colonies into the United States. The British government sent John Lambton, the Earl of Durham, to Canada in 1838 to study the causes of the rebellions and recommend policy changes in response to them. Durham was only in Canada for less than a year, but he produced the *Report on the Affairs of British North America* (1839), otherwise known as the *Durham Report*. The report recommended that Upper and Lower Canada be united into one province and be given a legislative assembly with tangible authority. The report's recommendations were accepted, Upper and Lower Canada became Canada West and Canada East, setting the stage for discussions on achieving dominion status and a wide degree of autonomy from Britain 28 years later.

Responsible government, meaning elected legislatures with the ability to make laws, finally came to Canada, but beneficial changes to work and labour regulations did not accompany it. A legal framework that was used across the British Empire was effectively employed in Canada to keep workers under control, regardless of the creation of a Canadian legislature. Master-and-servant laws were first passed in Britain, then across the colonies. The first such act was passed in Canada in 1847, well after the *Durham Report*. Master-and-servant laws outlined the obligations of both parties in the employment contract, but the rule of law favoured masters and disadvantaged servants. The Master and Servant Act delineated how recalcitrant servants would be handled.[13]

Workers had engaged in periodic work stoppages since the colonization of New France, but forming a union or mutual benefit society of any kind led to workers facing the wrath of militias and magistrates. Remembering that what happened in Britain influenced practices in Canada, there are two events in British history, one more well known than the other, that illustrate the fury the state and British law could direct at the working class.

The first case involved a demonstration that led to a massacre in Manchester, England, in 1819. Britain industrialized before any other country, a process aided by imperialism that created enormous social tensions. William Blake, when he referred to "dark Satanic Mills" in the preface to his epic *Milton: A Poem in Two Books*, may have been contrasting the possibility of heaven in England with the nature of workplaces that arose in the early stages of the Industrial Revolution. Later, the poem became a hymn entitled "Jerusalem" and was set to music by composer Hubert Parry and orchestrated by Edward Elgar. Blake may have been thinking primarily in religious terms when he wrote his poem, but as with most works of literature, its meaning was adapted by workers and industrial reformers. Workers felt threatened by new industrial machinery and the socio-economic change that it brought and resorted to deliberately breaking it in response. The term *Luddite* entered the English language due to the followers of a character named General Ned Ludd, who may not have actually existed, but his disciples did, and the British government responded by passing the Frame-Breaking Act in 1812, which outlawed the deliberate damaging of industrial machinery.[14]

Protests broke out across Britain, especially in the industrialized north, and culminated with a demonstration by 60,000 people in Manchester on August 16, 1819. The protestors were in St. Peter's Field listening to orators hold forth on the need for political reform. The city's authorities saw something seditious occurring. The Manchester Yeoman Calvary eventually charged the crowd and in the process killed 15 people and injured another 650, including women and children, all of whom were assembled for peaceful purposes. The incident was immortalized in George Cruikshank's savage cartoon as well as in an anonymous print published by labour activist Richard Carlile, one of the speakers at the protest. There was an official inquiry after Peterloo and calls in Parliament for political reform after the massacre, but that was cold comfort for the thousands of people who had witnessed it.[15]

The second case was directly related to Canada. It involved a group of workers in Dorset, England, in 1834 and shows what could happen to those who tried to organize to oppose their employers. Combination Acts had been passed in Britain in 1799 and 1800, in the aftermath of the French Revolution, to outlaw workers from organizing. The acts were eventually repealed, and a Combinations of Workmen Act was introduced in 1825 to prohibit unions from bargaining and engaging in strikes.[16] In 1834, six agricultural workers in the village of Tolpuddle in Dorset met to form the Friendly Society of Agricultural Workers. Their names were George and James Loveless, James Brine, James Hammett, Thomas Stansfield, and Stansfield's son, John. George Loveless initiated the formation of the organization.[17] Another worker named Edward Legg betrayed the group's existence to the authorities and the six men were put on trial, convicted of swearing secret oaths, and sentenced to seven years' transportation to Van Diemen's Land (Tasmania in modern Australia). A public uproar ensued in England, over 200,000 people signed a petition supporting the convicted men, and 30,000 marched in London to protest their convictions.

The Canadian connection emerged when all six men were given passage back to Britain and four of them chose to immigrate to Canada. That group included George Loveless, who lived in the London, Ontario, area and was buried there. The Tolpuddle Martyrs are still known in British labour history but receive much less popular attention in Canada. Loveless and his compatriots clearly viewed Canada as a place to restart their lives. Their journey was remarkable by 18th-century standards:

from Britain to Australia, back to Britain, and then to Canada firstly as convicts then as free men, all because they swore a benign oath.[18]

From the 18th century on, there was similar concern in Canadian colonial legislatures about workers. For example, the Nova Scotia legislature passed a law banning journeymen and workmen in Halifax from holding meetings and combinations to regulate wages. There was consequently worker militancy in the Canadian colonies, including the years after the creation of the Province of Canada (the union of Upper and Lower Canada) in 1841. This happened in the context of ongoing demand for labour of different types.[19]

Britain and Continental Europe experienced considerable social change in the 1840s. Chartism, which was a working-class movement, emerged in Britain in the 1830s with the objective of expanding voting rights and democratic participation. The movement peaked in the early 1840s. At that time, voting rights were still limited to men who were property owners, a requirement that disenfranchised vast swathes of Britain's population. There was also a wave of revolutions and political upheaval across much of Europe in 1848. Political changes that would appear in Canada were consequently part of a wider social and political transformation within the British Empire and Continental Europe.[20]

8 DOMESTIC WORK AND HARD LABOUR

Having a domestic worker in a home was a clear marker of social status for a family in pre-Confederation Canada. There were also never enough domestic workers to satisfy demand, they were usually women, and their wages were low. As historian Elizabeth Jane Errington notes, single and widowed women were part of the working poor in Upper Canada.[21] Ninety percent of women married, but usually not for love. Marriage was overseen by churches, and marriage vows aside, it often did not take death long to part people. Pregnancy and childbirth were extremely dangerous for women, and giving birth could take the life of a mother and a child. Women had numerous pregnancies, and a family could expect to have at least one child die before reaching adolescence.[22] Housekeeping was difficult and labour-intensive, with every meal prepared in kitchens that were cold in the winter and stifling hot in the summer. Laundry was scrubbed by hand, and clothes were often sewn and knitted in the house. Women's hands did all of that work and more. This was the only real time that women directed other women, since those from wealthy families with means to pay servants oversaw household activities. As professor of law Jeremy Webber describes, domestic servants were considered the same as farm labourers.[23]

The machines that were in use in Canada for much of the immediate pre-Confederation decades were rudimentary at best. Ploughs were pulled by horses or oxen, water power was employed to drive grain and sawmills, but human toil was the main contribution to the work process. For example, the first Welland Canal was constructed between 1824 and 1829, mostly by Irish labourers who dug it by hand. Canal work was back-breaking, and workers on the lowest rungs of the occupational hierarchy performed it. Working-class life involved long hours, straining muscles, and rough entertainment. Overseers on canal projects made ample use of barrels of whiskey to motivate men; they were placed ahead of work gangs to induce them to keep their shovels in the ground.[24]

The mortality rate of immigrant labourers was high, with up to 10 percent of Irish workers dying within two years of arriving in the Canadian colonies. Diseases that are now usually consigned to the dustbin of history ran rampant in pre-Confederation Canada. Cholera, a malady caused by eating food or drinking fluid contaminated with *Vibrio cholerae* bacteria, was a constant threat. Typhus, which is transmitted by ticks and fleas, was also a public health problem. Other biological threats, such as syphilis, occasionally turned into epidemics. These health threats faced little organized medical opposition because physicians often possessed only basic medical training.

Canal work was an example of seasonal employment, and that aspect of it disadvantaged immigrant labourers. Canals were important, since the Welland, in particular, connected Lakes Ontario and Erie and opened new routes for commerce and the movement of people. The Erie Canal, which linked Lake Erie to the Hudson River, also shaped economic activity in Canada while also transforming New York State's economy. Canals could not be dug when the ground was frozen with frost and covered in snow and ice. The harshness of Canadian winters brought a lot of paid work to a halt until spring arrived. Canadian-born workers who grew up in rural communities could return to farming when their other jobs ended due to a change in season, such as going back to the farm after a summer of logging. Immigrants could not resort to that pattern and faced periods of enormous hardship when they fell out of work due to no fault of their own.

Work was heavily influenced by ethnicity and race. Irish immigrants were viewed as racially distinct from other whites. They were also thought to be prone to drunkenness and licentiousness. The fact that most Irish immigrants were also Roman Catholic exacerbated public attitudes toward them even though their labour was a key part of the Canadian economy. The Irish Potato Famine from 1845 to 1849 led to a huge exodus of people from Ireland, with an estimated two million leaving the island and most of that number choosing to go to the United States. Ireland was a British colony at that time, and the famine was yet another British imperial event that had repercussions across the Atlantic.[25]

9 COLONIAL LIVING

The life of the average person living in the Canadian colonies was far from idyllic, bound as it was by rigid social norms and conventions. For example, there was a cultural practice called the charivari in English-speaking Canada that involved roving groups of mostly men who donned costumes or went around at night harassing people deemed to have violated unspoken social norms. A newly married couple who were vastly different in age could anticipate a knock on the door on their wedding night demanding a drink, along with a loud ruckus outside the house. The charivari came from Britain and was also practised in Holland. It was a method of enforcing unwritten social rules.[26]

The ability to engage in leisure activities in the early 19th century was limited by wealth and also by season. Mid-19th-century Canadians spent their winters indoors, cold as their homes were, and looked forward to spring and summer. Churches and fraternal orders were popular social spheres. Division between Protestant churches and the Catholic faith helped drive membership in the anti-Catholic Orange Order, a fraternal organization particularly active in Canada West (Ontario). Newspapers were printed across the Canadian colonies, and books were also available to those who could read them. The daily cycle of work and leisure was governed by the hours of the day, and anything that happened after dark had to be illuminated by candles or oil lamps. People rose in the morning and worked with the rising of the sun and went to bed with its setting in the evening, unless they had the means to burn candles and lamp oil.

There was nothing like modern consumer culture in the pre-Confederation decades. Working-class people ate at home, owned a limited amount of clothing, often made and gave practical gifts, and generally fretted about money. Their diets were plain and entirely based on local agriculture. Small delicacies like fruit were only available annually for a short period during the summer. Root vegetables were common and could be easily stored. Meat could rot quickly, since it could only be frozen during the winter months.

Falling ill from influenza, scarlet fever, tuberculosis, chicken pox, gonorrhea, or syphilis could still be as deadly in the five decades before Confederation as it was when Europeans first set foot in the Americas. Progress had been made in Europe when it came to inoculation against bubonic plague, but there was little defence against other widespread ailments. Medical treatments were perilous and costly, so home remedies were customary. A visit to a physician with a severely broken or shattered limb could easily lead to amputation and the risk of death from subsequent infection. The need to sterilize surgical instruments and use antiseptic did not gain currency until later in the 19th century. People still bathed infrequently as Confederation approached — it was becoming common among the upper class but much less so among the working class — and the link between personal hygiene and good health was still not widely understood.

10 PROFESSIONS, INSTITUTIONS, AND WORK IN EARLY CANADA

Irish workers and free African Canadians were effectively barred from the emerging professions in Canada and had difficulty entering the merchant class. The clergy was one occupation that Catholic immigrants could enter as a first real profession, and Catholic families aspired to seeing a son enter the priesthood. The church provided education of a calibre unavailable to the vast majority of Canadians, and having a priest in the family also earned prestige. Putting on a clerical collar involved taking vows of chastity and poverty, but the Catholic Church in Canada still became as wealthy and powerful as it was in Europe.

That power, great as it was especially in Quebec, was surpassed by the Anglican Church's. The British government designated lots of lands as Clergy Reserves, which entailed giving land to the Anglican Church for its exclusive use, including selling it. It was also land that had been expropriated, often by treaty, from the Indigenous Peoples already occupying it. The Anglican Church, known in Britain as the Church of England, was symbolically led by the reigning monarch and benefited enormously from Clergy Reserve land.

Religion played an understandably central role in the Canadian colonies. Belief in an unseen supernatural force that could provide salvation and a serene afterlife was about the only respite people had in a world of rudimentary medical care, possible exposure to a panoply of untreatable diseases, and a daily existence that was physically hard for most of the population. Pre-Confederation Canada was still a place of ever-present disease and death.

Immigrants who came to work and live in the Canadian colonies were Christians, and seemingly minute divides between denominations easily became chasms. This was particularly true of the gulf between Catholic and Protestant faiths. Differences in religious doctrine between Presbyterians, Methodists, and Anglicans were also well parsed. Religious difference certainly shaped who people married, but it also influenced the work and social spheres they inhabited. Being a good Christian meant being industrious, usually temperate, and constant in your religious faith.

The power of organized religion as it related to work was most clearly felt in education. None of the mainline 18th- and 19th-century religions was opposed to education, although with limits. The Jesuits, a Catholic religious order formally known as the Society of Jesus, advocated education and sent priests to the Americas when the first explorers began arriving. The Catholic Church overall was a keen education promoter and founded colleges, including Saint Mary's University in Halifax in 1802.[27]

The first universities and colleges in Canada were established to provide liberal arts education grounded in religious faith, and also to educate and foster a local Canadian elite and professional class. Those efforts largely bore fruit. Canada's first institutions of higher learning were started in the Maritime colonies in the late 18th century. The University of New Brunswick was founded in Fredericton in 1785, while Halifax's University of King's College was inaugurated in 1789. They were followed by McGill University in Montreal in 1821 and the University of Toronto in 1827. The latter was initially known as King's College and was affiliated with the Anglican Church and John Strachan, its influential bishop. Education promoters were interested in creating common standards for education and wanted to see the Canadian colonies populated by people with basic literacy who were taught to respect those in positions of power and who could contribute to the economy.[28]

The expansion of education in the Canadian colonies helped improve literacy and also nurtured the development of early professions, but there were negative aspects to it. Egerton Ryerson, a Methodist minister for whom a university in Toronto was later named, was an early pre-Confederation proponent of free public education. He also played a significant role in the founding of residential schools for Indigenous children, institutions that now occupy an infamous place in Canadian history. Residential schools were intended to assimilate Indigenous children and were a form of cultural genocide. They also placed a heavy emphasis on vocational training that was intended to make children into workers. Ryerson's efforts led to the creation of the first school boards in Canada West as well as to the establishment of normal schools that were dedicated to training teachers. However, another century would pass before teachers were regarded as close to equal with other professions.

Regardless of the religious denomination, the priesthood was the paramount profession, and in Canada it was followed closely by the military and the law. Officers who led local militia units in Canada were chosen because of social position and status as much as for military prowess. The Law Society of Upper Canada was founded in 1797 to regulate the colony's legal profession. Training to be a lawyer was principally an apprenticeship undertaking in the early 18th century, but the law eventually became part of university curricula. Learning to be a merchant was a vocational experience, and the first business education programs would not begin in earnest until later in the 19th century.[29]

The training of skilled craftsmen was much the same as Confederation approached as it had been since the start of the 19th century. Canada in the 1860s was a workplace of people such as cordwainers (shoemaking), wheelwrights (makers of wheels for carts and carriages), coopers (barrel makers), and carpenters, among others. Some trades, like cordwaining, eventually diminished and disappeared as Canada experienced industrialization later in the 19th century. Others, like carpentry and bricklaying, saw little if any change. New craft occupations appeared along with technological change. Young workers, usually boys, apprenticed in their early to mid-teenage years and had their lives essentially governed by the masters under whom they apprenticed. Someone who was a skilled tradesperson could find work that paid better than subsistence wages.

A workable steam engine was invented in 1776 by James Watt, enabling the start of the Industrial Revolution. Britain was the first country to industrialize, but its Canadian colonies did not initially run on steam power. There were railways in pre-Confederation Canada — the first one built in 1836. The colonies first relied on animal and water power rather than on machines. The profusion of rivers and lakes in the colonies facilitated water transport and explains why so many major cities, Montreal and Toronto, for instance, were on bodies of water. Flour mills were powered by water wheels, horses pulled carts and carriages, and oxen ploughed fields. With the widespread introduction of steam power and machinery, those same cities became industrial centres.

The work of running organizations was largely manual in the first decades of the 19th century. Canadian newspapers were printed on presses with movable type, but commercial typewriters had yet to be invented and administrative work was completed with pens and ink. Office work was overwhelmingly male.

11 ECONOMIC LIFE AND THE COMING OF CONFEDERATION

The foundations of Canada's economic development were notably described by political economist Harold Adams Innis and historian Donald Creighton. Innis devised the "staples thesis" of economic development, arguing that Canada's economic progress was based on the exploitation of a succession of staple goods beginning with the fur trade.[30] Creighton took a somewhat different approach, building on Innis's theory to present the Laurentian Thesis, which argued that Canada's economic development was rooted in activity around the exploitation of staple goods by merchants along the St. Lawrence River. The durability of those theses is periodically reconsidered by historians when looking at Canada's later history. The period from colonization up to Confederation does show that exploitation of natural resources was the central activity for Canadian workers, but the post-Confederation period would start to bring some changes to that pattern.[31]

Lord Durham's report led to the creation of a political system that afforded tangible democratic participation, but it also produced political deadlock between Canada West and Canada East. Each province had equal numbers of seats in the combined legislature, and there was little common ground for legislative initiatives. At the same time that this tension was worsening, the United States was divided by a four-year civil war that caused horrific casualties and divided the country. Canada was peripherally involved in the American Civil War as escaped enslaved people journeyed north to freedom where they could not be recaptured and sent back into bondage, and some cavalry from the Confederacy came north with the approval of the British government to slip across the border and harass the northern states.

The real problem with the Civil War involved early British support for the Confederacy. British textile mills purchased cotton from the southern U.S. states, and the Confederacy was heavily dependent on cotton to fuel its economy. The vastly greater resources of the Union forces in the war ensured they would eventually prevail, and by 1865, the U.S. Army was enormous. Not surprisingly, politicians in Washington turned irate eyes north to Canada in response to Britain's meddling in the conflict.

Britain was also reconsidering its future role in Canada, both due to relations with the United States and also because of other imperial commitments. India was a source of greater wealth than Canada, and Britain was also starting to acquire more colonies in Africa. The defence of Canada was no longer a priority in London. Granting dominion status to Canadians seemed like recognition of the colonists' maturity and ability to govern themselves, but it also placed Canada in a precarious position when it came to relations with the Americans. In the 1840s, U.S. President James K. Polk had already talked about annexing the entire Pacific Northwest, and there was no way to know if his successors would express the same sentiment. He famously said the United States would annex Canada to a latitude of 54 degrees, 40 minutes. The annexation never happened, but Polk later inspired a British Columbia rock band to name itself 54-40.

Tensions with the United States generated anxiety among Canadian politicians, but moving from one country to the other was relatively simple. The border was lightly guarded, and workers, especially craftsmen and sailors, travelled between the Canadian colonies and the United

States with comparative ease. The solution for Canadian policy-makers to address their concerns was to find a way to coexist with the United States, try to maintain close links with Britain, quickly build Canada's industrial capacity, and work to fill the vast underpopulated nation with immigrants who were gainfully employed and contributed to national prosperity.

The collection of colonies that were initially founded in the 16th and 17th centuries grew and formed themselves, with Britain's prodding, into a dominion within the British Empire in the summer of 1867. The meaning of work in those colonies had not fundamentally changed in the two centuries prior to Confederation. Masters — employers — felt they never had enough access to labour. Work was divided by gender and whether or not it was paid or unpaid. Most people were employed in some aspect of natural resource exploitation or agriculture. The legal framework was rooted in British common law that overwhelmingly favoured masters over servants. Finally, Indigenous Peoples were gradually forced off their land and expected to conform to European ideas of social organization as more colonists arrived from abroad. It was in those circumstances that Canadians began working in their new country.

NAME	PART II Confederation to the 1930s	
DAY	TIME IN	TIME OUT
1	7 48	16 17
2	7 45	16 15
	7 4?	

12 CONFEDERATION TO 1914

Canada became a self-governing dominion in the British Empire on July 1, 1867. Canadians welcomed what they believed was a significant measure of independence, but for anglophones, the country was still British. Francophones obviously had a different view of Canada's founding and future, and the opinions of Canada's many Indigenous communities were egregiously not considered when Confederation was conceived. Britain was concerned about the possibility of conflict with the United States in the aftermath of the latter country's Civil War and also wanted to redirect resources to the defence of India. Canada would have control over domestic affairs but would not have an independent foreign policy. The British North America Act was the name of the law that conferred dominion status on the country. It contained clauses that eventually had a profound impact on work and labour in Canada, such as how provincial and federal jurisdictions were outlined. The country would have a national labour market, and so would each province and region. Laws affecting work were enacted at both the federal and provincial levels.

The years after Confederation brought about legal and public changes that shaped labour in Canada. The country's first Trade Union Act was introduced in 1872 in response to workers who had been striking to win a nine-hour workday.[1] The law made unions legal and no longer criminal conspiracies, but it did not require employers to recognize unions and bargain with them. Workers' organizations were overwhelmingly craft-based at this point in Canada's history. The first steps toward organizing workers in Canada and the United States were taken at this time following the founding of the Noble and Holy Order of the Knights of Labor (KoL) in Philadelphia in 1869.[2] The KoL was ostensibly a craft-based union, but it did organize workers in semi-skilled jobs. Whereas work prior to the first wave of industrialization had been divided between skilled craft and unskilled labour, post-Confederation Canada witnessed the rise of jobs that ranged in terms of the skills required to perform them.

A KoL lodge led the 1886 strike against the Toronto Street Railway Company, even though international union leader Terence V. Powderly generally eschewed the use of strikes to solve labour disputes. Workers could be legally militant, but they also faced sanctions, since magistrates readily used local militias and police to confront worker demonstrations. That pattern continued to the beginning of the 20th century. The KoL reflected 19th-century social practices, since it was modelled after existing fraternal organizations in the United States and Canada. At that time, there were Masonic lodges, Oddfellows and Knights of Columbus halls, and a myriad of other fraternal and civic associations. It was not unusual that labour organizations assumed similar forms, since workers often belonged to one or more fraternal societies as well as unions. Canada's first labour federation, the Trades and Labour Congress of Canada (TLC), was founded in 1883.

Major Canadian unions organized workers in railways — a new and key form of transportation in the late 19th century — and work in that sector of the economy reflected broader tensions in Canadian society. The recently independent country had a small population concentrated in the eastern provinces. The Conservative government of John A. Macdonald, Canada's first prime minister, introduced the National Policy in 1878, which featured three main objectives that were all closely related to work and labour: the erection of high tariff barriers to foster the development of domestic industry, virtually open immigration from Europe, and the construction of a transcontinental railway. Labour shortages that had continually been a problem for Canadian employers would be resolved through mass immigration, the railway would bind the country together and help ward off the threat of American annexation, and new Canadian businesses were supposed to flourish under tariff protection. Canada experienced its first wave of industrialization in the 1880s as factory production expanded in Ontario, Quebec, and the Maritimes.

The reality of post-Confederation employment policy was somewhat different than what Macdonald planned. Contemporary scholarship has revealed that Macdonald's legacy is more controversial than Canadians have generally realized. He indeed played a crucial role in Confederation and was the principal architect of the National Policy, but he also held views on Indigenous people that were racist even by 19th-century standards. The National Policy was notable for what it included and who it benefited, but also for who it did not help. Later, Clifford Sifton, Canada's federal minister of the interior from 1896 to 1905, devised a strategy to promote Canada in Europe and encourage Europeans to brave the Atlantic crossing and unknown life in a new country, but similar recruiting efforts were not made in non-white countries. Nevertheless, people still came from those places regardless of the government's official disinterest in seeing them in Canada, something particularly true of Chinese labourers. The iconic photo of Donald Alexander Smith symbolically pounding the last spike of the Canadian Pacific Railway (CPR) into the ground at Craigellachie, British Columbia, in 1885 gave Canadians the impression that the great track across the country had been exclusively built by hardy white men. Indigenous and Chinese labourers were kept out of the photo. In fact, so many Chinese labourers toiled on the line that it was nicknamed the Chinese Pacific Railway, and it was also alleged that one Chinese worker died for every mile or so of track laid.[3]

The family lives of immigrant workers varied greatly depending on their countries of origin. It was much easier for people coming from the United Kingdom or Continental Europe to migrate as families than it was for those venturing from China. Chinese men were not permitted to immigrate with their wives in the 19th century, were subject to a head tax, and were limited in where they could live and work. The practice of sojourning, meaning people coming from their home countries to work, then returning, existed in Canada, but leaving home and sailing across an ocean was often a one-way trip for many immigrants. The country also began to see distinct labour markets develop within the wider national market.

Primary resource extraction and processing continued to be a central employment activity across Canada after farming, despite the best efforts of the government to encourage the expansion of domestic industry. Logging and mining were principal activities in British Columbia, while farming in the Prairie provinces, manufacturing and resource extraction in Ontario and Quebec, and farming and fishing in the Maritimes were paramount. Families were particularly essential to farming activities. As historian Sandra Rollings-Magnusson has shown, child labour was an important part of family farms. Children helped their parents and also learned skills to enable them in turn to operate farms of their own. This also meant their childhoods were dominated by work.[4]

Resistance to non-white immigrants and workers in Canada at the turn of the 20th century could reach a point whereby immigrants were not even permitted to disembark when they arrived at the country. In 1914, the Japanese ship *Komagata Maru* arrived in Vancouver carrying Sikhs from India, which was part of the British Empire the same as Canada. White nativist sentiment in British Columbia reached a fever pitch over the unwanted arrivals, and after spending considerable time languishing on the ship in port, they were compelled to sail back across the Pacific and away from Canada. The racial barriers of British imperial citizenship were on full display. The *Komagata Maru* incident was a shameful event that further illustrated that, while Canada wanted workers, not everyone need apply. Indigenous people could not be simply sent away on ships, but while their labour was also an important part of local economies across the country, they, too, faced colour bars.[5]

The environments in which people worked in the post-Confederation years were divided by gender, race, social class, and technology. They were also often quite dangerous. Images of late-19th-century factories in Canada show dark spaces with machinery that lacked guards to protect the workers operating them. The factories were places of boilers, steam engines, and open flywheels. There were no prohibitions on hours of work after Confederation, and achieving even a 10-hour workday was a major objective for craft unions. Industrialization began to occur in Canada in the 1880s, which was later than in the United States and Britain.

John A. Macdonald's National Policy worked in one sense, since it did foster industrial growth in central Canada and a railway was built across the country. Western farmers resented the fact that they could not access cheaper American-made goods that were subject to tariffs. The settlement of the West also meant the grievous displacement of Indigenous communities. Bitterness over government policy sparked the 1885 North-West Rebellion led by Métis Louis Riel. European immigrants who arrived on the Prairies were also in for a rude surprise when they discovered the Canadian West was different than what the federal government had advertised.

Men and women did not often work in the same organizations. Married women were generally not in paid employment, but their unpaid work was a crucial part of family economies. Families were also dependent on child labour, both in cities and on farms. Childhood, as recognized in the 20th century, did not exist in the early decades of Canada's history. Working-class families could not afford to have their children in full-time education and instead needed them to earn money. The optimal situation for a working-class family was to have grown children at home who worked and contributed to overall household costs. The death of the main breadwinner meant economic catastrophe for families.

Labour militancy rose in the 1880s, and government and businesses in Canada and the United States began to talk about the "labour question," which became an issue worthy of at least some policy scrutiny. The 1886 Royal Commission on Relations of Labour and Capital brought a series of people from different walks of life to testify about their economic challenges. This type of fact-finding entity became a default choice for Canadian governments that professed interest in comprehensive study of social issues, but the findings of some commissions were taken more seriously than others. The Macdonald government swung into action and established the 1886 commission largely in response to Knights of Labor militancy. The prevailing view among the Canadian upper and middle classes was that if working-class people had problems, it was due to moral failings and lack of industriousness. Testimony before the commission revealed something much different as workers recounted how hard they toiled without making any economic headway. Working people were not suffering from a lack of virtue; they were instead not paid enough for their labour.[6]

Alcohol was often cited as a working-class moral failing. Temperance movements, meaning groups opposed to booze, were first organized in the late 1820s and were out in full force in the 1880s and into the early 20th century. Working-class life often did include alcohol, but so, too, did middle- and upper-class social life. Nonetheless, it was common for middle- and upper-class social reformers to lecture the working class about alcohol consumption. Booze production became a major economic activity in the new dominion. Indeed, William Gooderham and James Worts built a windmill on Lake Ontario in 1832, which eventually grew to become, for a time, the largest distillery complex in the world (now part of Toronto's Distillery District) and the biggest corporate taxpayer in Canada.[7]

Late 19th-century labour militancy did bring a public policy change that became beloved by all Canadians whether or not they were unionized: Labour Day. In 1894, both the Canadian and American governments designated the first Monday in September as Labour Day. That choice of date was noteworthy because the established annual holiday in Europe was May 1 — otherwise known as May Day — and celebrating on that day had pre-industrial roots. Canadian and American governments certainly did not want to adopt a date associated with political radicalism, as was the case with May Day, so a workers' holiday that was more about leisure and transitioning from summer to fall was instead selected.[8]

The term *middle class* was in use in 19th-century Canada, but the members of that socio-economic group had yet to become numerous. Being middle class in late-19th-century Canada meant working in a professional or early managerial occupation, owning a home at a time when renting was more common, and having sufficient money to afford having your children stay in school into their teenage years. Professions grew during the decades after 1867. New organizations like the Canadian Medical Association were created to establish standards and regulate who entered a given professional occupation. Canada's universities, though small in number compared to later decades, began paying more attention to the education and training of professional workers.[9]

The public policy apparatus in Canada from 1867 to 1914 was dominated by moneyed interests. A significant working-class political movement had yet to appear in Canada prior to the First World War. Workers instead supported candidates from the two main parties — Liberal and Conservative — that seemed most receptive to labour concerns. Workers, through their craft unions, exerted political power but not yet in a clearly partisan manner. The late 19th century was a period when identity in Canada was shaped by a range of influences. Political affiliation was an important aspect of how workers of all types expressed themselves, but they also revealed their interests through other collective activities.

Intellectual trends began to change in the late 19th century as Canada and other countries entered the period of modernity. That era is often associated with evolutions in art, literature, architecture, politics, science, and overall culture. Canadians first had some experience of technological acceleration in 1879 when the Toronto Industrial Exhibition debuted (later renamed the Canadian National Exhibition). People came to marvel at the technological innovations on display, and they were also surrounded by change in their daily lives. For instance, horse-drawn streetcars were first used in Toronto and Montreal in 1861. An electric version was showcased at the Toronto Industrial Exhibition in 1884, and the process of mechanizing mass human transport was under way.[10]

Social and scientific understanding of infection and disease was also markedly transformed in the second half of the 19th century. British surgeon Joseph Lister lobbied for the use of sterile environments to conduct surgery — Listerine mouthwash was named after him — and his research on cleanliness and hygiene in medicine led to dramatic improvements in mortality in hospitals. Hospitals were converted from places to be feared to organized institutions that could save lives, while medical care became more specialized, as seen with the founding of the Hospital for Sick Children in Toronto in 1875.

Historian Mariana Valverde calls the period from 1885 to 1925 "the age of light, soap, and water," since Canadians were encouraged to think more about hygiene, slum clearance, and ending prostitution, among other efforts at moral reform. The cities in which Canadians lived and worked were better planned. The problem of open sewage and human waste running through streets and rivers was notably solved by Joseph Bazalgette who designed and constructed a sewer system for central London in England. Public works projects were thereafter constructed with public health in mind.[11]

Hygiene and good health practices were also advocated in people's homes. A commonly sold 1912 book entitled *Vitalogy* (the 1990s rock band Pearl Jam named an album for it and even used the book's cover for the album image) includes advice on topics such as the benefits of discreetly sunbathing, how to use mustard to remove freckles, remedies for croup, the "management of infants," the evils of masturbation, how to close wounds, and treatments for cholera. The book also helpfully listed a compendium of herbs and compounds that could be used for home cures. Canadians and Americans no longer had to resort to clutching their religious tomes and praying for salvation from illness, they could also peruse a home medical guide like *Vitalogy* to find a cure.[12]

Canadians living in the years leading up to the turn of the 20th century were employed in new jobs that previously did not exist as new technologies emerged. Electricity revolutionized working life more than anything since perhaps the first widespread use of water power. Nonetheless, there were negative aspects to the changes occurring. The creation of electric light meant work could be performed around the clock, regardless of the impact it had on the human body. Writers like American Henry David Thoreau wrote about the beauty and impact of the natural environment in which humans lived, but the environmental impact of factories, steam engines, and the greater use of coal were not fully understood.

The institutions and belief systems that people relied on for centuries also experienced new and vigorous challenges, most notably religion. Understanding of religious faith and the place of humans on earth was forever altered with the publication of Charles Darwin's *On the Origin of Species* in 1859. The idea that humans were created by a supreme deity and directly descended from a man and woman expelled from paradise over the seemingly innocuous eating of an apple was fundamental to the Christian world view. Christianity is a monotheistic religion, meaning one god, not many, and Islam and Judaism were also founded on the same premise. Indeed, the three religions are collectively known as Abrahamic because of the role the prophet Abraham played in their religious texts. Darwin's assertion that humans were part of the animal kingdom as much as any other creature and were even descended from other primates would surely have gotten him imprisoned if not executed if he had published his book 200 years earlier. Religious belief was shaken, but churches pushed back against Darwin and other new thinkers.

Darwin's book was followed in 1867 by Karl Marx's *Das Kapital*, which critiqued and challenged the free market capitalist economic system. Marx found inspiration in the attempted European revolutions of 1848 and devoted his life to studying capitalism and the working class. Canada did not experience the rise of a major new political party in the late 19th century, since the Liberals and Conservatives dominated electoral politics, but the seeds for new movements sprouted in Europe. This notably happened in Britain with the founding of the Labour Party in 1900, which quickly started to disrupt the two-party system then in place.[13]

Late-19th-century Canadians professed religious faith, were suspicious of radical thought coming from Europe, and took pride in being part of the British Empire. As historian Ramsay Cook argues, many people tried to reaffirm their faith in traditional beliefs in response to the rise of modernity. For the purpose of this discussion, *modernity* means a break from established beliefs in religion and social order, with Darwin and Marx being dominant representatives of the dramatic intellectual shifts happening in the second half of the 19th century.[14]

Religion did directly link to work and labour issues as the 19th century came to a close and the 20th century began. The poor conditions in which the working class lived in Europe and abroad were addressed by Pope Leo XIII in the 1891 "Rerum Novarum" encyclical. "Rerum Novarum" rejected socialism but supported the right of workers to organize unions. German sociologist Max Weber wrote about the Protestant work ethic in 1905. Leo XIII undoubtedly believed there was a Catholic work ethic, and people from other faiths surely would have felt they were as industrious as any Christian.

The decades following Confederation are often popularly portrayed as a period of national accomplishment, but the expansion of Canada came with costs. It was a wrenching process for Indigenous Peoples, involved mass movement of immigrants from other countries, and resulted in social change and conflict in Canada's cities. The faith that Canadians placed in traditional social structures and beliefs was about to be further shaken by the worst conflict the world had ever seen.

13 THE FIRST WORLD WAR

Canadians originally called the war that raged from 1914 to 1918 the Great War because they hoped there would never be another one like it. Canada had control over domestic policy, but its foreign affairs were still largely governed by Britain in the pre–First World War years and Canadian volunteers fought in the Boer War in South Africa from 1899 to 1901. The country's economy was gradually becoming more closely linked to the United States, although Canadian industry benefited from access to the enormous British imperial market. The First World War began with little influence from Canada, but the nation eventually played a significant role in it. As a dominion, Canada was part of the conflict as soon as Britain declared war on Germany. Soon, the Canadian economy experienced an entirely new phenomenon as it moved toward war mobilization and virtually all industries focused on military production.

Unemployment practically vanished as government and business rapidly moved to contribute to the war effort, which in turn led to major changes in the Canadian workforce. The long-established preference for employing men in industrial jobs was disrupted as the small

Canadian military swelled to include more than 600,000 people in uniform. Volunteers initially streamed into recruiting depots eager to don uniforms and beat Germany and its allies, the Austro-Hungarian and Ottoman Empires, by Christmas 1914. The number of volunteers declined as the war continued, and conscription was introduced to meet recruiting shortfalls. Women were employed in industrial jobs previously done by men.

Wartime production appeared across Canada, but not in exactly the same manner. A nation that was economically dependent on natural resource extraction and processing became a key part of the Allied wartime logistics effort. Many Canadians still lived and worked in rural communities in 1914, with a significant percentage of the workforce engaged in agriculture. Canada supplied food and raw materials, primarily to Britain, and also produced large quantities of finished goods.

Canada did not possess a domestic arms industry prior to the First World War, but one was in place by 1918. Canadian munitions plants in Ontario and Quebec produced vast amounts of shells that were fired on the Western Front and also manufactured armaments and supplies used to equip the four divisions that comprised the Canadian Corps. A shipbuilding industry had operated in Canada before 1914, but it was focused on civilian construction — the country had a small navy prior to the onset of war — but that changed as Canadian shipyards assembled vessels to support the war effort. Canadians built ships of different types during the war, which led to the expansion of shipbuilding facilities in Atlantic Canada, British Columbia, and Quebec.

The development of industrial capacity that had begun under the National Policy during the 1870s in many ways reached full maturity during the war. In Ontario, Hamilton's steel-making capacity had been created to give the country independence from the United States, and that city and its workforce prospered during the First World War. The raw materials utilized to fabricate steel, armaments, and other supplies were mined out of the earth in British Columbia, Ontario, and Nova Scotia and transported by rail and steam to mills in Hamilton and Sydney, Nova Scotia. The term *supply chain* had yet to be coined in 1914, but that is what was initiated in wartime Canada.

Relations between Canadian business, government, and labour were at times contentious during the war years. Organized labour finally obtained a modicum of legal legitimacy during the Great War, but union leaders could not contain growing rank-and-file militancy. Businesses profited enormously from wartime contracts and an overall climate of economic prosperity. Canada was led through the war by Conservative prime minister Robert Borden, who shrewdly formed a coalition government that included the Liberal Party. The message behind the unity government was clear: if the government was unified, then the country should follow its lead. That meant government expected business and labour to co-operate for the sake of victory in Europe. There were extensive efforts to coordinate different forms of production, and business and labour were involved in those discussions.

The problem of ameliorating labour-management conflict had been addressed immediately prior to the start of the war by William Lyon Mackenzie King through the publication of his book *Industry and Humanity*. King was hired by the Rockefeller family in the United States to resolve its employment-relations problems in the aftermath of the horrendous murder of coal miners during the Ludlow Massacre in Colorado in April 1914. Striking miners and their families were killed by the state's National Guard after the latter were deployed the previous year at the request of Colorado governor Elias M. Emmons. The Rockefellers, eager to avoid another massacre and public-image disaster, hired King to implement policies and practices to make sure there would not be another Ludlow. *The Colorado Industrial Plan* published by John D. Rockefeller reflected King's ideas and much of it involved the introduction of welfare capitalism programs to smooth worker resentment and blunt any efforts at unionization. Those same practices were used by Canadian employers during the First World War, although with mixed success.[15]

Patriotism and affinity with the British Empire were emphasized throughout the war years, and Canadian workers of all types were exhorted to do their bit for victory. Canadian businessmen played a key role in that effort, with John Craig Eaton of the famed retailing family serving as a leading example. Eaton paid to equip a unit that was deployed overseas out of his own funds, and Eaton's employees who donned uniforms were assured that their jobs would be waiting for them when they returned. The reality of actually being on the front was far different than what the Canadian public was led to believe. Being in the military is often not popularly construed as work, but the First World War Canadian military was a workplace and the employment terms and conditions were terrible. The country suffered close to 60,000 war dead out of a population of just over eight million in 1914.

Film director Peter Jackson's documentary on life for the average soldier on the Western Front vividly illustrates a working environment alternating between terror and boredom. It was also a situation enveloped in mud, blood, rats, and death. Many of the working-class men who volunteered in droves to join Canada's army initially had access to food and clothing that eluded them in civilian life. Volunteers were rejected in the first years of the war for medical reasons, many of which were not readily observable, and those who were turned down for service suffered from social stigma.[16]

As time passed and the need for reinforcements grew, fewer volunteers were rejected and conscription — forcing people to serve — was introduced. The Western Front was an overwhelmingly male environment with women only found in roles such as nursing. Pay was low, physical conditions were harsh, and even those who did not suffer physical injuries still came back to Canada dealing with the psychological effects from what they had endured. Soldiers who were traumatized by combat and unable to fight were labelled cowards and could be shot by firing squads. Those Canadian veterans who returned home suffering from what would later be called post-traumatic stress disorder carried their symptoms into their homes and workplaces.

The armies engaged in combat were also joined by another unseen foe in 1918. Early that year, a strain of influenza, A/H1N1, began a deadly tour around the world. Historians now believe the geographic birthplace of the disease was in the U.S. Midwest, but it still became known as the Spanish flu because Spain was neutral during the war and was the first country to report an outbreak of it. It was an ecumenical virus that killed people regardless of the side on which they fought in the war, and it also cut a grievous swath through civilians who contracted it. A third of the world's population was infected during the 1918–20 pandemic, and up to 100 million people died from the virus. Medicine and science made great strides during the war years, but scientists and physicians were ill-prepared for the flu pandemic that killed soldiers and workers with equal alacrity. The virus eventually diminished after a year of raging across the globe, but the human wreckage it left behind became part of social conditions in the postwar years.

One of the advances medicine made in Canada related to treating diabetes, a disease that caused a person's pancreas to stop producing insulin. Attempts were made to treat it through diet, since doing so could regulate blood sugar levels, but it was still often a death sentence. Canadian physician Frederick Banting and his collaborator, John James Macleod, were the co-discoverers of insulin and its therapeutic application in the treatment of diabetes. Working with Charles Best and James Collip, Banting first administered it to a diabetic patient in 1922 and was successful. Subsequently, Banting and Macleod were awarded the Nobel Prize for Physiology or Medicine in 1923. This triumph over diabetes meant that people faced one less major death threat in the post–First World War period.[17]

The first insulin produced in Canada came from Connaught Laboratories in Toronto. Connaught was an early example of an organization comprised of highly skilled staff who made a substantial impact on public life. It was founded in 1914 to devise a vaccine for diphtheria, which was the leading cause of death for Canadian children prior to 1920. Connaught succeeded and later contributed to other public health advances.[18]

There were diseases in early 20th-century Canada that could not yet be treated with vaccines or medication. Tuberculosis (TB), often called consumption until the early 1900s, was a bacterial infection that attacked a person's lungs. Starting in 1897, a network of sanatoriums were opened across the country to house quarantined TB patients. They were kept in those institutions until they hopefully recovered and could return home. Sanatoriums were also major workplaces staffed with medical personnel. Between TB, Spanish flu, and diabetes, working and living in the early decades of the 20th century could be a dangerous prospect.[19]

14 THE 1920s: ANTI-WORKER REACTION, ECONOMIC BOOM, AND WORKPLACE CHANGE

The end of the First World War brought a finish to official hostilities, but new conflicts ensued. Canada's economy grew and prospered from 1914 to 1918, but the cost of living also increased and wages did not always meet price rises. There was widespread discontent among Canadian workers, and their grievances manifested themselves through a militant period called the Workers' Revolt. Canadians are taught in elementary school about one of the major events of that period, the 1919 Winnipeg General Strike, but not that it was part of a broader pattern of protest. Canadian women gained the right to vote during the war, but married women could also still be denied employment.

The conciliatory practices of Prime Minister Borden were quickly abandoned by business and government after the guns fell silent in France, and strikes and protests were suppressed by force. The presence of competing labour organizations in Canada complicated responses to state and government hostility. Many unions were part of the American Federation of Labor and did not adopt the same level of militancy shown by movements such as the One Big Union or the Industrial Workers of the World. The more conservatively minded unions, like those in the Trades and Labour Congress, lost large swathes of their membership in the 1920s, but the militant workers' movements were almost completely marginalized. Labour played a central role in winning the war but found itself largely defeated after the peace was agreed to.

A second wave of industrialization started in the 1920s, and eventually stalled due to the Great Depression. The Canadian economy would eventually be regarded as characterized by "branch plants," which meant there were operations established by American firms to access the market north of the 49th parallel. In the context of 1920s and 1930s Canada, U.S. companies came north to jump tariff barriers and sell goods in the British imperial market. For instance, the Ford Motor Company set up Canadian operations in 1904 in Windsor, Ontario, and supplied vehicles to British imperial markets other than the United Kingdom itself. General Motors did the same thing when it purchased the McLaughlin Motor Car Company in Oshawa, Ontario, in 1918. The new branch-plant economy became popularly associated with the automotive industry, but it also included smaller products like home appliances, with companies such as Kelvinator coming to Canada to produce and sell their wares.

There were domestic Canadian firms that thrived during the 1920s, such as steel companies, but the arrival of American companies added a new dynamic to industrial production. The importance of post–First World War heavy industry did lead to Canada becoming a predominantly urban country in the 1920s. The country was still evenly divided between urban and rural populations, but the overall trend was moving toward more people living in cities. Canadian corporations such as Massey-Harris helped automate agricultural processes and make farming less labour-intensive. Farming continued to be a family-based undertaking, but farms increasingly sold their crops to large food-processing businesses. Food production and how it literally fed Canadians was linked to a further important post–First World War development: consumer culture.

The Eaton's catalogue helped European settlers populate western Canadian territory that was formerly occupied by Indigenous Peoples, and it was also symptomatic of the further creation of an economy that provided an ever-widening range of goods and services. Virtually every medium to large Canadian city had one or more department stores, with many of them family-owned enterprises. For example, Vancouver's Wosk family operated a large store, and the Eaton family expanded physical locations across Canada. The Kingsmill family in London, Ontario, continued with a store that had been founded in the 19th century, and Montreal shoppers could take in the wares at Simons, all of which meant the role of retail clerk increased in importance but in a highly gendered manner. As historian Donica Belisle has shown, retail operations were overwhelmingly staffed by women but overseen by men. A pattern of retail wages being comparatively low and jobs non-union was established. The post–First World War expansion of the retail industry was accompanied by the creation of a leisure culture that also shaped work and labour, something that was most evident with the opening of movie theatres across the country. There was a nascent film industry in Canada in the 1920s, but many films shown across the nation came from south of the border. The films were silent and linked Canadians to American media culture.[20]

The fact that the size and nature of organizations changed after the First World War also brought differences in how they were administered. The modern Canadian civil service really began as a result of the war, and the way that businesses were run markedly changed. For the civil service, the transformation was greater than what was occurring in the private sector. The impetus for change in the civil service was simple: there was widespread evidence of cronyism and a lack of hiring and promotion based on merit. People were hired for civil service jobs due to their connections to the government in power. Prime Minister Borden threw his weight behind the idea of civil service reform, and some key modifications were made in selection processes. The practice of hiring based on merit became the guiding principle when staffing federal government departments. The public service was not unionized in the 1920s, but employees still formed representative organizations, which was courageous considering that labour militancy was being suppressed right after the war. Professional organizations grew during the 1920s, and the idea of expertise became more common in everyday discourse. For instance, employees in the federal public service founded the Professional Institute of the Public Service of Canada in 1920 to advance professionalism and advocate for better wages, pensions, and other terms of employment.

This was an era in which the public service saw the rise of the "Ottawa Men" described by historian Jack Granatstein. The creation of the modern federal bureaucracy was headed by people such as Oscar D. Skelton. Other organizations, such as the Association of Professional Engineers of Ontario (now called Professional Engineers Ontario), were started to regulate occupational standards and licensing in both the public and private sectors under the Professional Engineers Act.[21] These changes were not limited to just the professional occupations, since skilled trades work also became more regulated after the First World War. In fact, Ontario's Stationary Engineers Act, passed in 1906, was one of the earliest laws governing skilled trades work.[22]

Regulation of trades and professions brought both benefits and limitations for workers. Laws like the Operating Engineers Act were passed because new technology was being used in different commercial and industrial applications and specialized skills were required to ensure that it would not fail. Boilers and other pressure vessels had to be monitored by competent people. The same was true of the imperative to regulate and license engineers, since they were the people designing all manner of buildings and machinery and overseeing the introduction of new processes.

Canadians in the 1920s increasingly lived in a mechanized and electrified country. For instance, the electrification effort in Ontario overseen by Adam Beck beginning in 1906 came to greater fruition after the First World War. In the 1920s, automobiles were more common, particularly since they were now mass-produced for widespread purchase. All of those technological developments required new trades and professions to keep them running. The auto mechanic job is a clear example of how jobs mutated. The first people working in that position, all men, were essentially self-taught amateurs. Historian Kevin Borg revealed that the chauffer-mechanics who repaired the cars that were driven gradually had access to formalized training through apprenticeship, which grew as the auto industry expanded and vehicles became more complex.[23]

Occupational groups altered the course of the war. As shown in

Table 1, the size of Canada's workforce increased between 1911 and 1921. Agriculture continued to be the main source of employment, with other areas broadening, including manufacturing and transportation. There was a marked rise in the number of people in professional occupations. However, close to half of overall employment was concentrated in agriculture and resource extraction. Also important to note is that in the 1921 census the Canadian government only counted women working in paid occupations when it thought about work. In reality, the overwhelming majority of women were working whether or not they were paid.

TABLE 1: OCCUPATIONS OF THE GAINFULLY EMPLOYED POPULATION OF CANADA BY SEX AND NUMBER, 1911 AND 1921

Industry	1911 Male	1921 Male	1911 Female	1921 Female	1911 Total	1921 Total
Agriculture	917,848	1,023,706	15,887	17,912	933,735	1,041,618
Logging	42,901	39,808	13	7	42,914	39,815
Fishing and Trapping	34,547	29,241	265	51	34,812	29,292
Mining and Quarrying	62,706	50,860	61	203	62,767	51,063
Manufacturing	384,606	441,249	98,345	105,408	482,951	546,657
Construction	162,502	184,577	218	625	162,720	185,202
Transportation	210,692	246,947	6,852	21,145	217,544	268,092
Trade	205,857	248,548	39,441	61,891	245,298	310,439
Finance	35,403	46,180	2,746	15,121	38,149	61,301
Service Domestic	75,612	81,504	139,064	134,766	214,676	216,270
Professional	57,081	82,064	47,649	99,327	104,730	181,391
Public Administration	72,531	81,959	4,073	12,582	76,604	94,541
Recreational	2,410	6,848	432	959	2,842	7,807
Unspecified Industries	94,117	119,528	9,775	20,153	103,892	139,681
Total	2,358,813	2,683,019	364,821	490,150	2,723,634	3,173,169

Source: Statistics Canada, *The Canada Year Book, 1927/1928*, www65.statcan.gc.ca/acyb02/1927/acyb02_19270729001-eng.htm.

The way employees were supervised on the job also changed after the First World War. The idea that organizations had grown to such sufficient size that they needed a cadre of trained managers became widely accepted in the 1920s. Although it originated in the United States, what was termed the *managerial revolution* gained currency in Canada. American business historian Alfred Chandler wrote about the rise of modern companies, describing the creation of the M-form corporation in which an organizational chart shows different functional areas and the associated department names and who is in charge of each one.[24]

Concepts about how to manage people altered during the 1920s, the decade when modern management techniques became more sophisticated. Canadian universities increasingly offered undergraduate business programs. The University of Western Ontario, the University of British Columbia, and École des hautes études commerciales de Montréal were pioneers in that type of programming. Academic business and management education were meant to marry theory with the practical application of business learning. There were two leading architects of workplace organization from the late 19th century into the 1930s: Frederick Winslow Taylor and George Elton Mayo. Taylor's work preceded Mayo's, and their influence resonated well beyond the periods in which they worked.

Taylor was American and hailed from a middle-class background. His family was initially somewhat outraged that he chose to pursue a machinist's apprenticeship rather than something that was not applied, but he nonetheless began an apprenticeship that he did not finish. He worked as a foreman — the term used for *supervisor* at the time — at the Midvale Steel Works in Philadelphia. Taylor's studies of work processes at Midvale inspired him to write *The Principles of Scientific Management* in 1911. He was obsessed with maximizing time to its best use and recommended breaking down jobs into their constituent parts — a process eventually called "work rationalization" — to enhance productivity. Taylor argued that his main objective was to "secure the maximum prosperity for the employer, coupled with the maximum prosperity for each employee" and "that in the past the man has been first; in the future the system must be first."[25]

For instance, the usual practice for someone making a pair of shoes was for the craftsperson, in the case of shoemaking a cordwainer, to complete all the steps required to assemble the footwear from start to finish. Taylor's idea was to have different workers perform each stage. Aside from productivity improvements, the other underlying concept was to diminish the power of skilled tradespeople and enhance the authority of management over the work process. Workers everywhere disliked Taylorism — the name given to Taylor's management practices — but management had an affinity for it. The stopwatch was Taylor's preferred measuring tool, and it became the foundation of time-and-motion studies. Thanks to Taylor, measuring the time workers took to complete the various tasks in their daily work routines became a permanent feature of workplaces. Taylor felt he had done a great service for business and workers, but he provided a system that greatly reduced worker autonomy and strengthened managerial control.

Taylor was one of two major management theorists who influenced Canadian workplaces from the turn of the 20th century; the other was George Elton Mayo, who used his middle name rather than his first. Management theory was in its infancy at the dawn of the 20th century. French theorist Henri Fayol wrote an early and quite brief book on management based on his observations of the operation of a single business. There were also people such as Seebohm Rowntree in Britain and Mary Parker Follett in the United States who promulgated ideas about how to better manage workplaces.

Elton Mayo is a key person in the history of management thought around the world, and his lasting influence rivals Taylor's. It is virtually impossible to pick up a textbook on organizational behaviour and not see Mayo mentioned in it, largely because he helped give the world a concept later dubbed the Hawthorne effect. Nevertheless, what he did and the school of management thought he contributed to are fundamentally misunderstood.

Born in Australia, Mayo earned an undergraduate degree in psychology and philosophy from the University of Adelaide. He was searching for a mission in life when he decided to sail across the Pacific Ocean, hoping to make a name for himself in the United States, and wound his way around the country before stopping at Harvard Business School (HBS). It was fortuitous for Mayo that HBS was invited to assist with a behavioural study the Western Electric Company was conducting at its Hawthorne Works in Cicero, Illinois. The company was looking for ways to increase worker productivity and wanted the business school's research assistance. Mayo was eager to find a foothold at Harvard, and the school chose to send him to Hawthorne. The Hawthorne studies were conducted between 1927 and 1932 and have had a lasting impact on management practice.

Western Electric, as its name suggests, made electrical components. The research team altered the working environment for selected groups of employees, one of which was entirely composed of women, who worked in one room. Lighting levels were raised and lowered and schedules adjusted, yet productivity seemed to increase regardless of the variable. These experiments yielded the conclusion that the study group of women were more productive because they were receiving positive attention from management and felt special. This assumption further led to the notion that there are intrinsic rewards other than money that motivate people to be more productive, producing the Hawthorne effect.[26]

The idea that people respond favourably to incentives other than money was heartily welcomed by corporate managers throughout the United States and Canada. Mayo made his name thanks to the Hawthorne studies, ushering in the human relations school's rise to prominence. The problem was that the methodology of the studies and their underlying deductions were false, and the people conducting them knew it. The Hawthorne studies employed methods that were questionable even for the 1920s and 1930s. There was a test group — the women working together — but there was no comparable control group against which it could be measured. The women also grew tired of participation in the studies as time passed, so they were offered more money to continue. This last point is absolutely crucial because by offering more cash to women, a central conclusion of the study was undermined. Money was indeed as important as ever when it came to motivation, and non-monetary incentives were not enough to placate workers when they had concerns.

The human relations approach to management did not displace Taylorism; instead, the two became linked. Indeed, Mayo helped give a veneer of humanity to Taylorist management practices. Workers were still monitored, measured, and made to adapt themselves to work processes, while management endeavoured to make them feel good about everything. Human relations became part of two other emerging 1920s management practices: employer paternalism and welfare capitalism. Those management methods put human relations into practice. Welfare capitalism involved initiatives such as providing social clubs, cafeterias, and limited benefit plans for workers. The family that controlled the Dofasco steel company in Hamilton, Ontario, was especially adept at using forms of welfare capitalism. The Eaton family was also devoted to paternalism, which essentially involved an employer presenting itself as the benevolent and responsible parent in the workplace family, with employees occupying the role of children. Their efforts succeeded, since long-service Eaton's employees referred to themselves as Eatonians. These efforts reflected broad employer determination to avoid unionization at all costs. Canadian management tactics to keep workers in line by using the Mayo carrot and Taylor stick were often successful in the 1920s, and they mirrored practices prevalent in the United States. For instance, the Swift meat-packing company in Chicago gave workers free sausages. Other firms, such as Kodak in Rochester, New York, practised elaborate forms of welfare capitalism, including a pension plan over which the company had full control.

The so-called company town was a frequent part of workplaces across Canada, the United States, and the United Kingdom. They were communities built around specific industries and employers. Baie-Comeau, Quebec, became dependent on the pulp-and-paper industry, and more specifically on newsprint sales to the *Chicago Tribune*. Oshawa, Ontario, was closely identified with General Motors. The Rowntree confectionery firm in Britain carefully constructed a community in York around welfare capitalism, which meant attempting to act in a humane fashion toward workers, but not all employers were as overt as the Rowntree family. Welfare capitalism and employer paternalism was increasingly popular from the first decade of the 20th century to the 1920s. The important point is that ideas about managing were in vogue in the early years of the 20th century, which helps explain the rise of the human relations school of management.

Canada was unique compared to the United States and Britain, since it was not home to employers who espoused religious or idealistic management beliefs. The Cadbury and Rowntree confectionery families of Britain were Quakers, and their religious doctrine influenced their management practices. Indeed, the British food industry included several Quaker-owned businesses. In the United States, Kellogg's Corn Flakes were invented as a dietary supplement served at a sanatorium in Battle Creek, Michigan. The Kellogg brothers, who were Seventh-day Adventists, eventually competed against each other in business, but their first product was intended to promote personal health.[27]

Using health and vitality to sell products was fine with Canadian businessmen, but profit was their main motive. The Kellogg brothers were not the only people trying to change Canadian and American diets. In 1884, a Canadian named Marcellus Gilmore Edson invented what he called peanut paste, while John Harvey Kellogg created the first peanut butter in 1895.[28]

The Canadian economy performed reasonably well during the 1920s. New jobs gradually began to appear, but wage inequality expanded during the decade. Canadian business was in an advantageous position, although, as historian Don Nerbas has shown, the country's business elite felt threatened. Leftist thought was still current in Canada despite the furious business and government response during the Workers' Revolt. The Communist Party of Canada was founded in 1921, a vigorous critique of free market capitalism was in place, and business leaders preferred a return to pre–First World War social norms.[29]

Changes in the workplace were accompanied and shaped by wider trends in Canadian society. Canadian leisure culture expanded during the 1920s, since people were able to go to early films by the end of the decade, and more importantly, listen to radio broadcasts. Later, the Canadian Broadcasting Corporation (CBC) was founded in 1936 to provide a national radio network, and soon radio rivalled traditional forms of print media. Sports competition in Canada was becoming more professionalized and popular during the 1920s, even if the players were not making much money. Disposable incomes were sufficient to enable middle-class families to enjoy at least some leisure pursuits. The term *precarious* was not used to describe the job market in the 1920s, but work was often insecure. Men were still far more likely to be in the paid labour market than women. Workers overall had little legal protection in the workplace, women were usually expected to leave their jobs if they married, and the balance of power in the workplace still favoured employers. Immigrants continued to arrive in Canada in the 1920s, but immigration from Europe was still favoured while immigration from Asia was almost impossible. For example, the 1923 Chinese Immigration Act barred virtually all potential Chinese immigrants.[30]

Joining unions remained legal in the 1920s, but employers were still under no obligation to recognize or bargain with them. A significant change did occur with the issuing of the *Toronto Electric Commission v. Snider* decision in 1925 by the Judicial Committee of the Privy Council (JCPC). The JCPC was in England and was the final court of appeal for Canadians at that time. The case was related to the perennially thorny issue of federal versus provincial authority. Workers at the Toronto Electric Commission went on strike in 1923 and sought dispute resolution under the Industrial Disputes Investigation Act (IDIA), and the employer challenged the constitutionality of the IDIA on the grounds that Ontario's Trades Disputes Act should take precedence. The case wound its way through the legal system before the JCPC ruled that the IDIA did not apply in provincial jurisdiction. The federal government accordingly amended the IDIA so that its scope was limited to federal-regulated industries. *Snider* was important because it caused a majority of workers in Canada to be covered by provincial labour and employment law, with the role of the federal government circumscribed. It also put Canada into significant contrast with other countries, most notably the United States, where federal law continued to predominate in the private sector.

The political culture of the country still alternated between Conservative and Liberal governments. A Conservative administration led by Prime Minister R.B. Bennett was elected in 1930, while William

Lyon Mackenzie King was still in charge of the Liberals. Bennett soon found himself forever associated with the economic cataclysm that ended the Roaring Twenties. The two parties remained closely aligned with business interests, but the next decade brought major political changes within the context of substantial economic and social unrest.

15 THE 1930s: ECONOMIC TURMOIL AND SOCIAL UNREST

C anadians who enjoyed prosperity during the 1920s were largely unaware they were living in an economic system that was governed by little regulation and was ultimately highly unstable. The financial crash that occurred in October 1929 had been preceded by other economic downturns in the 19th century, but this one was different due to its scope, severity, and duration. The crash initially began with enormous losses on the stock market on Wall Street, and the ensuing contagion spread beyond America's borders. Public policy-makers did not know how to respond to what happened.

Most people around the world, including Canadians, did not own stocks in corporations. The idea of companies being owned by shareholders had existed since the formation of the British East India Company and later firms like the Hudson's Bay Company, and that form of business ownership had become dominant by the 1920s. Major companies like General Motors were owned by collections of shareholders who did not actually exert managerial control over the firms they owned. Instead, companies were run by cadres of professional managers who did not always have ownership stakes in the organizations that employed them. Most Canadians, if they knew anything about the stock market, were unaware of the financial house of cards in which joint-stock companies operated.

This change in the nature of corporate ownership and management drew concern from public commentators in the years prior to 1929, and the crescendo of criticism increased after the October 1929 stock market crash. Authors such as Americans Adolf A. Berle and Gardiner C. Means argued that corporate ownership and management needed to be reformed to ensure companies did not focus solely on shareholders and instead thought more widely about stakeholder capitalism. The main problem was that the financial system was in a tenuous if seemingly profitable state in 1929, and nobody was ready for what occurred. Grievous job losses were the first impact of the crash on Canadians in the aftermath of October 1929, and governments at all levels were unprepared for what transpired.

The way corporations operated also changed in the 1920s and 1930s. That evolution was clearly seen in the expansion of General Motors, which was formed through successive takeovers of independent auto companies, including Chevrolet, Oldsmobile, Buick, and Cadillac. Those firms became brands under the General Motors corporate umbrella, along with Pontiac, and they were intended to represent successively more expensive and opulent levels of car ownership, with Chevrolet as the entry-level brand and Cadillac at the top. The Ford Motor Company was supplanted by General Motors largely because of the latter's brand differentiation.

Ford founder Henry Ford once famously said that people could buy any colour of Model T they wanted as long as it was black. General Motors president Alfred P. Sloan in contrast promised a car for "every purse and purpose" and also introduced the idea of planned obsolescence. Cars were remodelled every few years to spur renewed consumer interest. The rise of General Motors drove the overall growth of automotive industry employment and also contributed to the rise of consumer culture. Wider economic concerns were on the minds of Canadian workers in the 1930s, particularly if they felt marginalized economically.[31]

The Depression gave impetus to a major political development in Canada. In 1932, a collection of urban intellectuals, labour activists, and Prairie populists met in Calgary to form a new movement called the Co-operative Commonwealth Federation (CCF). The members of the CCF had high ideals of creating a just society and codified them in the Regina Manifesto the following year at their first convention. The manifesto was a call to action against free market capitalism and opened by stating: "We aim to replace the current capitalist system with its inherent injustice and inhumanity." This was a radical objective and demonstrated that the militancy of the Workers' Revolt period persisted. The people who gathered in Regina were not revolutionaries, but they did want a clear role for government in Canada's economy and their objectives included a national labour code and public health care. The manifesto showed interest in socialism and social democracy rather than the all-encompassing state ownership and collectivization associated with communism. In subsequent years, it would sometimes prove difficult for the CCF and its successor, the New Democratic Party, to convince Canadians of the distinction between the differing ideologies.[32]

Many of the people behind the CCF and the Regina Manifesto were part of an influential group called the League for Social Reconstruction whose members included Frank Underhill, F.R. Scott, Eugene Forsey, David Lewis, Jean Palardy, and Jori Smith. Their emphasis on social and economic justice was markedly different from the more market-oriented policies of the other main parties in Canada. The CCF, first led by J.S. Woodsworth, a former church minister and member of the Social Gospel Movement, endured and grew across Canada. The country's first female federal Member of Parliament, Agnes Macphail, was initially elected in 1921 for the Progressive Party of Canada. After winning a number of elections representing that party, she briefly joined the new federal CCF but broke with it in 1934 and continued to serve as an MP with the United Farmers of Ontario and other affiliations until being defeated in 1940. She maintained a strong relationship with the CCF and by 1943 rejoined the party and won an Ontario provincial seat, which she held off and on until 1951. The fact that a new progressive political movement emerged out of the depths of the Depression did not bring immediate improvements for workers in Canada, but the new party's program eventually had a profoundly beneficial effect for all Canadians.

Canada was quite ill-prepared for an economic downturn in 1929, even as the political sands began to shift in the country. There was no national unemployment system at that time. Unemployment was still considered a result of personal moral failing, and people who lost their jobs had to apply for relief through their local municipalities. The western provinces were overwhelmingly dependent on agriculture and resource extraction in the 1920s and 1930s. The West was also the first region to acutely feel the impact of the Depression. Cities such as Winnipeg, Calgary, and Edmonton were soon overwhelmed and clamoured for relief assistance as ever-larger groups of unemployed men moved into urban areas. The western Canadian provinces were not as fiscally robust as Ontario and Quebec, and it quickly became evident that Ottawa would have to become involved in providing financial relief.[33]

Prime Minister Bennett's government recognized the severity of the unemployment problem, but instead of introducing a national system to provide unemployment support, a network of relief camps was built in Canada's North to provide work for unemployed single men. The ostensible reason for erecting the camps was to give men meaningful employment. The real reason for the relief camps was that unemployed single men were viewed as potential sources of social unrest by government and polite society. The fact that they were emblematic of bias against the working class was not recognized, nor was the fact that the government basically forced men to work in the camps if they did not want to starve. Unemployment was treated as a social ill, and the apparent solution was to remove the problem via remote camps to get it out of sight and mind. It was almost as though unemployment were a disease like tuberculosis and the work camps were sanatoriums.

Workers began leaving the camps two years after they were opened to protest the conditions they endured, and many joined what became the On to Ottawa Trek to directly challenge the government over unemployment. The people on the trek did not make it to the nation's capital. A group of 1,500 men travelled to Vancouver from northern British Columbia, then moved east to Ottawa before being stopped at Regina, where they were challenged by police. Dealing with the men on the trek was one of the final acts of Bennett's government.[34]

William Lyon Mackenzie King spent the first half of the 1930s out of power, but it may have been fortuitous for him, since Bennett's Conservatives dealt with the onset of the Depression rather than the Liberals. King returned to the prime minister's office for the third time in 1935 and displayed his usual abhorrence of social disorder and suspicion of radicalism. Canada's economy gradually improved into the late 1930s, but there were also storm clouds on the country's horizon. It was clear even by the early part of the decade that a war could break out in Europe. For King, there was also the more immediate matter of what was happening on the other side of the border with the United States.

The Bennett government had resisted implementing a comprehensive public policy response to the Depression, while the administration of Republican president Herbert Hoover largely avoided the same impulse in the United States. The situation in America markedly changed when Franklin Delano Roosevelt was elected in 1932. Roosevelt was a U.S. president, but his policies resonated beyond the borders of his own country. He initiated a series of policies collectively known as the New Deal, which included a range of public works projects such as the Tennessee Valley Authority, Social Security, and labour law reform. American historian Jefferson Cowie has argued that the New Deal was made possible due to a unique set of social, economic, and political conditions, and that view is correct.[35] Canada did not get a version of the New Deal because King initially looked aghast at what Roosevelt's policies involved. Nevertheless, free market economic principles were increasingly challenged in the 1930s.

The origins of the economic crisis have been traced to decisions made in the immediate aftermath of the First World War. The Treaty of Versailles, which imposed ruinous reparations payments on a vanquished Germany, fuelled social unrest in that country. New economic thought emerged to deal with unfettered capitalism. British economist John Maynard Keynes published *The General Theory of Employment, Interest and Money* in 1936 and the idea of Keynesian economics was born.[36] Keynes advocated for government intervention in the economy to ensure social stability, a view he had held since attending the Versailles Treaty negotiations in 1919, and while his book was published after the New Deal started, Roosevelt was doing what Keynes suggested. Mackenzie King, ever cautious, eventually had to grapple with what the American president was doing south of the 49th parallel, and commented in his famed diary that "I shudder to think what may yet come about as a consequence of it all."[37]

Canada in the 1930s was a country that did not want to be dependent on Britain for foreign policy and gained further autonomy following the First World War. The 1931 Statute of Westminster gave the dominions, including Canada, authority over all aspects of state operation unless a country chose to stay subordinate under Britain. For example, the Judicial Committee of the Privy Council remained the final court of appeal for Canadians until 1949. The strain of the war and the fundamental fact of geographic proximity gradually drew Canada away from Britain and toward the United States in the 1930s. There were few substantive border controls from Confederation to the 1930s, and Canadians could easily move to the United States to live and work.

Canadians watched American films, heard radio broadcasts from the United States, and worked for companies headquartered in cities like Detroit. Charlie Chaplin's 1936 film *Modern Times* is a commentary on the alienating aspects of factory life and the society that modern capitalism has created. American playwright Clifford Odets produced *Waiting for Lefty*, which brings to life the 1934 New York City taxi strike. The 1930s were also prime years for protest music that focused on work and labour themes in the United States. Woody Guthrie wrote the lyrics to "This Land Is Your Land" in 1940, while African-American actor-singer Paul Robeson penned and performed politically driven songs throughout the 1930s and 1940s. John Steinbeck's 1939 novel *The Grapes of Wrath* was made into a powerful film starring a young Henry Fonda, and both the book and movie illustrate the grinding poverty of migrant farm workers in California.

The film industry in Canada was small in the 1920s and 1930s, but domestic silent movies were made by people such as Ernest Shipman. Canada was also referenced in U.S. films such as the 1936 feature *Rose*

Marie starring Nelson Eddy and Jeanette MacDonald. That movie forever associated the Royal Canadian Mounted Police (RCMP) with Eddy, but his performance is at best a caricature. However, the founding of the National Film Board (NFB) in 1939 by John Grierson began the process of more Canadian films, especially documentaries, being made.

Themes relating to work and labour appeared in unlikely places in the 1930s. The famous board game Monopoly is an example of an unexpected commentary on capitalism and social class. The game was released by Parker Brothers in 1935 after being ostensibly invented by Charles Darrow. It originated in 1903 as The Landlord's Game and was created by Elizabeth "Lizzie" Magie, who wanted to show how wealth concentration occurs under capitalism. Darrow essentially stole Magie's idea and held the patent for Monopoly. The game went from being a critique of capitalism to a celebration of it, becoming a family favourite in Canada and the United States.

The close links between the two countries drew more interest from American labour organizations in the 1930s. One of the more remarkable aspects of the New Deal era was that it witnessed the rise of industrial unionism at a time of high unemployment. The militancy of the Workers' Revolt endured in the United States, and workers grew disillusioned with the existing economic order. The American Federation of Labor (AFL) operated in Canada prior to the Depression and was principally interested in organizing workers into craft unions. The AFL's leadership was less focused on organizing all workers in a given industrial workplace, or what was known as wall-to-wall unionism. In 1933, a group of new industrial unions was formed in the United States and became known as the Congress of Industrial Organizations (CIO). The CIO's leaders, personified by United Mine Workers union president John L. Lewis, were far more confrontational than the leadership of the AFL. It was only a matter of time before the CIO began organizing in Canada, and auto workers would provide the opening.

The 1930s auto industry featured low-wage jobs, dangerous working conditions, and heavy-handed management. Founded in 1935 in Detroit, the United Auto Workers (UAW) became synonymous with industrial unionism as it quickly set about organizing the major American automakers and their supplier firms. There was often violence when UAW organizers attempted to reach out to line workers, and the auto companies dispatched security staff to harass union activists. Arguably the most important strike occurred in 1936 at General Motors' assembly plant in Flint, Michigan. Workers occupied the factory to win an agreement from the company, and the Flint Sit-Down Strike entered the lexicon of American labour history.

Canadian auto workers also struggled with Detroit automakers, a conflict that climaxed at the General Motors works in Oshawa, Ontario, in 1937. The strike in Oshawa can be easily conflated with the earlier dispute in Flint. Oshawa workers did not sit down in their factory like their American counterparts, but they were still engaged in something momentous. The English-Canadian labour movement had two main umbrella organizations in the 1930s: the Trades and Labor Congress of Canada (TLC) and the All-Canadian Congress of Labour (ACCL). The former organization was aligned with the AFL, while the latter was independent. Canadian union activists wanted to bring union membership to more workers, but there was disagreement about how best to pursue that goal. The arrival of the CIO unions in Canada further complicated the debate, since the resources of unions like the UAW were welcomed but there was apprehension about American influence over Canadian workers.

The Oshawa strikers, like workers at other American branch plants owned by the Detroit automakers, joined the UAW because of the organization's ability to support their struggles. Backing from a larger union was needed because of employer hostility and also due to threats from the state. The federal government did not become involved in the Oshawa conflict, but the Ontario provincial government led by Liberal premier Mitchell Hepburn vociferously opposed the strikers and their union. Hepburn verbally sparred with Homer Martin, the UAW's president, over the union's successful recruiting in Oshawa and its plans to continue organizing 40,000 auto workers in Ontario. Hepburn's ire was surely raised higher when he saw the ACCL merge with the CIO unions in Canada to form the Canadian Congress of Labour (CCL) in 1940.[38]

The CIO unions played a critical role in expanding industrial unionism in Canada, particularly Ontario, but there was one drawback for workers. In the United States, the CIO unions enjoyed dramatic membership gains because of the passage of the National Labor Relations Act in 1935. The law was commonly known as the Wagner Act, so named for the American senator who shepherded it through the U.S. Congress, and it created a legal framework that enabled workers to engage in collective bargaining through their unions while also requiring employers to take part in the process. The Wagner Act also conferred legal protection on workers participating in union organizing and prohibited employers from interfering in their activities.

All of these events meant that the American industrial labour movement was far better organized and stronger than its Canadian counterpart. Being in an industrial union in Canada usually came to mean membership in a CIO union headquartered in the United States, and those unions did not always see much difference between Canadian and American workers. That situation was often grudgingly accepted in the 1930s, but it would emerge as a significant point of contention in later decades. On the other hand, American workers may have gotten the New Deal, but their Canadian peers benefited from the creation of the pro-worker CCF. Time would tell which development would have the most enduring legacy.

16 FROM CONFEDERATION TO GLOBAL WAR

anadian workers experienced a great transformation from the heady days of July 1867 to the coming storm of war in the summer of 1939. Laws that regulated workplaces and workers organizations were passed and altered in that 72-year period, workers demonstrated considerable militancy, and the organizations that employed them markedly changed. Management theory became more sophisticated, especially because of Frederick Winslow Taylor and Elton Mayo. Canada's post-secondary education institutions turned their attention to the teaching of business subjects. New occupations in both professional and trades classifications were developed and regulated, while other jobs disappeared due to industrial change.

Canada experienced waves of industrialization before and after Confederation, which accelerated during the First World War. The country moved away from Britain economically and politically and closer to the United States. Canadians were increasingly urban people and now often lived in communities and regions associated with one industry or employer. Social class shaped work and was influenced by it. A new consumer and leisure culture emerged in Canada, but it varied depending on class. The working class got by economically while the middle and upper classes earned enough to enjoy leisure pursuits.

Women and children occupied key roles in the Canadian economy, whether performing paid or unpaid work, but the domestic sphere continued to prove crucial to male breadwinners and the paid workplace was a highly gendered environment. Women were virtually absent from managerial jobs, and those who worked were clustered into a limited group of occupations such as teacher or nurse. In the latter case, as shown by historian Kathryn McPherson, women were thought to possess empathy that made them good at nursing, but physicians were overwhelmingly male and at the top of the medical occupational hierarchy.[39]

Canadians did not always welcome immigrants, especially if they came from non-white countries, but Canada continued to be heavily dependent on their labour. Indeed, as illustrated by historian David Goutor, organized labour was often hostile toward immigrants.[40] Canadians who rode trains across the Prairie provinces may have been blissfully ignorant of the sacrifices of Chinese labourers, but they would not have been on trains had those sacrifices not been made.

Throughout the 1930s, the nation continued to be divided by region. Francophone Canadians were not racially distinct from their fellow anglophone citizens, but they faced a degree of workplace discrimination. Much of the Quebec business community was anglophone and so was the Canadian managerial class. The 1930s were a decade when a family of quintuplet baby girls from Northern Ontario, the Dionnes, became an unfortunate public spectacle. That family would not have lived through that wrenching experience had they not been working class, nor if they had been English- rather than French-speaking.

The Maritime provinces had been economically depressed compared to central Canada since they had joined Confederation, but Newfoundland was still a British colony. Maritimers became another important source of labour, especially for Ontario, as industrialization carried on. Indeed, Maritime Canadians were part of an internal economic diaspora that would be an enduring aspect of the country's working life.

The Depression exacted a terrible toll on Canadian workers. The photographs taken by Americans Dorothea Lange and Mike Disfarmer eventually became the images linked with the Depression in popular culture. Both Lange and Disfarmer added to the photographic legacy of American sociologist and photographer Lewis Hine, who took pictures of child labourers in the early 20th century. Canadian author Morley Callaghan also wrote about the Depression's impact in his 1934 novel *Such Is My Beloved*, while W.O. Mitchell's later novel *Who Has Seen the Wind* is a commentary on Depression-era life on the Canadian Prairies. Canadians did not have many anti-hero cultural icons during the Depression on the scale of American criminals Bonnie Parker and Clyde Barrow or John Dillinger, but they still lived in a society that was on edge for a decade and knew what was going on in the United States because of popular media. However, Red Ryan, a 1930s Toronto bank robber, was one example of a Canadian anti-hero.

Canada was not yet equal to its southern neighbour when it came to labour rights or industrial progress. The rise of fascism in Europe was watched with growing anxiety during the 1930s, but people did not rush to military recruiting depots in 1939 with the same enthusiasm shown in 1914. Their country and the jobs they performed were about to again go through a sharp period of accelerated change.

NAME	PART III The Second World War to the 1960s	
DAY	TIME IN	TIME OUT
1	7 48	16 17
2	7 45	16 15
	7 42	

17 THE 1940s: ONCE MORE INTO THE BREACH

Historians once looked at the two world wars as conflicts divided by 21 years of economic and political upheaval. In fact, the Second World War was in many ways a continuation of the first. Germany was blamed for starting the First World War by the victorious Allied Powers and was forced into paying ruinous reparations payments. British politician Eric Geddes famously stated, "We shall squeeze the German lemon until the pips squeak," such were the terms that were imposed on Germany. There were people, including economist John Maynard Keynes, who warned that the Allied Powers were making a mistake at the 1919 Versailles conference that mandated peace terms, but their voices were drowned out by those who wanted to assign blame for what had happened during the preceding years of war.[1]

Canadians reacted much differently to the start of the Second World War than they had in 1914 when the previous world war began. The onset of hostilities was, in fact, greeted with quiet resignation. The rise of fascism in Europe had signalled that war again loomed on the horizon, but there were no public celebrations as Canadians learned of the country's entry into another global conflict in 1939. Canada had not rearmed prior to 1939, but it had industrial capacity that could be expanded.

The jobs Canadians performed in the 1940s were more weighted toward manufacturing and transportation than services. As Table 2 shows, there were slightly over 2.8 million people working for wages in Canada in 1941, which included almost 2.1 million men and 700,000 women. Manufacturing was a dominant sector and slightly exceeded services in terms of overall employment numbers. Many of the jobs in which people were employed would not exist for many more years. For instance, the 1941 census counted people such as newsboys, coopers, and housekeepers and matrons. There were clear divisions on how men and women worked: men were dominant in manufacturing and women in services. There were also huge disparities in wages, since an average male worker earned $993 per year while an average woman made $490.[2]

TABLE 2: EMPLOYMENT IN CANADA IN 1941

	Men	Women	Totals
Manufacturing	517,998	120,698	638,969
Services	243,229	328,380	568,609
Total All Sectors in Canada	2,117,357	699,441	2,816,798

Source: Dominion Bureau of Statistics, *Census of Canada 1941*, vol. 5, *Earnings and Employment*, Table 4.

There was grudging acceptance across Canada that the country was again at war — and some dread over what it would mean. The Canadian economy had begun to improve in 1938, with the problem of Depression-era unemployment ended almost overnight once war was actually declared. Canada's economy was again put on a war footing, manufacturing was labour-intensive, and virtually every manufacturing facility was converted to wartime production. The federal government obtained provincial agreement to introduce an unemployment insurance system with the passage of the 1940 Unemployment Insurance Act. The new law established that unemployment insurance would be funded through a combination of worker and employer contributions.

Appliance factories switched from making stoves and refrigerators to rifles and machine guns, while Canada's shipbuilding capacity was directed toward assembling warships. Agricultural production was expanded across the country, the country's vast natural resources were vital to the Allied war effort, and steel mills in Hamilton, Ontario, and Sydney, Nova Scotia, toiled around the clock to turn iron ore into steel for vehicles and ammunition.

The First World War had brought enormous technological advancement to Canada, and the second global conflict further accelerated the influence of technology on people's lives. It was a war of science as much as it was of logistics and firepower. Canadian workers were already divided by social class in the 1930s. Possessing even a high school education was a significant academic achievement for those living during the war, which was largely fought by soldiers who did not possess much education. Furthermore, the military was able to meet its recruitment objectives in the first four years of the war, but the country had to move to conscription in 1944.[3] The Canadian officer class was more often comprised of men who possessed some level of post-secondary education or who had completed high school. Young men who worked in places such as paper mills in Thorold and Merriton, Ontario, put down their tools and joined local army units like the Lincoln and Welland Regiment and deployed to Britain. Women donned uniforms in the Second World War, but they more frequently found work in traditional male jobs on the home front, with factories such as those owned by General Motors of Canada employing women on assembly lines.[4]

The role of workers in the war effort often seems underappreciated in Canadian history. There were 1.2 million Canadians in uniform from 1939 to 1945.[5] Of that total, 45,000 died in combat and 55,000 were wounded. Another 900,000 people, a third of whom were women, were employed in war work. Those are astounding numbers, considering the country only had a population of 11 million in 1939. The Canadian economy grew in often novel ways. For instance, as historian Matthew Bellamy describes, Canada's chemical industry was essentially founded in Sarnia, Ontario, with the creation of the Polymer Corporation to produce synthetic rubber. That firm was a Crown corporation, a type of organization that played an important role in the postwar decades. Prewar vehicle tires and other products were made from natural rubber, which was not easily available during the war and also not especially durable. Canada's minister of munitions, C.D. Howe, spearheaded the establishment of the Polymer Corporation to address that strategic issue.[6]

Canadian companies profited during the war, but those earnings were not necessarily shared with their workers. As in the First World War, the new conflict brought increased wages but also higher prices due to inflation. The operation of Canadian firms had changed since 1918, becoming more sophisticated as the new human relations school of management was melded with Frederick Winslow Taylor's scientific management to control workers. The war years were the period when Canadian firms adopted the organizational form that carried on into the 1950s and 1960s. Some businesses, such as Labatt and Eaton's, continued to be large and family-owned. The joint-stock company, such as the American-owned automobile company General Motors or the domestic banks, was a dominant institution in the economy. Those enterprises were run by senior executives under whom were descending layers of management down to the factory or office floor.

The federal government hoped leaders of the country's unions would ensure labour peace during the war, but workers had other ideas. The restiveness that workers had shown in the mid-1930s gave way to workplace militancy by the mid-1940s. Strikes occurred across the country, including the one in St. Catharines, Ontario, in 1941 at McKinnon Industries, which supplied wartime equipment to the Canadian military.[7] Communists had long been the most effective labour organizers in Canada, but their militancy was somewhat tempered by a desire to see fascism defeated following the Nazi invasion of the Soviet Union in 1941. The industrial unions that grew in Canada in the 1940s, such as the UAW and the United Steel Workers of America (USWA), were based in the United States. The major labour federations — such as the AFL, the CIO, and the TLC — were led by people who were generally amenable to the government's expectation of labour peace, but they could not make any lasting guarantees about worker militancy.

Prime Minister King was concerned about the prospect of social unrest during the war, but politics interfered with his inclinations. In the 1930s, to stimulate the economy and provide relief, U.S. president Franklin Roosevelt had quickly implemented a vast array of policies, part of his New Deal, that included old-age pensions and non-union employment regulations created through the Fair Labor Standards Act, as well as a huge array of federally funded building and employment initiatives such as the Public Works Administration and the Works Progress Administration/Work Projects Administration. Most importantly for U.S. unions were the rights they gained through the passage in 1935 of the National Labor Relations Act, otherwise known as the Wagner Act.

In many ways, King was the opposite of the patrician and urbane Roosevelt. Ever the champion of non-confrontational labour relations policies such as conciliation, King was not interested in considering a Canadian version of the Wagner Act, which guaranteed workers the right to form unions and engage in collective bargaining without risk of reprisal and required employers to bargain with those unions. It was a remarkable change from the days when workers faced often deadly reprisals for even contemplating unionization. However, a shift in the political environment coupled with wartime labour militancy spurred King into his own action.

The founders of the Co-operative Commonwealth Federation were motivated by idealism and a desire to change the free market capitalist system they felt harmed average citizens. Led by Tommy Douglas in Saskatchewan, the provincial version of the party enjoyed growing electoral success and formed a government in 1944. The rise of the CCF at the provincial level was vexatious for King, but an event that happened in Toronto in 1942 was even worse. In that year, a CCF candidate named Joe Noseworthy defeated federal Conservative Party leader and former prime minister Arthur Meighen in a by-election.[8] The CCF hailed this improbable victory, but it also led King to worry that the CCF could surpass his Liberal Party and win a national election. So he implemented Privy Council Order 1003 in response to labour militancy and to blunt the growing popularity of the CCF. PC 1003 extended Wagner

Act–style labour rights to Canadian workers. The spirit of the order was further codified with the passage of the Industrial Relations Disputes and Investigations Act in 1948.[9] In subsequent years, similar laws were passed by each of the provinces.

Labour historians have long debated the legacy of the introduction of a Wagner-based labour relations system in Canada, since it illustrated the influence of American labour and employment policy on Canadian workers and business. Not only were Canadians employed by American firms in branch-plant operations, they were also members of American-based unions and engaged in collective bargaining under the auspices of a legal framework informed by American legislation. Practices utilized in Britain, such as the Whitley Council model that featured workplace councils and sectoral bargaining, were only eventually implemented in the Canadian federal public service.

Unions gave up the right to strike when a collective agreement was in force as a result of PC 1003 and later legislation, and employers were prohibited from locking out workers from their places of employment. Spontaneous work stoppages were declared illegal "wildcat" strikes and anyone engaging in them could face legal sanction. The system that came after PC 1003 created a framework of laws, labour relations boards, conciliators, mediators, arbitrators, and an expanding legal sub-field filled with labour lawyers. That system established the boundaries of industrial legality, which meant union behaviours and practices that were accepted by the state.

On one hand, there is a view that the postwar labour relations system, or postwar compromise, represented a surrender by organized labour. On the other hand, unions generally embraced it because it gave them stability. The idea of striking at any moment obviously rests on the willingness of workers to form picket lines and be out of work for indeterminate amounts of time. The Wagner-based system also crucially provided mechanisms for dispute resolution, while prior to the 1940s, violent disputes happened between unions and employers with considerable frequency.

The postwar labour relations system was dominated by three key players: the state (government), capital (employers), and labour (unions), with the last acknowledged as the junior partner in the triumvirate. The nature of the labour relations process is understandably arcane to outside observers; it even confuses people who work within its boundaries. It can be compared to a baseball game whose basic rules are easily identified. A union, as one team, shows up and brings its ability to play the game along with gloves and bats. The rules of the game are established by government, and the umpire is there as the rule enforcer. An employer is the other team, but it also owns the diamond, bases, backstop, seating, concession stands, and scoreboard.

Employers maintained enormous power even after having some guardrails placed on them through labour relations law. Managers across all unionized industries spent the postwar decades bemoaning the presence of unions in their workplaces, but their objections were usually baseless. Managers could continue to run organizations as they saw fit unless they signed collective agreements with unions that placed some limitations on them.

The labour and employment laws introduced in Canada, shaped by the Wagner Act and other national and international influences, had some uniquely Canadian aspects to them. The *Snider* decision issued by the Judicial Committee of the Privy Council in 1925 already gave the provinces principal jurisdiction over labour and employment law in the country. A majority of Canadian workers fell under the purview of new employment and labour relations acts after the Second World War, but most were covered by provincial rather than federal laws. This was a major contrast with the United States where private sector workers were covered by federal laws and public sector workers by both federal and state laws. It was also a marked departure from the model found in the United Kingdom where workers were governed by national laws. The centrality of provincial labour and employment legislation continued to differentiate Canada from other major industrialized countries well into the postwar period.

The lasting impact of the new labour employment laws enacted across Canada in the 1940s should not be interpreted as a complete win for all workers. Employment standards laws were passed to provide bare minimum working conditions, but they did not cover everyone in the workforce. The same was true with labour relations acts, since they excluded a significant group of workers — anyone working in management. There had been efforts in the United States to organize front-line supervisors, most notably with the formation of the Foreman's Association of America (FAA), but the U.S. Supreme Court ruled in 1947 that the National Labor Relations Act (Wagner Act) had not given foremen the right to unionize.

The FAA was actively resisted by employers, and labour laws in Canada and the United States were subsequently crafted to ensure that managers could not organize. This meant that anyone working in a managerial or supervisory job had no protection on the job other than what was afforded by the minimums indicated in whatever employment standards act covered them. Moreover, managers were also often exempted from key employment standards provisions such as overtime pay. The overall effect of the emerging postwar labour and employment system was to make sure that a significant number of people would not be able to join unions, and those who could not would only have basic legal protections and wages.[10]

Leisure culture in the 1940s was not markedly different than it had been immediately before and during the war years. Workers of all types had access to radios, and all manner of shows and sporting events were broadcast over the nation's airwaves. The first hockey game was broadcast over radio in 1923, and in later years the voice of Foster Hewitt calling games became ubiquitous in Canadian living rooms.[11] Sports became more professionalized with the advent of mass communication and was also central to the working-class male experience. Movie cinemas were found in communities great and small, but the films that were viewed were often from the United States. The emerging popular culture was often dominated by American forms of entertainment, which would become a cause of much concern among nationalist Canadian intellectuals such as George Grant.[12]

Where Canadians lived and worked did not significantly alter between 1939 and 1949. Living in a suburb in a city like Toronto meant residing in a place like Riverdale. Cities and towns were often closely associated with specific industries and thus with the workers employed in them. Communities such as Thorold, Ontario, and Baie-Comeau, Quebec, were still synonymous with the pulp-and-paper industry, while those in northern British Columbia were dominated by the logging industry. Some cities were unexpectedly transformed in the late 1940s. The discovery of vast oil reserves at Leduc in 1947 began the inexorable process of transforming Alberta from a have-not province to one that would be an economic powerhouse.[13] That transformation led to the rise of an oil patch that would employ tens of thousands of Canadian workers in coming years. Employment patterns in other parts of Canada were still much the same as they had been in previous decades.

The Maritime provinces were still dependent on resource extraction: mining, fishing, and logging. Those provinces were also unique as they were the source of a huge internal Canadian migration. Unemployment was high in the Maritimes compared to other provinces, so the jobs available were often seasonal. The addition of Newfoundland to Confederation in 1949 expanded the country's size, but it also added another province that was economically depressed. For example, commercial fishing was governed by specific seasons and not all fishers went after the same species of sea life. As a result, Maritimers migrated across Canada, often to Ontario, in search of better economic prospects.

The 1940s were a time when the role of government changed in Canadian life. A 1942 report written in the United Kingdom by William Beveridge, officially titled *Social Insurance and Allied Services* but known as the *Beveridge Report*, recommended the creation of social welfare programs, including public pensions. A 1943 report authored in Canada by Leonard Marsh called *The Report on Social Security for Canada*, known as the *Marsh Report*, made similar recommendations. The United Kingdom would implement many of Beveridge's recommendations after 1945, but it would take Canada somewhat longer to act on Marsh's.

The Canada that emerged from the Second World War in 1945 was a much different country and workplace than it had been in 1939. Worker demographics had markedly changed: more people were members of unions, women had worked in traditionally male occupations in huge numbers, and the ranks of managerial and professional employees had increased. Consumer culture began to expand, and returning veterans eagerly pursued well-paid full-time work so that they could enjoy what their country had to offer. The next generation of Canadian workers born between 1946 and 1964 — the baby boomers — would not yet exert their full influence on society and the workplace, but change would only accelerate in the 1950s.

18 THE 1950s: FULL-TIME JOBS, CONSUMER CULTURE, AND ANOTHER ECONOMIC BOOM

C anadians may have feared a return to pre-1939 economic austerity when the Second World War ended, but they need not have
been concerned. Immigration played a role in transforming
the country, with the immediate postwar wave of immigrants coming
from Europe. The Canadian soldiers who left their working-class jobs
to fight fascism experienced life far from home for the first time, and
some of them married while overseas. Their spouses became the 48,000
war brides from the United Kingdom, Holland, Germany, and Italy who
came to live and work in Canada.[14] British immigrants were more readily
accepted into Canadian society than people from some other European
countries. There was often discrimination against European workers
based on ethnicity. For instance, as historian Franca Iacovetta has described, Italian men were often employed in dangerous and physically
demanding work.[15]

Europe was teeming with millions of people after the war who were
commonly called displaced persons. That term was the basis for the

abbreviation DP, which became a derisive epithet for East European refugees. The term *war bride* was occasionally associated with the idea that British and European women who married Canadian soldiers were somehow morally loose when, in fact, they were not.

Many refugees braved perilous journeys across the Atlantic Ocean much as preceding immigrants had done in earlier centuries. The case of one group of Latvian immigrants shows the challenges that could be faced. A ship named the *Amanda* left Gothenburg, Sweden, on July 7, 1949. It carried Latvians who had fled their homeland as the Soviet Union initially moved to reoccupy the Baltic republics. The two-masted schooner sailed south to Falmouth, England, then to the Azores to take on provisions before continuing west across the Atlantic.

The *Amanda* was only 30 metres long, and its engine failed shortly after it left the Azores. Its skipper, Jekah Andersen, was described in the press as the "only full-fledged sailor on board." The sails of the *Amanda* were shredded in an Atlantic gale while it made the crossing and it was in dire straits 644 kilometres from Canada when its call for help was heard. A rescue mission was mounted, and the U.S. Coast Guard cutter *Unimak* was dispatched to find the distressed schooner. The *Unimak* was in turn met by the RCMP cutter *French* 193 kilometres from Halifax. The *French* towed the *Amanda* into Halifax's harbour where the latter's 31 passengers were processed at the Canadian government's Pier 21 facility. The *Amanda* had been at sea for six weeks, the experience of its passengers was dramatic, and the *Halifax Mail-Star* chronicled the vessel's remarkable journey.[16]

The Liepins family from Latvia was on the *Amanda* when it was saved by the *Unimak*. The family — parents Karlis and Olga and children Gunars and Velta — welcomed a third child named Silvia while living in Sweden. Once in Canada, they settled in Southern Ontario. Karlis was an accomplished tradesperson with carpentry skills and worked as a contractor on the interiors of new homes. All three children attended university, with Gunars training as a professional engineer, while Velta and Silvia became teachers. Olga died young from cancer.

The postwar refugee experience has often been misunderstood in Canadian society. People often think that immigrants come to Canada and quickly get on with their lives, and it may be that a family like the Liepins had little difficulty prospering as they settled and the children became well-educated participants in the Canadian workforce. In fact, the wrenching aspects of the immigration experience are poorly understood. That one particular family and the other people on the *Amanda* could have encountered a far different fate if the ship's engine had failed earlier or if the *Unimak* had not met it in time.

The jobs in which Canadians were employed were different than those in the 1940s. As shown in Table 3, the workforce expanded and services were becoming a significant portion of overall employment in the country. In 1951, new jobs were listed in the Canadian census for the first time, including those related to professional careers such as mechanical engineering and electrical engineering, expanding what was covered in the census 10 years earlier. Remarkably, slightly over three million women were listed as not in the labour force in 1951 because they were "keeping house" (only 5,000 men were similarly classified), even though domestic labour was crucial to family economies.[17] A man working in 1951 earned around an average of $1,500 per year, while a woman brought home around $1,000.[18] Wages increased substantially from the early 1940s, but women's incomes still seriously lagged behind men's.

TABLE 3: EMPLOYMENT IN CANADA IN 1951

	Men	Women	Totals
Manufacturing	668,556	171,412	839,968
Services	271,743	245,039	516,782
Total All Sectors in Canada (Except Agriculture)	3,329,901	1,168,823	4,498,724

Source: Dominion Bureau of Statistics, *Census of Canada 1951*, vol. 4, *Labour Force — Occupations and Industries*, Table 5.

Canadian author Barry Broadfoot called the 1950s the "veterans' years."[19] Servicemen and women wanted a prosperous return to civilian life and came back to a confident country that yearned to move beyond total war. One of the first steps forward was unfortunately a step backward as women were displaced from the manufacturing jobs they had been performing while men were overseas. Gender roles had shifted somewhat from 1939 to 1945, and a reset to prewar norms seemed in order to men who wanted their jobs back. Where everyone would live was a second problem. As historian Doug Owram has noted, a lot of new families eagerly moved into new suburbs.[20] The Canadian government provided funding for home construction and made it far easier to obtain mortgages. Whereas prewar Canadians were more likely to rent their homes than own them, postwar citizens gradually moved to reverse that ratio. The problem of how to pay for mortgages was thus a challenge.

Full-time work became the preferred postwar norm. Canadians did not realize it at the time, but they aspired to something called the standard employment relationship (SER), which involves working 40 hours per week and receiving some paid vacation, a modicum of protection from job loss, and wages that meet or exceed the cost of living. By and large, men working in 1950s Canada achieved those aims, especially if they worked in unionized jobs. Canadian collective-bargaining agreements included provision for annual wage increases and also began to incorporate cost-of-living allowances, which meant wages would not just rise on a percentage basis but also along with increases in the consumer price index.

Canadian workers were able to enjoy access to a much more varied consumer culture than they had known in the prewar years. American historian Liz Cohen describes the postwar United States as a "consumer's republic," and Canada can be viewed in similar terms.[21] Norgate, Canada's first strip mall, began construction in 1949 in St. Laurent, Quebec, and opened the following year, but consumer spending still largely revolved around bustling downtowns and main streets featuring mixes of major department stores and smaller retailers.[22] Those companies both sold to consumers and employed them in an era when Canadian retail was dominated by domestic firms such as Eaton's, Simpsons, and Hudson's Bay.

Consumer credit did not exist in 1950s Canada. The first credit card appeared when the Diners Club offered one in the United States in 1950.[23] The Second World War generation, Depression-era hard times still on their minds, shied away from easy credit and preferred to pay cash.

The retailing sector was a shining example of the growth of service industry employment. Services assumed many forms, including health care and retail, and eventually exceeded manufacturing in the number of people they employed. There were some key aspects of service work already evident in the 1950s: it was often low paid and women were usually working in it. At this time, women were under-represented by unions and encountered ferocious resistance when they did try to unionize. As Eileen Sufrin vividly describes in her book *The Eaton Drive*, the struggle to organize Eaton's in the late 1940s and early 1950s showed retailers were one group of employers who did not tolerate unions in their stores.[24]

The employment experience of blue-collar workers became more complex in the 1950s as those in manufacturing toiled in factories carefully organized to maximize productivity and minimize worker discretion. The factory is sometimes viewed as an entity essentially created by industrialists such as Henry Ford that remained more or less the same as time passed. Canadians at the time who lived near Michigan might have had occasion to visit the Detroit Institute of Arts and see the famed frescoes of Ford's River Rouge plant painted by Mexican artist Diego Rivera and concluded that it depicted what factory work was like. In fact, as revealed by historian David E. Nye, factories were continually evolving. Brute strength was a key requirement for factory work, but workers did not surrender all of the discretion they had over the jobs. There was a constant contest between workers and management, but the managers were changing.[25]

Workers usually saw pre–Second World War management embodied through the ubiquitous foreman, who was usually promoted off the shop floor, often had about as much education as the men he supervised, and employed unsophisticated methods to control the work process. Often clad in white shirts, black ties, and sporting close-cropped hair, foremen were interested in ensuring production and were not usually worried if the working environment was rough for employees. Historian

Jeremy Milloy has documented the high level of violence in auto assembly plants in the 1960s and 1970s, and the 1950s could not be viewed as much more peaceful. The people above foremen, also virtually always men, were somewhat more sophisticated. Universities began offering a greater range of management education programs in the 1950s, and companies were eager to see such programs established and gladly enrolled their middle- and upper-level managers in them. The University of Western Ontario was an early developer of such programs and was followed by other schools, including the University of British Columbia. Management education was developed in both languages, since École des hautes études commerciales de Montréal had already been founded in the early 20th century to offer commerce education in French and expanded in the postwar years into a wider array of undergraduate and graduate offerings.[26]

The ideology that drove management started to change in the 1940s. As noted earlier, management theory existed prior to the Second World War, but it became more sophisticated and mainstream in subsequent years. The autodidact theorists of the 1920s and 1930s gave way to academically trained specialists. People such as management academic Peter Drucker began to exert outsized influence on how corporations operated. He published a book called *Concept of the Corporation* and later devised "management by objectives." *Concept of the Corporation* was based on Drucker's research on General Motors and was widely read, with people believing that its lessons could be applied across different firms and industries.[27]

Books like Drucker's became bestsellers, and management theory entered mainstream discourse. Having people such as Drucker author books about management and ensuring that they were taught in universities demonstrated that corporate executives wanted to achieve the same level of social respect as other reputable professions. Whether or not that level of public respect, or social legitimacy, was achieved is hard to confirm. Other professions such as law and medicine required defined stages of training, apprenticeship periods, and the successful completion of licensing exams. Managers did not have to complete such tasks. The term *manager* actually originates in two Latin words: *manus* (*hand*) and *agere* (*act*) and was initially associated with handling tools or horses in Italy and keeping house in France. Much like the term *boss*, which can be traced to the Dutch word for *master*, *manager* can signify a lot of different things, depending on who does the job and where.

The postwar evolution of management and the training of managers were other Cold War trends. Canadians may have thought their main contribution to the Cold War was to station the bulk of the Canadian Army in Western Europe to help repulse a feared attack by the Soviet Union, but, in fact, many other institutions in Canada and the United States were enlisted, often unwittingly, to the anti-communist cause. Harvard University's business school was a leading example, since it trained academics who later taught at Canadian universities and also successfully exported its business-case teaching method. Major American philanthropic organizations, such as the Ford Foundation, donated huge sums of money to fund the expansion of management education across North America and around the world. Business and management education helped spread the gospel of free market capitalism and kept the dreaded but imaginary communist hordes of aggression at bay.

The rise of management was part of a wider pattern of credentialization that creeped into Canadian society in the postwar years. This trend had a major impact on how Canadians worked. Having degrees, diplomas, and licences became increasingly important. Nonetheless, most workers in 1950s Canada were not exceptionally well educated, although those who completed high school or even had a couple of years of high school education were still able to get in the door of major employers. For example, the unemployment rate in 1950 was less than 3 percent, so it was a seller's market for labour. People found work through want ads in newspapers and often by word of mouth. They filled out basic paper applications in person and listed how much education they had and their previous work experience. An average worker did not usually walk into a personnel office carrying a résumé.[28]

Where people lived in the 1950s began to be much different from where they were in the 1940s and that in turn shaped how they worked. Automobile ownership expanded in the 1950s, with cars giving rise to a new type of urban dweller: the commuter. It might seem mildly amusing to contemporary eyes, but the highways constructed in 1950s Canada were considered monuments to prosperity and engineering prowess. The Queen Elizabeth Way in Southern Ontario, built largely between the 1930s and 1950s, most clearly exemplified that view. It was followed by the vast Trans-Canada Highway, officially dedicated in 1962 and completed in 1971. On a smaller but equally important scale, urban expressways were constructed such as Toronto's famed, or perhaps infamous, Gardiner Expressway, started in the mid-1950s and finished in 1966.

Consumer culture in the 1950s was markedly different from what Canadians had known during the war years. The idea of working in and studying mass media was something new, and Canadians had access to an ever-expanding popular culture that continued to be heavily influenced by the United States. Previously, they only saw depictions of work in films, if they went to the cinema, but could now see work appear in televisions shows. Humour was often part of how work was portrayed. From images from *I Love Lucy* of Lucille Ball and Vivian Vance working frantically on an assembly line in a chocolate factory to Jackie Gleason's job as a bus driver on *The Honeymooners*, depictions of working-class life beamed into Canadian and American households every week.[29] The characters in those shows did jobs that were easily identified — everyone knew someone who worked in a factory or did something like drive a bus. The way in which professional and managerial workers were portrayed was much different than how blue-collar workers appeared in popular culture. For a start, it was not always clear what managers and professionals actually did at work. People sitting in front of their televisions watching *Leave It to Beaver* or *The Adventures of Ozzie and Harriet* knew the fathers played by Hugh Beaumont and Ozzie Nelson had jobs, but it was never entirely clear what they did for a living.[30]

The images people saw of women and men at work revealed enormous power imbalances. The 1960 Billy Wilder film *The Apartment* is one such example. It features a character played by Jack Lemmon who aspires to be promoted in a corporate personnel office. His boss, played by Fred MacMurray, and three other corporate managers are interested in conducting extramarital affairs with women, and Lemmon's character lets them use his apartment as a venue for trysts. The film was marketed as a comedy but has a tragic aspect, since a woman with whom MacMurray's character has an affair, an elevator operator played by Shirley MacLaine, takes an overdose of sleeping pills and almost dies before Lemmon's character saves her. The movie is fictional, but there were surely men in positions of workplace power all over North America who would have dearly loved access to an anonymous apartment for an afternoon or evening.

There was one common aspect of how working life was portrayed in popular culture, whether or not it was about the working class: the role of women's labour. In television shows, women were either stay-at-home mothers or did low-paid work. Viewers might have thought men's work was the only real work being done in the shows they watched, but the work of women was just as evident. Domestic relations were not always shown in a positive light. People perhaps laughed when Jackie Gleason's character Ralph Kramden barked out "Bang, zoom, to the moon, Alice," to his wife, but lots of Canadian and American women would have known what he was really saying meant domestic violence. It was not unusual for women in the 1950s and early 1960s to suffer from domestic violence and then be asked, even by other women, what they had done to provoke their husbands to hit them. It was not until the 1980s that marital rape was considered a crime.[31]

Gendered differences about work appeared in other forms of media that seemed outwardly very benign, including children's books. Hungarian-American illustrator Tibor Gergely compiled a story collection called the *Great Big Book of Bedtime Stories*, which was published from 1943 to 1970. It found its way onto bookshelves in many North American homes. Work was a remarkably common theme found throughout its pages, as though it was overtly intended to socialize young readers about jobs and the need to be industrious.

This was most clearly shown in a poetic story called "Daddies" written by Janet Frank, which began by asking, "What do daddies do all day? Daddies work while children play." It went on to show men working in a variety of occupations, mostly involving physical strength or manual dexterity, with the exception of a picture of a father singing opera on-stage. There was even an image of a man teaching a primary school class, an occupation usually done by women in the 1950s. There was no mention of work performed by mommies, although the first illustration in the story showed two women with a baby pram sitting on a park bench at a playground. The message was clear: fathers performed paid work; women gave birth and looked after children. Indeed, at the time this story was published, women in Canada could be fired from their jobs when they became pregnant.[32]

The baby-boom generation, and even some members of Generation X who came after it, grew up internalizing messages like the one in the Gergely book. Similar "lessons" were conveyed in other children's media. For instance, the main characters in Warner Brothers and Disney cartoons were almost always male and often engaged in some kind of work. Women were invariably beautiful damsels in distress or evil witches. Work was a frequent theme even when it failed, as when Wile E. Coyote's incessant mail ordering from the Acme Company falls short of providing him with the means to finally catch the Road Runner. The relentless rise of television made it possible to widely transmit such images.

There was a key shift in popular culture in the 1950s. Whereas a singer like Frank Sinatra was a major celebrity in the 1940s and the airwaves were dominated by big band music, a gyrating white guitar player named Elvis Presley was the biggest performer of the 1950s. Presley played rock and roll, an amalgam of rhythm and blues, country, and other influences. He was white, but rock and roll's roots were Black. Presley was one of many new musicians with working-class origins, regardless of race. Chuck Berry, Little Richard, the Big Bopper, Buddy Holly, Ritchie Valens, Chubby Checker, Don and Phil Everly, Bill Haley, Dion, Frankie Valli, and numerous others came out of cities and towns across the United States, and their music initially horrified many radio listeners. The television medium added a new dimension to music listening, and camera operators were forced to broadcast Presley from the waist up lest the viewing public be offended by his lower-body gyrations.

Communication technology, like television, changed workers' leisure time in the 1950s and also transformed their work experiences. The Binary Automatic Computer, or BINAC, built by the Eckert-Mauchly Computer Corporation in 1949, was the first stored-program electronic computer intended for commercial use in the United States, though only one was ever built and sold. By the end of the 1950s, later developments of such machines became increasingly common in large organizations.[33] Punch-card technology had already been invented in 1890 by Herman Hollerith and put into widespread use by International Business Machines (IBM) in the early 1920s.[34] Tabulating equipment was utilized in the Second World War by Germany and the Western allies and dovetailed into the introduction of computers. This change led to new occupations. For instance, computers needed to be programmed, and one of the first programming languages was called common business-oriented language, or COBOL. After its introduction in 1959, it became ubiquitous across public and private sector organizations throughout Canada and the United States.[35]

Working and having a family in 1950s Canada presented challenges that had always bedevilled parents. For example, they were often anxious about their children playing in large groups with others, especially on beaches and in public pools, out of fear they might contract polio, a much-dreaded disease that caused muscle weakness, possible paralysis, and even death. Some children who suffered it spent their lives living in an apparatus called an iron lung, which helped them breathe. Franklin Roosevelt contracted polio as an adult in the 1920s, something the American public was largely unaware of during his long tenure as the president of the United States, though he had to use leg braces, crutches, and a wheelchair. In 1952, Jonas Salk developed the first effective polio vaccine, which became available for general use in 1955.

Canada was one of many countries that suffered the effects of the Asian flu (H2N2) pandemic of 1957–58 that led to an estimated 7,000 deaths in Canada. In the late 1950s, a German drug called thalidomide first appeared in many countries outside Canada to treat women experiencing morning sickness during pregnancy as well as for other ailments. Samples of the drug were distributed by Canadian doctors as early as 1959, with formal approval to sell it given by the federal government two years later. Thalidomide soon proved to cause birth defects, especially shortening and deformity of limbs. The drug was taken off the Canadian market in 1962 once its effects were evident even to Canada, although it had already been banned in other countries and the United States never did allow it for sale. Thalidomide was yet another example of medical perils faced by Canadian families in the 1950s and early 1960s. Polio and thalidomide also contributed to the creation of physically challenged workers who would face serious hurdles in the labour market.

A vast majority of workers did not use computers in their daily work lives; technology instead wove its way into their jobs in other ways. Large companies employed enormous typing pools in the 1950s, which were usually staffed by young women. Those women would have learned to type in the early 1950s on typewriters equipped with manual carriage returns. By the end of the decade, they may well have tapped away on the keys of one of the three models of electric typewriter introduced by IBM.[36] Service jobs performed by women, such as working in restaurants and hospitality, did not become much more technologically advanced than they were in the 1930s and 1940s. For instance, historian Dorothy Sue Cobble has shown waitressing to be an example of a postwar job done by women that was physically tiring and low paid.[37]

The jobs men performed were also altered by technology during the 1950s, and not just in large factories. Civilian automotive production ceased in Canada as soon as war began in 1939, but the vehicles produced following the war years became more sophisticated. Most cars still came with manual gearboxes and did not have power brakes or steering, but the gradual introduction of automatics and other conveniences like automotive air conditioning indicated how much more complex cars became in the 1950s. Designing, building, and repairing new vehicles required more education and training and new occupations. Other jobs predominantly done by men, such as construction, did not markedly change.

There were definite economic rewards from work in the 1950s, even if there were problems of gender discrimination. This was clearly seen in housing policy. Most Canadians lived in rented homes prior to the Second World War. Mortgages were principally offered by banks for commercial and industrial properties and not for residential homes. Large Canadian cities had prewar suburbs, but they were not built for commuting. Huge increases in postwar car ownership made it possible to commute, and cities expanded outward into new suburbs.

Federal housing policy in both Canada and the United States facilitated postwar home ownership, especially for returning veterans. Wartime or veterans' housing was built across both countries. The building of Levittown, New York, the first of many sprawling communities of veterans' housing constructed in the United States, commenced in 1947. The houses were often identical, but they represented a huge advance in socio-economic status for every family that purchased one. People no longer just worked to spend their lives paying rent; they could now spend a couple of decades paying off a mortgage, then have debt-free ownership of the roofs over their heads. A well-paid industrial job, preferably unionized, made that dream possible.

The 1950s were a period of growth and prosperity across Canada as the country moved confidently into the postwar period. One major conflict happened after the Second World War when Canada contributed troops to the Korean War, fought from 1950 to 1953, but it did not require mass mobilization on the scale of 1939 to 1945. However, the threat of nuclear war loomed in the minds of every person who knew what it meant. Canadians nonetheless looked confidently toward the 1960s, but they were in for some surprises.

19 THE 1960s: CULTURAL, POLITICAL, AND ECONOMIC CHANGE

The baby-boom generation started the decade as children and ended it by entering adulthood, and, by extension, the labour force. It was a decade when the role of women in the workforce markedly changed. The corporations that operated in the country began pursuing different business strategies, and government implemented significant policies that impacted the broader working lives of Canadians. The post-secondary education system was vastly expanded to educate the baby boomers as they left high school, and it was particularly oriented to training young people for the workplace. Management continued to become more sophisticated and organized labour was also increasingly powerful in Canadian workplaces. What it meant to be a union member in Canada would also be transformed as collective bargaining rights were extended to public sector workers and workplace technology became more advanced. The 1960s were generally good years for Canadian workers, but they also marked the beginning of the closure of a particularly prosperous period in post–Second World War history.

The jobs Canadians performed and the wages they earned changed from the early 1950s. As Table 4 illustrates, men still far exceeded women in manufacturing employment. What is most striking is that total service sector employment was outstripping jobs in manufacturing. The 1961 census did not ask anyone if they were working as computer programmers, but electronics workers were mentioned for the first time.[38] Average wages had improved since 1951, with a man earning $3,679 and a woman taking home $1,195.[39] An egregious gender difference in wages had widened since the 1950s.

TABLE 4: EMPLOYMENT IN CANADA IN 1961

	Men	Women	Totals
Manufacturing	862,417	174,525	1,036,942
Services	599,069	789,150	1,388,219
Total All Sectors in Canada	4,705,518	1,766,332	6,471,850

Source: Dominion Bureau of Statistics, *Census of Canada 1961*, vol. 4, *Earnings and Employment*, Table 4.

Industrial work in postwar Canada was often associated with the automotive industry and companies such as General Motors. The Canadian government, while generally eschewing the idea that it had an overall national industrial policy, still assiduously pursued policies that enhanced industrial expansion. Canadian business had long benefited from trade tariffs and other policies that limited foreign ownership of Canadian firms. Canadian nationalists may have looked nervously at the fact that the country had become a branch-plant economy, but the country's financial sector was overwhelmingly dominated by domestic firms, including banks, trust companies, and insurance firms. The major railways were also Canadian-owned, and the country had a robust commercial maritime sector. There were some domestic technology firms such as Northern Electric (later Northern Telecom), but people worried about the possibility of economic domination by the United States were still smarting over the February 1959 cancellation of the Avro Arrow interceptor jet by John Diefenbaker's Conservative federal government.

The Arrow program is still looked back upon wistfully by aviation enthusiasts who feel it would have transformed military aviation. The plane had a major impact on employment in Canada when it was conceived and built — and when it was terminated. Canada was part of a continental air defence alliance with the United States called the North American Air (now Aerospace) Defense Command. Both countries feared attack by Soviet bombers armed with nuclear weapons, and high-speed jets were the best early option to counter such a threat.

The A.V. Roe Company was founded in Britain, eventually purchased an existing Canadian aircraft factory, and made it a subsidiary. A.V. Roe Canada, abbreviated to Avro, built Canada's first and only jet fighter — the CF-100 Canuck — in 1946, but it was ill-suited to shoot down bombers. There were fears that the United States would dominate the aircraft market, military and civilian, so Avro resolved to develop a domestic supersonic interceptor. Earlier, in 1949, the company had also built the second commercial passenger jet — the Jetliner — which was only beaten into the air by 13 days when the British launched the Comet. The Jetliner met a fate similar to the Arrow when production on it was arbitrarily shut down in the early 1950s.

The CF-105, as the Arrow was formally designated, first flew in 1958 and had remarkable performance characteristics. It was powered by two Orenda Iroquois engines, designed in Canada, and could fly at twice the speed of sound. The problem was that it was expensive and there were no export markets for it, which were the official reasons for the Arrow program's demise. Avro had built a remarkable industrial base at its facilities in Malton, Ontario. The company employed almost 15,000 highly skilled workers who represented the nucleus of a possible Canadian aerospace industry when the Arrow program was shut down. Thousands of other workers in the supply chain for Avro outside the firm also lost employment. Furthermore, it is now widely recognized that the ending of the Avro program led to Canada's first major brain drain when many people who worked on the interceptor moved to the United States and contributed to that country's space program.[40]

The worst coda of the Arrow's abrupt discontinuation was the Canadian government's decision to purchase an American fighter — the

CF-101 Voodoo — that was not equal to the Arrow. The U.S. Bomarc missile was also purchased to shoot down bombers. It was meant to be armed with a nuclear warhead — destroying enemy planes with nukes — but Prime Minister Diefenbaker did not want such weapons on Canadian soil. So, in the meantime, sandbags were placed in the tips of the missiles in place of the usual apparatus.

The Canadian government sought to embrace the United States economically while also trying to make sure it would not get squeezed by the superpower below the 49th parallel. Historian Dimitry Anastakis revealed that this effort was quite clearly evident in a piece of negotiating legerdemain known as the Auto Pact. That agreement, concluded in 1965, guaranteed that American automakers would manufacture at least as many cars in Canada as they sold. At that time, imported cars were only thought to come from the United Kingdom and Germany. Nobody seriously thought American automakers would lose their domination of the Canadian and U.S. markets. The Auto Pact stabilized and expanded employment in the auto industry and solidified the status of cities such as Oshawa and Windsor, Ontario, as being inextricably linked to the fortunes of a single industry.[41]

In western Canada, natural resources and agriculture remained central to provincial economies, while Atlantic Canada was also still heavily dependent on fisheries and continued as a source of labour for the rest of the country, with baby boomers from the Maritimes quickly realizing by the end of the 1960s that they, too, would have to leave home to find work. Quebec became more unique within Canada at the onset of the decade with the election of the Liberal government of Jean Lesage in 1960, marking the advent of the Quiet Revolution. Prior to 1960, francophone Quebecers faced discrimination in the job market. The Canadian business community was still largely headquartered in Montreal and spoke English. Companies such as Sun Life, Royal Bank of Canada, Bell Canada, and Molson were based in Montreal. A desire for greater status in their own province was manifested by francophone workers of all types in Quebec. By the end of the 1960s, a francophone managerial class had been developed, while for workers, Quebec had separate federations for its own unions inside and outside the Canadian Labour Congress, which had been formed in 1958 as the main umbrella organization for unions in the rest of Canada.

Canadian business has historically declared that it only wants minimal government involvement in economic affairs, but in reality, government influence and resources are most welcome if business believes it will bring benefits. Business wished 1960s Canada to be an environment that improved profitability and wealth without necessarily redistributing any of it. One of the first steps was to ensure there was a sufficient supply of workers capable of contributing to the economy. The supply part of the equation was solved with the arrival of the baby boomers; the education part would be resolved through deliberate and large-scale public policy decisions. The federal and provincial governments across the country made substantial investments in post-secondary education in the 1960s. Universities in Canada in the immediate postwar period had mostly been founded in the late 19th or early 20th centuries and were largely oriented to liberal arts and professional education. Those forms of education were still thought to have merit, but it was also believed there was a dire need for vocational education.

At the time, a patchwork of vocational colleges existed in the provinces, and it was common for vocational high schools to be home to extensive night school programs specifically geared to the workplace. The operation of education systems was a provincial domain. The federal government lacked a national department of education and instead provided funding and attempted to corral the provinces into something resembling a national education strategy. There were national and provincial task forces and studies on how to address the country's perceived skills shortage that identified a new kind of institution as a solution to the problem — the community college. That type of education facility was already found across the United States and was intended to serve the needs of students in specific cities and areas.

Founding community colleges, such as Vancouver Community College, was considered a crucial socio-economic matter. Ontario opened more than a dozen community colleges between 1966 and 1970. Quebec went even further and created its version of community colleges — the Collège d'enseignement général et professionnel or CEGEP — as a distinct step after high school that either led to entry into the workforce or into university. New universities were established across Canada from the late 1950s into the 1960s, including Simon Fraser, Waterloo, York, Lethbridge, Brock, and Trent, yet they represented an expansion of an existing university system even if they were meant to educate the burgeoning teenage population. They were not oriented toward career training with the exception of professional schools such as law, medicine, and engineering.

Community colleges, regardless of the form they took, were something new for Canada, but they also represented a certain continuity in education policy because they emphasized practical skill and were specifically meant to get baby boomers ready for work. Egerton Ryerson would probably have approved of them. Community colleges, especially those in English Canada, were closely linked to the business community and crafted their programs with business needs in mind, which meant that students would acquire presumably marketable skills. Critiques of business and its role in Canadian society were not often heard in the colleges.

There were key differences between how colleges and universities were run that shaped them as educational institutions and workplaces. Universities had systems of shared governance, which meant having senates with representatives elected by the faculty who voted on policies, programs, and practices. Shared governance was far less common at community colleges, especially in Ontario. They were instead overseen by appointed boards. Community colleges were initially organized along the same lines as secondary schools, while new universities were modelled after other institutions like themselves.

There were some epic labour struggles in Canada in the 1960s, most notably the 1965 wildcat strike by postal workers. People employed in the private sector had enjoyed collective bargaining rights for over 20 years when the wildcat started, and the federal government's seeming response was to quickly pass the Public Service Staff Relations Act (PSSRA) in 1967. There is often a belief in the labour movement that the PSSRA was all about the postal strike, but the government had, in fact, been mulling the extension of collective bargaining rights to public sector workers for some time. The PSSRA granted public sector workers the right to bargain with employers, but it did not ultimately give them the exact same rights as their union brothers and sisters in the private sector. The provinces granted public sector collective bargaining rights, as well, but there were restrictions on what workers could pursue at the bargaining table and also on their ability to strike. This was largely because of the unique role of governments as employers.

Governments are able to employ people and also alter laws governing the employment relationship. For instance, postal workers gained the right to bargain with the postal service, but they also found themselves routinely legislated back to work by Parliament when they went on strike. Workers such as nurses were also prohibited from striking. Anyone working in a role considered an essential service could be sure they would face impediments to going on a picket line. The PSSRA also transformed the organizations that represented public sector workers. Unions such as the Public Service Alliance of Canada (PSAC) and the Professional Institute of the Public Service of Canada (PIPSC) had been set up as employee associations, but the PSSRA transformed them into unions.[42]

Women joined unions in increasing numbers in the late 1960s, and their entry into the workforce was due to certain key factors. Families benefited from the income of a second wage earner. More importantly, women wanted autonomy from their husbands. Unpaid domestic work was still as central to Canadian society as it had ever been, but women wanted lives beyond the house and that meant access to paid work. They encountered flagrant sexism, but they also proved to be ardent trade unionists.

The entry of women into the job market was also shaped by other social changes. The service sector, which continued to expand in the 1960s, was the leading employer of women. Services still meant different types of work — health care to retail and beyond — but women were often in lower-paid service occupations. A further landmark in the history of women and work in the 1960s occurred when a uniform divorce law was passed in Canada in 1968. That law made it easier to end marriages. CBC Television reported that people lined up at courthouses to file divorce papers as soon as the new law was passed. One woman had been waiting 38 years to start the process. Women wanted and needed jobs that paid decent wages, and many made the entirely rational decision to work at unionized companies to make it easier to free themselves of stale or even violent marriages and get on with their lives.[43]

The expansion of service work and management and professional occupations came with expectations of how people in those fields should behave on the job. Sociologist Arlie Russell Hochschild writes that the toll of emotional labour was really a problem that existed from the time the service sector became a source of employment.[44] Workers, especially women, were increasingly required to adjust their emotional responses to fit the workplace and always be pleasant. There was widespread expectation that workers should check their personal problems at the workplace door.

That notion was particularly true for people in management. Unionized workers generally viewed work as a means to an end. They could be active in union affairs such as running for leadership roles, or they could simply go home at the end of the day with the assurance their unions were looking after their best interests. Managers were more or less compelled to adapt themselves to the needs and attitudes of their firms. In 1956 in *The Organization Man*, journalist William H. Whyte noted the rise of what he called the "collectivist ethic" in companies and the expansion of corporate bureaucracy.[45] Whyte was writing from an American perspective, but Canada created its own "organization" man (and woman) as time progressed. Working in corporations, even as an executive, was also portrayed as oppressive as shown in Sloan Wilson's novel *The Man in the Gray Flannel Suit*.[46] Postwar organizations were still dominated by men, even if they felt alienated by it, and they controlled formal and informal workplace relations. As U.S. historian Julie Berebitsky has ably shown, women have long dealt with unwelcome advances from men in the office.[47]

By the early 1960s, women doing both paid and unpaid work were beginning to publicly object to their socio-economic conditions. American writer Betty Friedan published her seminal book *The Feminine Mystique* in 1963. She describes the stifling nature of suburban domestic life for women, something certainly not represented on television at the time. Friedan was at the forefront of first-wave feminism, and her book blazed a trail for women who came after her, one of whom was Gloria Steinem.[48]

Steinem began her career as a journalist and turned her investigative skills on a leading 1960s icon — *Playboy* — which mattered for many reasons, mainly because it brought softcore pornography to masses of men. Pornographic photos were taken as soon as photographic technology made it possible, meaning almost immediately after it was invented, but distribution of it was a largely underground activity. Many men devoured it when they could find it, but the production quality of porn magazines was little better than that of an average comic book. Full of grainy photos and crude, lewd cartoons, underground porn left much to a reader's imagination. *Playboy* upped pornography's clarity and attractiveness.

The magazine was founded by an outwardly reserved man, Hugh Hefner, who gradually shed his shyness along with any inhibitions he might have had early in life. *Playboy* shot into North American popular consciousness when it featured a nude photo of movie star Marilyn Monroe, the leading sex symbol of the 1950s and early 1960s. The magazine spawned a media empire, including a string of eponymous men's clubs in major cities, so Gloria Steinem resolved to find out what it meant to work in one of those clubs.

Steinem worked as a bunny in *Playboy's* club in New York City. The job involved women serving drinks, waiting tables, and conversing with customers while wearing form-fitting, sleeveless, legless, low-cut outfits with sets of bunny ears on their heads. Steinem used her work experience as the basis for a 1963 magazine article entitled "A Bunny's Tale," which chronicled the harassment and sexism women encountered on the job at the New York club. The piece did not lead to the downfall of *Playboy*, but it put a crack in the veneer of respectable fantasy cultivated by Hefner and also encouraged other women to share their workplace experiences.[49]

Personnel management grew during the 1960s, although with variability across organizations. Some companies devoted time and resources to recruiting new employees and developing comprehensive policies and techniques to keep them motivated. More commonly, senior managers viewed personnel's chief job as making sure people were paid on time. The professionalization of personnel management began in Canada when the Montreal Personnel Association was established in 1934. Its founders included Leonard Marsh, one of the creators of the Regina Manifesto, which meant its members had at least some interest in social reform. By the early 1960s, though, reformist zeal had dissipated.

The decade started with media representations of work that altered significantly by the end of the decade. The 1950s seemed quaint from the perspective of 1968, especially when it came to music. Much of the change was due to youth culture. Rock and roll was first greeted with horror by adults, but teenagers loved it. It at first conveyed coded content about sexuality, then changed as sexuality became more overt. Black artists such as Chuck Berry became popular with white audiences, but it was more often white artists who climbed the record charts.

The 1960s witnessed the rise of American counterculture, which influenced youth lifestyles in Canada. Teenagers grew long hair and took recreational drugs, all the while listening to music and watching films that perplexed their parents. Those trends reached their apogee in August 1969 when the Woodstock music festival was held in Bethel, New York. Counterculture then took a darker turn a few months later when an audience member was killed, three people died accidentally, and chaos ensued at a free concert headlined by the British band The Rolling Stones in December 1969 in Altamont, California.

Bands were marketed to sell music and their backgrounds were not usually revealed early in their careers. The Beatles were young working-class men from Liverpool, England, yet were made to look middle class. In contrast, The Rolling Stones were essentially middle class yet cultivated a tougher, more working-class demeanour. Songs from both bands, such as The Beatles' "A Day in the Life" and The Rolling Stones' "Factory Girl," touched on work and labour themes. Later, in the 1970s, The Beatles' John Lennon wrote and performed "Working Class Hero." Music also linked to the wider social and cultural turmoil happening around the world, especially in the United States.

Canadians looked on with a mix of sadness and disapproval at America's involvement in the Vietnam War. Canada was not riven by conflict over that war or because of civil-rights struggles like those in the United States. Montreal hosted Expo 67, Liberal Pierre Trudeau was elected prime minister in 1968, and the country seemed prosperous. Although 1960s counterculture still seeded the soil of social change, bosses did not want men showing up at work with long hair. The Second World War generation often only heard grating noise when 1960s bands such as The Rolling Stones or The Doors were heard on the radio. Younger workers grew up in a much more materially abundant society than their parents had experienced, and they had different expectations. They were not involved in the great union organizing drives of the 1930s and 1940s and often viewed union leaders with the same level of suspicion as they did people in any leadership role.

The 1960s brought major changes in government policy that profoundly altered working life in Canada. John Diefenbaker's Conservatives were defeated by the Liberals led by Lester Pearson in 1963. Pearson was only able to form a minority government and was supported by the New Democratic Party (NDP), which had been formed in 1961 with the support of the Canadian Labour Congress and the Co-operative Commonwealth Federation. The NDP forced the Liberals toward the political left, and two new social programs were created: the Canada Pension Plan (CPP) in 1965 and the introduction of universal health care in 1966.

CPP was meant to be a supplement to workplace pensions and public savings, but it still helped alleviate poverty among senior citizens and was guaranteed to all Canadians who worked and paid CPP premiums every pay period. Universal health care was an even greater achievement. Canadians had previously relied on health insurance provided through work or that they purchased themselves, which was the pattern in the United States. Many people had no health insurance and paid out of pocket for medical services. Universal health care eventually provided high-quality medical services to anyone who needed them, and it decoupled medical coverage from employment. Canadian workers were not tied to employers by health insurance. Insurance companies and physicians opposed universal public coverage, but good public policy ultimately prevailed. The difference between public and private health insurance had a major impact on labour relations. In Canada, wages were usually the lead collective bargaining issue, with medical and dental benefits being a secondary bargaining item. In contrast, health insurance often became the main bargaining concern in the United States.

The 1960s came to a close with the meaning of work changed from what it had been at the start of the decade. Baby boomers were entering the workplace, women were increasingly leaving domestic toil for paid jobs, and wages generally increased. A vast new education infrastructure had been put into place to educate people for jobs, and governments were actively pursuing policies to make the country more economically competitive and prosperous. The meaning of union membership changed as public sector unions acquired collective-bargaining rights. However, Canada was still an economy of economies, with central Canada concerned with manufacturing and the western and eastern provinces striving to further utilize natural resources.

20 THE 1940s TO THE 1960s: A GOLDEN ERA?

The way Canadians worked changed from 1900 to the 1930s, but it was nothing compared to what happened from the Second World War to the 1960s. Canada suffered losses during the war but still emerged relatively unscathed compared to other countries. Workers across Europe and Japan were either living in victorious or defeated countries with weakened or destroyed economies. Not so in North America, where Canadian and American workers of all types resided in nations that had boomed economically during the war years.

Canada was one of four countries along with the United States, the United Kingdom, and Australia to experience a huge demographic transformation as returning veterans married and created the baby-boom generation. Canadian business expanded, new educational institutions were established, and women began entering the workforce in significant numbers by the late 1960s. Technology shaped people's lives in entirely new ways, from the manner in which they worked to the ways they played. The 1940s to the 1960s were years when government was viewed as a positive force in people's lives. Social programs were expanded at the federal and provincial levels, and new labour and employment laws were passed.

Wage increases met or exceeded the cost of living, a shift from renting to owning homes occurred, and a bustling consumer culture was developed. Youth tastes flourished with new forms of art, music, literature, and film dominating public discourse. Immigration to Canada increased in the two decades after the war as weary Europeans left their damaged countries for a new start across the ocean, continuing a long tradition of Europeans going westward. Unions became key parts of Canada's politics and economy, although within the boundaries of what was legally permissible.

There were people for whom the postwar decades were not idyllic. Women were still confined to low-wage jobs and were usually paid less than men doing equal work. People of colour were marginalized into low-paid jobs, and Indigenous people often lived in poverty. Living well from the 1940s to the 1960s could mean attaining a middle-class lifestyle for many people, but there were other Canadians who continued to be on the edge of the economic abyss. Those two decades were transformative for Canadian workers, regardless of where they lived and what they did for a living.

People in the 1970s, and certainly the 1980s, would often look back on the 25-year period after the end of the Second World War and conclude that it was a golden era for Canadian workers. That view was true if factors like wages, benefits, education, housing, and social mobility are considered. The material circumstances of people's lives had markedly changed since the end of the war. Canadians participated in a consumer culture quite unlike what they had previously known in the prewar years. On the other hand, prosperity was experienced within the context of the Cold War and its related anxieties. Technology improved work processes, but it also further forced people to adapt to machines instead of the other way around. Work became more complex and required new skills and training to deal with it. Canadians increasingly lived in cities, and the urban environment was their overall workplace. Demographic change led to the development of transportation systems, suburbs built around automobiles, and new infrastructure programs.

There was still a clear class divide in Canada between blue- and white-collar workers, although it was possible to bridge the divide and move from one sphere to the other. The role of women in Canadian working life changed more than the position of men. Women were beginning to break free of bad marriages and stultifying domestic work and make their way in society, but they still faced barriers from governments, companies, and unions. It would take many more years before women could realistically say they had the same occupational opportunities as men. The Second World War generation that had donned uniforms, saved the world from totalitarianism, then returned to build postwar Canada gave birth to a huge new generation but unfortunately did not always understand their baby-boomer children.

Another problem revolved around who was generally portrayed as a worker in postwar Canada. Every one of the daddies in the previously mentioned Tibor Gergely storybook was white. Workers of colour made huge contributions to Canada's society and economy but were invisible to white people. A 1965 National Film Board of Canada documentary called *High Steel* reveals the lives of Kanien'keha:ka men working on the steel skeletons of buildings in Manhattan, but images of Indigenous workers in 1950s and 1960s Canada were otherwise scarce.[50]

Sociologist John Porter argues that in the mid-1960s Canada was stratified by social class and that occupations played a key role in that process.[51] Being on the lower end of the class structure could be difficult. James Lorimer and Myfanwy Phillips have written about their experience of living on a working-class Toronto street in the late 1960s and describe people who faced difficult socio-economic challenges.[52] A 1967 National Film Board of Canada documentary called *The Things I Cannot Change* also exposes what it means for a family to not be part of the prosperity supposedly existing in postwar Canada.[53] That film profiles the Bailey family of Montreal and shows people living in hard poverty. The documentary was critiqued for some of the images it included, such as the father of the family being beaten in a fight without the camera crew trying to intervene.

Books such as Porter's and Lorimer and Phillips's, along with films like *The Things I Cannot Change*, expose the problems with regarding the two decades after the Second World War as a golden age for all Canadians. Considerable poverty remained in Canada, with many people barely hanging on economically. The poor and working class continued to be studied as a social problem, and the idea of them failing because of a lack of moral fibre was often as prevalent as it had been in the 19th century.

Wages clearly increased between 1941 and 1961, and the country's workforce dramatically expanded. It was still not necessarily a golden era for everyone unless they had access to decent work. Canada's economy was far stronger at the end of the 1960s than it had been at the start of the Second World War. The country became much more industrialized, although many of the manufacturing firms in Canada had American owners. American influence loomed large in Canadian workplaces as business and management practices easily crossed the border. Natural resources continued to be important to Canada's economic growth. New labour and employment laws were enacted, but they often provided minimum rather than maximum benefits for workers.

Canadian workers ended the 1960s with mixed feelings of hope and trepidation. The country had a young, charismatic prime minister and the economy was robust. Public sector workers gained the right to unionize and bargain collectively. Workers had access to public pensions and health care, enjoyed wage increases that met or exceeded the cost of inflation, especially if they were unionized. There was justified social unrest in Quebec, America was fighting a losing war in Vietnam, and the Cold War brought the spectre of nuclear holocaust. Things would get even more interesting as the country moved into the 1970s.

| NAME | PART IV **The Tumultuous** | |
| | **1970s and 1980s** | |
DAY	TIME IN	TIME OUT
1	7 48	16 17
2	7 45	16 15
	7 4	

21 TWO DECADES OF TRANSFORMATION: THE GOOD AND THE BAD

From the late 1940s to the end of the 1960s, times were generally good for Canadian workers, but the 1970s and 1980s were a marked departure for many reasons. The baby-boom generation entered the workforce in significant numbers, including many more women, and postwar economic prosperity began to decline. Technological change altered work from the 1940s to the 1960s, but few alarms were raised about what it might do to jobs. Attitudes toward technology shifted in the 1970s as the predictions of society's future morphed from utopian to dystopian. Portrayals of work in popular culture — movies, television, music, and books — were different in the 1970s and 1980s than they had been in the previous three decades. It was not quite a return to the pessimism of the 1930s, but popular sentiment about work revealed more anxiety than had been seen in years.

Public policy was transformed after 1970 when it came to labour and employment issues. Canadian governments were more concerned with controlling inflation than job creation and demonstrated a greater propensity to side with employers than with workers. The underlying ideology of government became harder in the 1970s. Whereas Keynesian economic policy shaped the 1950s and 1960s, the 1970s and 1980s brought neo-liberal economic thought into mainstream policy-making. Government was viewed as playing a positive role in people's lives during the Second World War and after the conflict ended, but the role of government in public life came under attack in the 1970s and those critiques intensified in the 1980s. Many ideas about problems with government originated in the United States and Britain. Ronald Reagan famously claimed that "the nine most terrifying words in the English language are: *I'm from the government, and I'm here to help.*" That was a sentiment that became widely shared. The term *privatization* was coined in Britain while Margaret Thatcher was that country's prime minister.

The organizations that employed Canadians markedly changed in the 1970s and 1980s. Canadian business continued to be closely linked to the United States, and even closer economic links were forged by the end of the 1980s. Corporations became more focused on short-term economic gains such as quarterly increases in stock prices, and management compensation was also adjusted as corporate executives received stock options and other incentives to pursue immediate increases in profits.

Training and education programs to prepare people for the job market were yet another aspect of work and employment that adapted in the 1970s and 1980s. Community college programs continued to expand in both decades in response to the latest developments in the job market, while new occupations appeared — especially anything related to computers — along with the training programs created for them. University management education gradually lost its connection to the liberal arts and became dominated by quantitative analysis. Traditional skilled trades jobs such as electrician, plumber, and auto mechanic were still key parts of the job market, but they were soon accompanied by new occupations.

Existing professional organizations evolved during the 1970s and 1980s and were joined by new groups representing emerging occupations. The voice of business grew more prominent in popular discourse. Groups such as the Canadian Federation of Independent Business and the

Business Council on National Issues were routinely mentioned in popular media. At the same time, the influence of groups on the left, like organized labour, waned. Canadians had access to more news media messages by the end of the 1980s than in past decades, but the message was generally pro-business, since media were usually money-making operations.

Canadian newspapers once had reporters who specialized in labour issues, but they were mostly gone from newsrooms by the end of the 1980s, though business sections proliferated. The CBC was publicly owned and operated regional and national television and radio programs, but virtually all other media in Canada was in private hands. There was policy debate in the press, but it was less about critiquing business than the types of economic policies that government should pursue. For example, the *Globe and Mail* ardently advocated for free trade in the late 1980s, while the *Toronto Star* was more suspicious of it.

The transformations in unionization that began with the introduction of PC 1003 in 1943 continued to reverberate in the 1970s and 1980s. The impact of the Public Service Staff Relations Act became fully evident within 10 years of its passage as public service union membership mushroomed vastly while private sector membership slowed and eventually stalled. This modified the overall objectives of the wider labour movement as public sector unions exhibited growing interest in social issues such as education policy, minimum wages, and pay equity, while industrial unions, and those in construction, often hewed more closely to a focus on making economic gains for their members through collective bargaining. The postwar labour relations system that originated with PC 1003 began to come apart in the 1970s, with the situation worsening in the 1980s.

Changes in work and employment shaped wider socio-economic trends in Canada from the start of the 1970s to the end of the 1980s. Whereas the nuclear family model that featured two married heterosexual parents with two or more children was the accepted social norm in the 1950s and 1960s, there were more single-parent families from the 1970s onward. The increase in the divorce rate that began in the late 1960s carried on in the next two decades as more women sought escape from bad marriages and entered the workforce. The value of overall family incomes declined in the 1970s, so women also entered the workforce to make up for the relative decline in the value of their husband's wages. Children born in single-parent or dual-income families often found themselves coming home from school to empty houses, thus becoming latchkey kids.

The greater influx of women into the workforce did not lead to quick improvements in gender equity. It continued to be common to find entire workplaces full of women workers with management that was overwhelmingly male. Women earned less money than men while working in the same jobs. The idea persisted that men were out winning the bread while women just earned extra cash to supplement family incomes. Women workers, beginning with those who were activists in unions, made it clear they would fight for equal pay. It was also quite clear that women were as capable of setting up picket lines as men were, indeed, even more so in one famous strike in Huron Park, Ontario, in the late 1970s.

The baby-boom generation had moved into the labour market, but another important demographic shift was under way as members of Generation X started being born in the late 1960s and early 1970s. They, in turn, began entering post-secondary education and the workforce by the mid-1980s. Generation X workers eventually found themselves chafing at the dominance of the baby boomers, but would also have their own societal impact. While the baby boomers entered the workforce when computers were still mainframes and electric typewriters were ubiquitous in offices, Generation X workers arrived in jobs that were quickly being computerized.

The messages Canadians received about work and labour through news media shaped public perceptions of what it meant to be an employee, but other popular media outlets such as television, film, and music had a more profound impact. The depictions of seemingly domestic life that were prominent in 1950s and 1960s television programs and movies gave way to more realistic portrayals in the 1970s. Many of the attitudes Canadians received came from American sources. Archie Bunker in *All in the Family* might have been a blue-collar worker from Queens, New York, but Canadians still often saw someone they knew in Carroll O'Connor's portrayal of his character.

Canadian women joined their American counterparts in watching a young working woman portrayed by Mary Tyler Moore in her eponymous television comedy. *The Mary Tyler Moore Show* was a departure from previous depictions of women in the workplace because it presented the lead character functioning well without relying on a man. She often spars with her boss, played by Ed Asner, and routinely solves problems that confront her co-workers.

The period from 1970 to 1989 also witnessed Canada go through periods of heightened tension during the Cold War to that long conflict's ending with the fall of the Berlin Wall. It was a time of enormous change for Canadian workers, the organizations that employed them, and the governments that sought to regulate the labour market. The entire complexity of what occurred was further accentuated by socio-economic trends that both affected employment and were influenced by it. In time, Canadians would look back at the years prior to 1970 and see them as somewhat dull compared to the years that followed them.

22 THE 1970s: GOODBYE TO THE 1960s

In Canadian history, 1970 was a difficult year. The wave of enthusiasm that returned the federal Liberal Party to power in 1968, dubbed "Trudeaumania," began to sour by 1970. The Canadian economy was still churning out new jobs, and possessing a high school diploma was usually sufficient qualification for someone to find a job that paid decent wages, but the political situation was considerably different as tensions emerged that worsened as the decade unfolded.

The country faced a serious political crisis in the fall of 1970. A terrorist organization called the Front de libération du Québec (FLQ) kidnapped British trade commissioner to Canada James Cross and Quebec deputy premier and minister of labour Pierre Laporte. Cross was eventually released by his captors, but Laporte was murdered. The Quebec provincial government, led by Liberal Robert Bourassa, was paralyzed, and Prime Minister Trudeau responded by implementing the War Measures Act, which essentially meant martial law. The events of autumn 1970 became known as the October Crisis. The Canadian military was deployed in Quebec, but the crisis was also used as a pretext to investigate and detain other people across the country who were considered suspicious. The Royal Canadian Mounted Police were very active during October 1970.

There are several reasons why the October Crisis helped to influence Canada's economy as well as the nation's work and labour. The FLQ wanted Quebec independence and that cause grew stronger even though the FLQ itself disappeared. In the past, if English Canadians thought about Quebec at all, they likely did so as a province with a strong hockey team — the Montreal Canadiens. Francophones were not thought to be equal to their anglophone peers, and people across the country did not dwell on what happened in La Belle Province. The October Crisis changed perceptions and focused Canada's attention on Quebec.

The political climate in Quebec underwent a seismic shock when the separatist Parti Québécois (PQ) won the 1976 provincial election. Anglophone Quebecers were already worried about the province's future in the aftermath of the FLQ crisis. Montreal had been founded by French colonists, but it was still largely an anglophone city in the early 1970s.

The 1976 Quebec election and rising sovereigntist sentiment had a considerable impact on business in the province. Leading firms, including Sun Life and the Royal Bank of Canada, transferred their corporate head offices to Toronto. Whereas Montreal had long been viewed as the home of corporate Canada, Toronto began assuming that mantle, a process that continued into the 1980s. Quebec still remained the home of major francophone-owned companies such as Bombardier and Desjardins, while foreign firms such as Rolls-Royce maintained operations in the province. The idea that corporate Canada felt compelled to move to Ontario was a major shift in corporate policy.

Government labour and employment policy was transformed in substantial ways beginning in the mid-1970s. The short period from 1970 to 1973 was not a significant departure from the late 1960s in economic terms. The political situation altered in 1972 as the Trudeau Liberals won two more seats than the Conservatives to form a minority government with NDP support. It was a remarkable fall from political grace, considering the excitement that had surrounded the Liberal victory in 1968. The Liberals did come back to win another majority in 1974 but within the context of a grave economic crisis.

The expansion of the global oil industry that started with the ramping up of production in the Middle East's reserves in the late 1940s and 1950s literally fuelled economic recovery and growth in Western Europe, North America, and Asia. American and European companies such as Exxon, Shell, and British Petroleum dominated the oil business and usually prevailed in negotiations with Middle Eastern governments, since the firms were supported by the governments in their home countries. Countries that tried to defy the major oil companies usually found themselves receiving unwanted attention from the United States or Britain. This fact was most clearly seen in 1953 when American and British intelligence services initiated a coup in Iran against a government led by Mohammad Mosaddegh, who dared to prioritize his country's interests by nationalizing its oil industry.

The principal oil-producing countries created the Organization of the Petroleum Exporting Countries (OPEC) in 1960 in an effort to set global prices for the commodity. In 1973, OPEC announced an embargo against countries perceived as supporting Israel. The 1973 Arab-Israeli war was the ostensible reason for the embargo, but Arab countries in particular were interested in changing the balance of power in the oil industry. They largely succeeded, but the embargo had a major impact on the economies of Western nations. Canada had its own thriving oil and gas industry, but eastern Canada still imported Middle Eastern oil. Canadians who were used to purchasing relatively cheap gasoline and other petroleum products were subjected to price sticker shock in 1973.

The 1973 OPEC oil embargo essentially brought the post–Second World War economic boom to a halt. Unemployment rose across Canada, inflation soared, and government policy toward workers became more punitive. The postwar economic boom had largely confined the Great Depression to the past, and public policy-makers, the business community, and organized labour were poorly prepared for the 1970s economic slowdown. The first two groups became harsher toward the last one.

The Trudeau Liberals campaigned against wage-and-price controls during the 1973 election, then promptly introduced the policy once safely re-elected with a majority. The business community responded to the different economic environment by working to limit wages and pushing unions to accept concessions such as the elimination of collective agreement clauses that benefited workers but were considered costly for companies. For instance, unions had successfully negotiated the inclusion of cost-of-living allowance (COLA) clauses in collective agreements by the end of the 1960s. COLA clauses were based on increases in the consumer price index and provided wage boosts beyond annual percentage hourly raises that were also part of collective agreements.

Unionized workers could earn greater wage increases through COLA clauses than they did from regular percentage house raises. For instance, a manufacturing worker in the 1960s could have been covered by a collective agreement that provided 3 percent hikes every year over three years. A COLA clause could provide another 1 or 2 percent or more per year on top of that 3 percent increase depending on the annual consumer price index hike. COLA clauses enabled workers to earn raises that met or exceeded the cost of living even more than annual wage increases, which explains why companies were determined to eliminate them in the 1970s.

Strikes had occurred in Canada during the 1950s and 1960s, but there was a significant strike wave in the 1970s. Unions were determined to hold on to the gains they had made in the first two decades after the Second World War but doing so proved difficult. Canadian unions responded to wage-and-price controls by mounting a national day of protest on October 14, 1976. That event was the closest Canada has ever come to a national general strike. The struggle to hold on to postwar bargaining gains was also fought at the local level.

Immigration markedly changed in the 1970s. The Trudeau Liberals announced in 1971 that multiculturalism was official government policy based on the recommendations of the Royal Commission on Bilingualism and Biculturalism. The 1976 Immigration Act was designed to align with Canada's public policy goals, including economics, and the number of immigrants from Europe declined while arrivals from other regions of the world increased. That profound shift inevitably resulted in changes in Canada's workforce. The adoption of official bilingualism at the federal level also meant that being proficient in French and English was a definite asset when seeking employment in the public sector.

In the summer of 1977, a UAW local in Huron Park, Ontario, went on strike at a medium-sized auto parts plant called Fleck Industries. The strike drew national attention because a majority of the strikers were women. There were some men who initially went on strike, but they eventually crossed the picket line while the women remained. The company owner, James Fleck, was so determined to break the strike that he appealed for police assistance to maintain order on the picket line. At one point, there were more Ontario Provincial Police officers in Huron Park than there were strikers on the picket line.

The advent of stagflation — meaning high inflation and overall flat economic growth — in the 1970s further accentuated economic trends that had been brewing since the 1960s. Corporate management began to abandon a stakeholder model of governance by the late 1960s. A stakeholder model involved thinking about the role of employees, communities, and the wider society when making business decisions and not simply considering the interests of corporate shareholders. That decision was originally made because profits were not as great as they had been starting in the late 1940s, so shorter-term gains became a more pressing objective than taking a longer-term view of a company's future. Management and labour also faced 1970s headwinds beyond their ability to counter.

Canadian and American postwar prosperity was largely predicated on the reality that Canada and the United States had emerged from the Second World War in comparatively good economic health. Japan and much of Western Europe had been levelled between 1939 and 1945 and were not in a position to challenge North American economic strength until the 1960s. The United States was still the world's titan in virtually all respects, and Canada benefited enormously from close economic links to it, but the Western Europeans and Japanese were making impressive economic and technological strides by the 1970s. That fact was particularly true of West Germany and Japan, both of which had seen most of their infrastructure and industrial capacity destroyed by 1945.

There was little that labour and management in North America could do to prevent competitor nations from regaining economic strength. The United States was the architect of the postwar global economic system, including the monetary structure created through the Bretton Woods agreement concluded in 1944. The progenitor of the European Union was founded in 1958 when Belgium, the Netherlands, and Luxembourg signed the Benelux Treaty, which was followed later by the European Economic Area and the European Community.

Some free trade was pursued in the 1970s, although not with the same vigour with which it would be implemented in later years. The Western European trading bloc was often cited as an example of successful tariff elimination. Canada continued to reap rewards from close economic ties to the United States. Tens of thousands of well-paid industrial jobs depended on the auto industry, and all the auto assembly facilities in Canada were operated by American manufacturers. The 1965 Auto Pact continued to bring benefits to Canadian communities.

The term *globalization* — coined by Harvard Business School professor Theodore Levitt in 1983 — described a process that was still not widespread, but its roots were beginning to form. Manufacturing jobs were gradually lost to lower-cost countries such as Mexico, and imports from Asia similarly escalated. Successive Mexican governments began to actively court Canadian and American businesses to relocate to enterprise zones known as maquilas. A plant in a maquila zone operated on a largely tax- and duty-free basis. Mexican labour and employment laws were not nearly as rigorous as those in the United States and Canada, and Mexican wages were much lower than in the other two countries. The benefits of locating in Mexico were also extolled to European companies. Volkswagen was one of them, and it commenced assembling cars in Mexico in 1967 and expanded production in the 1970s.[1]

The fact that the world was still divided between Western- and Soviet-dominated spheres in the 1970s limited the reach of free market capital. There were some worries among public policy-makers about the permanent loss of manufacturing jobs in the 1970s, but Canada appeared to be faring well in comparison to the United States. Nevertheless, the fact that much of the country's economy was dominated by American branch plants was a topic that bothered some Canadians, though there were a few major Canadian manufacturing firms such as Northern Telecom (telephones and telecommunications), Bombardier (recreational and transportation equipment), Stelco (steel), and Dofasco (steel).

Companies that provided services of different types, and the accompanying jobs, were becoming more important. Canada's banks, trust companies, and insurance firms were few in number compared to other countries, but they were large and employed tens of thousands of people. Health care grew in economic importance during the 1970s after the creation of universal public health insurance. Education services of different types became more significant as the full impact of the establishment of community colleges became apparent, along with the expansion of universities.

Major Canadian cities continued to be associated with specific industries as they had been in preceding decades. Hamilton was known for steel, Windsor and Oshawa for automotive, Calgary and Edmonton for oil and gas, and Vancouver, Toronto, and Montreal for a variety of industries. It is important to note that it was common for large Canadian cities to have major manufacturing sectors in the 1970s. Everyday items like clothing, toys, and household appliances were stamped "Made in Canada" and were easily found on store shelves. Furthermore, Canadian department store chains such as The Bay, Eaton's, and Zellers sold those products and were major employers.

The way Canadian firms were run shifted in the 1970s. Western European management practices were different from those employed in the United States and Canada. Laws that mandated works councils, a form of worker representation, were customary in countries like Germany even if workers were not formally unionized. In contrast, unionization was the only method of gaining a voice at work for Americans and Canadians. U.S. employers often showed extraordinary hostility toward any form of worker representation, and labour law in Canada and the United States largely prohibited non-union representation schemes, since they were considered a form of company union.

Japanese business adopted new management methods devised by American statistician and engineer W. Edwards Deming that led to marked increases in product quality. Japanese workers were members of unions, but it was a type of enterprise unionism, which led to organizations more like the company unions banned by most labour laws in Canada and the United States. The reputations of Japanese businesses and their products benefited considerably from the introduction of quality management practices.

American companies felt the impact of more aggressive Japanese competition by the mid-1970s, and that effect was most evident in the automotive industry. General Motors alone controlled half of the North American automobile market in the 1950s. Ford, Chrysler, and an assortment of smaller firms like Studebaker accounted for most of the remaining market share. The imported cars that entered the United States and Canada in the 1950s and 1960s were usually built in British or Western European factories and did not pose a serious threat to North American automakers. General Motors chief executive Charles Wilson opined in a 1950s U.S. congressional hearing that what was good for America was good for General Motors and vice versa, such was the central role his company played in the U.S. economy.[2]

The place of General Motors and other automakers in the American business pantheon was under serious assault by Toyota, Nissan, and Honda by the late 1970s. A combination of poor product quality, overreliance on large gas-guzzling vehicles, and rancorous labour relations coalesced to gradually hobble the three Detroit-based auto companies. This fact had serious ramifications for Canadian workers and their communities, since there were several Big Three auto plants in the country and an extensive network of suppliers that depended on them. Losing market share to Japanese imports furthermore posed a threat to auto assembly jobs.

Anyone prior to 1973 who drove a car powered by anything less than a large eight-cylinder internal combustion engine was thought to be in a small and perhaps underpowered car. The V8 engine was the marque of a real car and was found in everything from pickup trucks to muscle cars. The OPEC embargo made the V8 engine an expensive option, and the Detroit automakers started building and marketing smaller cars that required less fuel and could challenge the flood of Japanese imports flowing into the United States and Canada. American vehicles regrettably suffered from flaws that were glaringly obvious by the 1970s, and that reality was entirely evident in the case of the Ford Pinto.

The Pinto was Ford's answer to OPEC and Japan. Reasonably stylish by 1970s standards, meaning stunningly average, it was a two-door hatchback coupe produced from 1971 to 1980. A Canadian factory in Talbotville, Ontario, was one of the places in the Ford network where it was assembled. The Pinto was an outwardly decent car but suffered from a potentially fatal design flaw. The car's gas tank could explode if it was hit from behind by another vehicle. This defect was grievously compounded by the fact that Ford management discovered it late in the car's development and decided, in a remarkable instance of risk-management rationalization, that it would be cheaper to absorb the cost of any lawsuits filed over the Pinto's flaw rather than devote resources to redesigning the vehicle.

The malaise that seemed to permeate much of North American business in the 1970s was reflected in the decade's popular culture. Television, film, music, and literature all experienced extensive changes as 1960s counterculture was displaced by new images, sounds, and narratives. Canada's cultural industries were protected by so-called CanCon regulations administered by the Canadian Radio-television and Telecommunications Commission that required radio and television broadcasters to have Canadian content in their programming, which enabled Canadian artists to create music and television programs that commented on work and labour in the country.

The way Canadians were prepared for the workforce and the jobs they performed changed considerably in the 1970s, something especially true when it came to educational credentials. Table 5 shows the changes that happened in Canada between 1951 and 1975. Canada's population increased by 62 percent during that 24-year period, and the number of people in school grew by 227 percent, which reflected the birth of the baby-boom generation. Major shifts occurred in post-secondary education attainment in those years. The number of people pursuing non-university credentials increased by 789 percent, and those engaged in university degrees swelled by 580 percent. Overall, whereas only 0.7 percent of Canada's total population in 1951 was in some form of post-secondary education, university or non-university, 2.4 percent were enrolled in post-secondary programs by 1975, which was a huge increase. The overall trend was clear as Canada's workers became much more educated by the mid-1970s.

TABLE 5: CHANGES IN EDUCATION ENROLLMENT IN CANADA, 1951 TO 1975

	1951	1975
Total Enrollment Elementary to Post-Secondary	2,716,000	6,186,000
Elementary and Secondary Enrollment	2,625,000	5,594,000
Non-University Post-Secondary Enrollment	28,000	221,000
University Enrollment	64,000	371,000
Total Population	14,009,000	22,697,000

Sources: Statistics Canada, Table W1-9, "Summary of Total Full-Time Enrollment by Level of Study, Canada, Selected Years, 1951 to 1975," www150.statcan.gc.ca/n1/pub/11-516-x/sectionw/4147445-eng.htm#1; and Statistics Canada, Table A1, "Estimated Population of Canada, 1867 to 1977," www150.statcan.gc.ca/n1/pub/11-516-x /sectiona/4147436-eng.htm.

Some sectors of the economy grew substantially by the early 1970s while others experienced more modest expansion. For instance, the number of people working in education in Canada more than doubled from just over 266,000 in 1961 to slightly less than 569,000 in 1971. The number of people working in health and welfare services increased by 66 percent over those 10 years. In contrast, the number of people working in textiles and clothing rose by less than 2 percent and there was a 25 percent decline in the number of people working in agriculture. The 1970s economy was heavily oriented toward the service sector, and many of the jobs in it required more education, which helps explain the expansion in community college and university education.[3]

The education programs available to young people in the 1970s reflected changes in the job market. The various provincial community college systems founded in the late 1960s offered a wide variety of programs by the end of the 1970s. For example, francophone students in Montreal could attend an institution like Collège Ahuntsic and study programs in areas such as veterinary medicine, dietetics, and social services. All these programs were intended to prepare young people for work.[4]

A similar set of learning prospects existed on the other side of the country in British Columbia. Students at Langara Community College in Vancouver also had access to an array of programs, including data processing and business management. There were also social services training programs such as early childhood education and welfare assistance. Langara was conveniently located in the city and also charged reasonable tuition fees.[5]

Ontario eventually became home to 24 community colleges. One of them, George Brown, is located in Toronto, and like its fellow institutions, it offers a lot of part-time courses on evenings and weekends. In the mid-1970s, George Brown's programs ranged widely from a diploma in addictions counselling to technical subjects such as blueprint reading, a variety geared to appeal to a huge number of potential students.[6]

Community colleges were careful to market their programs in such a way that they attracted both men and women. The term *diversity* was not widely used in the 1970s within the context of workforce composition, but some colleges tried to ensure that people from a range of racial and ethnic backgrounds were shown in their program guides. For example, the administration and faculty at George Brown College clearly thought about the demographics of Toronto's citizens when fashioning and marketing its programs.

Learning about the workplace involves acquiring applied skills and knowledge in full- or part-time education institutions and also means learning on the job. There are always distinctions drawn between academic learning and vocational training, but the line between the two can be difficult to clearly demarcate. This tension was evident when comparing the missions of Canada's universities and colleges in the 1970s. The influence of both academic and vocational approaches was evident in how managers were educated and trained during the decade.

The 1970s were years when people were still promoted from entry-level roles into managerial positions, with the colloquial expression "promoted from the ranks" often applied to describe the process. Front-line supervisors and even middle managers were selected from the ranks of their organizations, and a lot of their training was either conducted within their companies or through night school courses. That was where part-time community college offerings made their main contribution.

Companies made extensive use of internal training materials and programs to prepare people to manage. Those efforts often focused on personnel matters, including how to deal with recalcitrant employees, ways to impart customer service skills, and how occupational health and safety should be implemented. The last issue came to the forefront of employment relations in Canada in the 1970s with the introduction of provincial health and safety acts. Ontario notably created the Royal Commission on the Health and Safety of Workers in Mines in 1976, headed by James Ham, which led to the passage of the province's first occupational health and safety law.

The problem with internal corporate training methods was that they treated any form of worker dissent as deviant, if not dangerous. The messages that managers received about the workplace were heavily shaped by gender. Workplace issues of concern to women were not differentiated from those pertaining to men. For instance, the term *sexual harassment* was first coined in 1975. Women finally had a name to give to the treatment that too many of them experienced on the job, yet references to any type of harassment were largely absent from management training materials in the 1970s.[7]

The education that aspiring managers received in universities in the 1970s was increasingly focused on quantitative skills. Graduate business programs like those offered at the University of British Columbia's Faculty of Commerce, the University of Western Ontario's business school, and the École des hautes études commerciales de Montréal included more content on topics such as finance and accounting. There was less emphasis in curricula on human issues in organizations. Universities were often concerned with teaching theory and that approach was unsurprisingly found in business and management programs.

Trends in education reflected changes happening in Canadian workplaces, and education in turn influenced workers and their jobs. Management education and training were part of that process. Blue-collar workers, like those who came out of colleges, loomed larger in aspects of popular culture than people who wore white collars to work. Canadians only had to switch on their radios to hear it.

The study of work and labour was revolutionized in the 1970s. American political economist Harry Braverman published *Labor and Monopoly Capital: The Degradation of Work in the Twentieth Century* (1974) and detailed how workers became alienated from the jobs they performed. Canadian sociologist James Rinehart built on Braverman in

The Tyranny of Work: Alienation and the Labour Process (1975), while British sociologist Michael Burawoy explained in *Manufacturing Consent: Changes in the Labor Process Under Monopoly Capitalism* (1979) how workers were induced to consent to workplace regulation. There was also a marked shift within university history departments toward social rather political or economic research. Historians such as Irving Abella began transforming scholarly understanding of the working-class experience in Canada. Abella was followed in the 1980s by other historians, including Greg Kealey, Bryan Palmer, Craig Heron, and Ian McKay.[8]

Music in 1970s Canada often had a working-class background. Bachman-Turner Overdrive (BTO), founded in Winnipeg in 1971, enjoyed considerable success and produced two songs closely associated with being on the job: "Taking Care of Business" and "Blue Collar." BTO's poignant lyrics in the latter song are a commentary on the nature of blue-collar work and class difference. Guitarist and singer Randy Bachman revealed that "Taking Care of Business" started as "White-Collar Worker" and was supposed to be about a recording engineer working on a song for Bachman's first band, The Guess Who. "Taking Care of Business" eventually became a staple of classic rock radio.

The working-class experience was also portrayed on CBC Television, Canada's national broadcaster. Two shows — *The King of Kensington* and *The Beachcombers* — depict daily life, respectively, in an old Toronto neighbourhood and in a logging community in British Columbia. Al Waxman's character in *The King of Kensington* is a small business proprietor, and the show is a comedy/drama that touches on aspects of urban life such as immigration. *The Beachcombers* also has comedic moments, often revolving around Robert Clothier's character Relic, and also includes Indigenous actors. Neither show is explicitly about work, but both present workers who earn low or average wages.

The nature of living and working was thoroughly satirized in Canadian popular media in the 1970s, especially by the Second City comedy troupe based in Toronto. The group, which included Rick Moranis, Dave Thomas, John Candy, Eugene Levy, Andrea Martin, Martin Short, and Catherine O'Hara, performed in a comedy television program called *SCTV*. The premise of working at a fictional television station provides fertile ground for lampooning the behaviour of bosses, co-workers, and the overall nature of working in a media company. The actors starring in *SCTV* were employed in a Canadian entertainment industry that was enthusiastic about promoting the country's culture, but the industry, unfortunately, was not always especially robust, and being a Canadian entertainment industry worker often meant wondering where the next paycheque would be found.

Working life was the focus of many Canadian documentaries in the 1970s. For instance, Denys Arcand's 1970 film *On est au coton* (*Cotton Mill, Treadmill* in English) depicts working conditions in the Quebec textile industry. The film was suppressed for several years because two members of the FLQ appeared in it, and the production was financed with help from the National Film Board of Canada (NFB). The NFB's founding in 1939 predated the development of Canadian content regulations in media, and the board benefited from those regulations as it financed documentaries that would have encountered difficulty finding financing if they lacked ready commercial appeal.

Work and labour themes were also depicted in Canadian theatre. Michel Tremblay wrote *Les Belles-sœurs* in 1968, and its portrayal of working-class women had a profound cultural impact in Quebec. David Fennario authored a commentary on his experiences working in factories and warehouses in the 1975 play *On the Job*. Plays such as those revealed the work that was on the minds of artistic people labouring in Canada's creative industries. They also filled a cultural space that was not being met by the type of fare on display at venues such as the Stratford and Shaw Festivals.

Canada's proximity to the United States meant that American cultural messages about work easily found their way north of the border. American films, television, music, books, and magazines were, as in previous decades, avidly consumed by Canadians, and many ideas were received about the nature of work life. A lot of the perceptions about work and labour in American popular media were full of pessimism and even anger, and the recent past became pastoralized. The same trends were found in American music heard by Canadians.

Like *SCTV*, the 1976 film *Network*, directed by Sidney Lumet, is also based on a fictional television network, and its most famous scene involves a character screaming, "I'm mad as hell and I'm not going to take it anymore!" The movies of the 1970s were darker in tone than what had been released in the 1950s and 1960s. The 1970s were the so-called "Directors' Decade," and films by Brian De Palma, Francis Ford Coppola, Michael Cimino, and Martin Scorsese brought gritty realism to cinema screens. Scorsese's *Taxi Driver*, also released in 1976, features lead character Travis Bickle working a marginal blue-collar job while descending into insanity. Cimino's 1978 film *The Deer Hunter* depicts the involvement of three main blue-collar characters in the Vietnam War and the impact it has on people in their working-class Pennsylvania community.

Rocky also premiered in movie houses in 1976. The viewing public did not realize that Sylvester Stallone's screenplay was based on a real 1975 fight between a journeyman boxer named Chuck Wepner and world heavyweight champion Muhammad Ali. Wepner's fight with Ali lasted just seconds short of a full 15 rounds, but the fictional Rocky Balboa does go the distance against make-believe champion Apollo Creed. Rocky is a sympathetic hero rather than an anti-hero, and the character gave hope to working-class men everywhere who felt they were gradually losing socio-economic ground in the 1970s.

Actress Sally Field plays a union activist in a Southern textile mill in the 1979 film *Norma Rae*. Based on the true story of North Carolina textile worker Crystal Lee Sutton, that movie has a more positive message than those focused on the impact of the Vietnam War, and it shows a working-class woman fighting for her rights on the job. It is a film intended to depict the reality of factory work without the benefit of union protection. The American movies that Canadians watched in the 1970s presented workers under siege, challenging management, fighting a losing war, and perhaps even going crazy in the process.

The messages about work conveyed in American television were somewhat less dark than those in motion pictures, with workplace dynamics often represented as humorous ironies. Depictions of working women and workers of colour became more common in television programs. *One Day at a Time* influenced how people viewed single working mothers when they saw a confident woman in a leading role living an independent, fulfilled life while raising two daughters. *Laverne & Shirley*, a show rooted in 1950s nostalgia, features two young women at a brewery in Milwaukee, Wisconsin. *Taxi* shows a diverse working-class group of characters making a living driving cabs in Greenwich Village in New York City. *Good Times* focuses on an African-American family living in Harlem. *Sanford and Son*, starring noted Black comic Redd Foxx, hilariously depicts the daily travails that he and his son encounter while running a junkyard in the Watts neighbourhood of Los Angeles. *Good Times* and *Sanford and Son* both employ humour to reveal aspects of the Black working-class experience to a wide viewing audience.

Silence speaks volumes, and work and labour were almost entirely absent from some television programming. The first television soap opera, *These Are My Children*, premiered in 1949. Daytime dramas appealed to a specific demographic — women doing unpaid domestic work at home — and it was often entirely unclear what many of the characters in soap operas did for a living. However, they were very popular throughout the 1970s. Canadian viewers did see people working in a soap opera if they tuned in to the imported British program *Coronation Street*, but soap operas were an escape from work rather than principally a commentary on it.

BTO's "Taking Care of Business" was accompanied by other songs that were commentaries on work and labour in North America and beyond. In 1976, Gordon Lightfoot released "The Wreck of the *Edmund Fitzgerald*," his tribute to the sailors who perished on a lake freighter that sank in Lake Superior the year before. In the late 1960s, Lightfoot had already produced his tale of the Canadian Pacific Railway's building with the "Canadian Railway Trilogy," while Stompin' Tom Connors wrote many songs in the late 1960s and 1970s that spoke of hard work, including "Tillsonburg," "Sudbury Saturday Night," and "Jack of Many Trades." In 1977, American country singer Johnny Paycheck released a working-class anthem called "You Can Take This Job and Shove It." Three years earlier, the Canadian band Rush launched a song called "Working Man," while the U.S. band Styx unveiled "Blue Collar Man" in 1978. Most importantly, the 1970s saw the rise of Bruce Springsteen, a performer who chronicles the working-class American Rust Belt experience more fully than any other songwriter. Springsteen's songs nonetheless resonated north of the border.

The 1970s witnessed the rise of a music form that was almost incomprehensible to adult listeners, but it spoke volumes about white worker alienation. Three British bands — Led Zeppelin, Black Sabbath, and Deep Purple — are often credited with being the foundation of heavy metal music. They were followed in the late 1970s and into the 1980s by additional groups such as Motorhead, Judas Priest, Iron Maiden, and Metallica. Heavy metal lyrics were often dark and fatalistic, and many young working-class men grew their hair long and formed close connections to their favourite bands. Canada produced heavy metal acts such as Anvil, Helix, and Lee Aaron, but they usually did not attain the same stature as their U.S. and British counterparts. Steppenwolf was an exception because, while it was not necessarily a heavy metal band, its music was forever associated with biker subculture due to its song "Born to Be Wild" being featured in the soundtrack of the film *Easy Rider*.

Canadian workers ended the 1970s differently than they had embarked on the decade. The excitement of the country's centennial celebrations in 1967 waned by 1970, and new economic and social realities changed the future for workers. They were more educated than they had ever been but also felt economically threatened. The 1970s were a disappointment after the 1960s, somewhat like the day after a long party.

23 THE 1980s: ALMOST EVERYTHING CHANGES

In Canada, the 1980s brought some key departures from the 1970s. The decade started off with a Liberal government, but almost halfway through was replaced by a Conservative administration. The economy became less regulated and more unequal in terms of who benefited from growth and who did not. Technological transformation accelerated during the decade, especially as computers became more ubiquitous in all workplaces. The change in immigration policy introduced by the Liberal government in the early 1970s had a substantial impact on the demographics of the Canadian workforce. Canada started admitting more immigrants from Asia, and migration levels from Europe decreased. Canadians liked to think their country mattered on the international stage, and the decade ended with a major shift in international relations. It was a decade of both soaring optimism and deep cynicism for all workers.

Electoral politics in the 1980s commenced in ways similar to the previous decade. The rather feckless Conservative minority government led by Joe Clark lasted six months in 1979 before it was brought down on a non-confidence motion moved by NDP MP Bob Rae. Pierre Trudeau did not signal if he was going to definitively say he was staying on as Liberal leader after the 1979 election but still chose to lead his party into the 1980 contest. He won another majority government and dealt with two landmark events in Canadian political history, both of which had repercussions for work and labour.

The Parti Québécois government held a sovereignty referendum in 1980. Uncertainty about Quebec's future with Canada had a negative economic impact, since businesses were understandably concerned about what it could mean to invest money anywhere in a country that might eventually be split apart. Quebec's unemployment rate was often higher than in neighbouring Ontario, although the PQ introduced better legal protections for unionized workers, including a ban on the use of replacement workers during strikes. The PQ lost the referendum, with 40 percent of voters supporting sovereignty and 60 percent against it.

The sovereignty movement was poorly understood in English Canada, but the PQ also did not understand English Canada. The PQ talked about "sovereignty" and English Canadians heard "separatism." The fact that Quebec was governed by a party that wanted a different relationship with English Canada did not prevent the province's economy from growing. It also turned out that the exodus of anglophone companies in the 1970s did not necessarily impair business growth. Québécor, a major media conglomerate extolled as an example of a significant business in the province, was owned by Pierre Péladeau, who was also a PQ supporter.

The PQ pursued interventionist economic policies, with the government playing an important role as an investor and employer. Hydro-Québec was owned by the provincial government and was regarded as a shining example of what the Québécois could accomplish without the assistance or interference of English Canada. The fact that Hydro-Québec's electric-generating projects had serious environmental impacts and damaged the livelihoods of Cree communities was not factored into the business equation. American firm General Motors continued to employ Quebec workers at a factory in Ste-Thérèse, which built the Chevrolet Camaro and Pontiac Firebird.

There was growing anxiety in English Canada about the sovereigntist movement in Quebec, and Pierre Trudeau, arguably the most cerebral of Canada's prime ministers, embarked on the process of patriating the country's Constitution from the United Kingdom. The 1867 British North America Act was still in force in 1980, so Trudeau was determined to rectify that historical anomaly and finally shake off the remaining vestiges of Canada's colonial status. The new Constitution would have a profound impact on work and labour across the country.

Legal documents, especially national constitutions, are as important for what they do not include as they are for what they specify. The British legal tradition was based on an unwritten constitution that was the ongoing accumulation of legal precedents and laws dating back to the 12th-century Magna Carta. A written constitution was a clear move away from the British model toward what was used in the United States. The 1982 Canadian Constitution also recognized the legality of the treaties Britain and Canada had signed with Indigenous communities across the country.

The Constitution crucially included a Charter of Rights and Freedoms that banned various forms of discrimination. Organized labour wanted a right to unionization and collective bargaining included in it but was unsuccessful. The 1982 Constitution had some flaws, most notably a notwithstanding clause that enabled a provincial or federal government to set aside a legal decision for a five-year period. It was also not ratified by Quebec.

Organized labour attempted to use the charter to expand the rights of unionized workers, but as political scientists Larry Savage and Charles Smith have described, the Supreme Court of Canada opposed those efforts in the 1980s. In April 1987, the court ruled on a collection of cases that became known as the "Labour Trilogy." The right to strike was central to those cases, but the court held there was no such constitutional right. Business groups were surely satisfied with the outcome of labour's initial efforts to utilize the charter to expand workers rights, but their contentment would prove unwarranted in later years.[9]

The early 1980s brought Canadians a serious workplace tragedy and blow to the country's energy sector when the oil rig *Ocean Ranger* sank in the Atlantic Ocean in February 1982. The rig was portrayed as a shining symbol of the energy renaissance of Newfoundland and

Labrador. Public policy-makers hoped that the province's economic decline and loss of people would be reversed because of offshore oil reserves. A royal commission was established to determine what led to the loss of the *Ocean Ranger*. All 84 crew members died, 56 from Newfoundland. The Canadian energy industry learned a lot from that disaster, but it came at a terrible cost.[10]

Management in many ways became more punitive in the 1980s. Corporate executives up to the end of the 1970s were supposed to be conservative in appearance, demeanour, and political outlook. The last trait persisted into the 1980s, but the former two took major departures from past practice. The public profiles of corporate chief executives began to change in the 1980s. For instance, corporate executives often looked staid if not stern in photographs taken in the 1950s and 1960s, but by the end of the 1980s, they were being accorded the same reverence as rock stars, especially the new leaders emerging from California's Silicon Valley.

Chrysler Corporation chairperson Lee Iacocca was one example of a CEO as celebrity. He was a long-time veteran of the auto industry when he took the helm of Chrysler in 1978. His résumé included advocating production of the Pinto and the Mustang while he was employed by Ford. Chrysler was in serious financial difficulty in the late 1970s and received a loan from the U.S. government in 1979. Major job losses would have occurred in Canada had the firm gone bankrupt. Iacocca was feted for his assumed business acumen, and he duly produced an autobiography that served to cement his image in the eyes of the North American public. His emphasis was on saving Chrysler and acquiring failing American Motors Corporation in 1987, not on the deadly Pinto that was designed during his tenure at Ford.[11]

There were Canadian business leaders who sought public recognition with varying degrees of interest. The term *establishment* is commonly used in the United Kingdom within the context of the class divide that exists there. It appears less in everyday usage in Canada, even though social class is also a factor in Canadian society. The business and wealth elite that ran Canada's economy and shaped the lives of its workers did receive some scrutiny in the 1980s.

Peter C. Newman wrote a three-volume series of books called *The Canadian Establishment*, the first published in 1975, which chronicled the business holdings and interconnected networks of Canada's wealthy. The Eatons, the Desmarais family, the Molsons, the Rogers family, the McCains, the Irvings, and others fill the pages of Newman's analysis. He followed up with another book entitled *The Establishment Man*, which details the life and career of one particular member of the business community who has little affinity for working people.

The subject of *The Establishment Man* is Conrad Black. He was born into wealth in Toronto and eventually accumulated a substantial business empire largely centred on newspapers while cultivating relations with luminaries such as British prime minister Margaret Thatcher. Black generally shows enormous disdain for working people, having raided a pension fund when he took control of the Dominion supermarket chain. He also likes having a public image, and while not of equal global stature to Lee Iacocca, Black became a Canadian celebrity. Like many celebrities, Black professes contempt for most of Canada's media, yet assiduously courts its attention. He eventually married contrarian *Maclean's* columnist Barbara Amiel and renounced his Canadian citizenship so he could formally be called Baron Black of Crossharbour in Britain, since Canadians could not legally use such titles. Black was later convicted of fraud in the United States in 2010, spent more than three years in prison, and was pardoned by U.S. president Donald Trump in 2019. Black's public profile was unique for a corporate leader, since he clearly loved media attention, but his contempt for wage workers did not make him particularly unique among the ranks of chief executives.[12]

The meaning of management further changed during the 1980s as it encompassed a wide range of occupations and sectors. The corporate CEO continued to be the most visible of them, even though there was a sizable increase in people employed as managers or in similar jobs. There were 814,000 people in the Canadian workforce in 1980 who were classified as managerial and administrative, a 118 percent climb from 1970. That occupational group grew larger than any other surveyed by Statistics Canada. Technical, social, and cultural occupations swelled by 89 percent during the same period. The overall workforce expanded by

39 percent between 1970 and 1980, but there was clearly considerable growth in jobs overseeing the work of other people.[13]

The proliferation of management and supervisory education programs at universities and colleges was part of further escalation in post-secondary education. Community colleges like George Brown in Toronto increasingly offered courses relating to computers, including introductory data processing and the COBOL programming language described previously. The commonality of vocational courses and programs of various types reflected the fundamental fact that post-secondary education had in many ways turned into a business by the 1980s. George Brown was just one of many community colleges in Ontario, and it offered courses in 18 different subject areas in just one night school term in 1985. Extrapolate that across all of Canada's various community colleges and the scope of post-secondary education in the 1980s becomes clearer.[14]

The level of educational attainment grew further still in the 1980s compared to preceding decades. As Tables 5 (see page 166) and 6 show, Canadians became much better educated between 1951 and 1981. Overall student enrollments increased over a three-decade period, but the most remarkable growth was in secondary and post-secondary schooling. Demographic change drove the rise, but it is also clear that earning a secondary school diploma became the norm rather than the exception when it came to educational attainment. Baby boomers exhibited a pronounced inclination to go to college and university, but their higher education did not necessarily translate into higher incomes.

TABLE 6: EDUCATION LEVELS IN CANADA, 1981

Total Population Age 15 and Over	18,605,285
Grades 9 to 13 Without a Diploma	3,731,305
Secondary School Diploma	2,421,505
Trade Certificate or Diploma	1,842,975
University or Other Non-University with Certificate or Diploma	2,007,875
University Degree	1,490,180

Source: *1981 Census of Canada*, Census Highlights, 35.

The postwar era of rising wages and a better standard of living stalled as economic uncertainty set in during the 1970s and proceeded into the 1980s. The patriation of the Constitution coincided with a short but sharp recession that was the worst economic downturn Canada experienced since the end of the Second World War. The standard employment relationship frayed as it became more difficult to cover the costs of a family of four on one full-time wage. This fact was evident in federal government statistics from the early 1980s.

Statistics Canada tracked family incomes from under $5,000 per year to over $45,000. Only 25 percent of women in dual-income households earning more than the latter amount worked, obviously because their spouses were earning decent wages. The picture was different in lower-income families, such as those earning $10,000 to $15,000 per year and in which close to half of women were employed. The number of families in which both spouses worked increased by 83 percent between 1970 and 1980, but average family income only grew by 28 percent. People entered the 1980s working longer and harder hours, especially on the lower-income scale, than they did at the start of the 1970s. It did not take long for worker advocates to notice what was going on with Canadian incomes.[15]

Organized labour seemed strong heading into the decade, but it came under more attacks than it had faced in the previous 20 years. Shifts in management attitudes toward workers were one part of labour's challenges, but major changes in government policy also made life more difficult for unionized workers. Unions became more nationalistic in the 1980s as interest in gaining independence from American-based international unions intensified. In the 1960s, unions felt as if they owned collective bargaining, while management had it under control by the 1980s.

Canadian workers were economically linked to their American counterparts in the 1980s, but the two groups differed when it came to collection action. Union density levels in both countries were equal from the 1950s into the 1960s, but began diverging in the mid-1970s as Canadian union membership grew to over 30 percent of the non-agricultural workforce and American levels declined into the low 20 percent range in the 1980s. That was an important trend, and there were key reasons that it happened. Political ideology and economic policy were factors in both countries.

Canadian workers did not face any influenza pandemics in the 1970s and 1980s, but a new unstoppable disease did occur that had a peripheral impact on labour and employment. The mysterious sickness began taking the lives of gay men in the early 1980s. It attacked a person's immune system, which then made the patient susceptible to infections that would otherwise not appear. In short, it was a death sentence. Science eventually called the deadly affliction acquired immune deficiency syndrome (AIDS), which was caused by contracting the human immunodeficiency virus (HIV).

There was an early Canadian connection to the AIDS epidemic, since scientists long thought that a Canadian flight attendant named Gaëtan Dugas was the first person to bring the disease to the United States. He was referred to as Patient Zero. Time would reveal that Dugas had perhaps not been the initial person to bring AIDS to America, but the AIDS epidemic cast further negative scrutiny on the gay community in Canada. People would viciously joke that gay meant "got AIDS yet?" AIDS led to gay people being further ostracized from their families and co-workers.[16]

The late 1970s ushered in a long period of neo-liberal political thought that had been germinating for more than 30 years. Neo-liberalism essentially meant allowing free market capitalism to operate in an unfettered manner without interference from government, as well as minimizing the state's involvement in people's lives. The widespread belief in the United States was that the New Deal era marked a new trajectory in that country's history. In fact, reactionary groups in the United States, such as the John Birch Society, hated the New Deal and bided their time for conditions to appear that would enable an assault on the programs and structures put in place by Franklin Roosevelt. The election of Richard Nixon in 1968, the same year Pierre Trudeau came to power in Canada, initiated the gradual postwar ascendancy of the Republican Party in the United States. That rightward shift on both sides of the Atlantic accelerated in 1979 when Margaret Thatcher became prime minister of the United Kingdom, and more so in 1980 with the election of Ronald Reagan as American president.

Britain entered the European Community in 1973. Margaret Thatcher wanted to shrink the postwar welfare state that had been created by the Labour Party, deregulate industry and capital, and move Britain politically to the right. She also waged an unremitting assault against British unions, which in turn led to a ferocious and often desperate response from them. The climax was an epic strike by the National Union of Miners from 1984 to 1985. Not surprisingly, British union density declined during the Thatcher years.

Social and political progressives frequently described Ronald Reagan as a hard-right ideologue, but his world view was malleable and his policies were often driven by people around him. He was different from Thatcher in that regard. Reagan was the first U.S. president to have been a union president — the Screen Actors Guild in his case — and did not run on a platform of outright animosity toward unions. He nonetheless became forever associated with a 1980 strike by the Professional Air Traffic Controllers Organization (PATCO), which represented staff in the federal public service. Contrary to popular belief, Reagan wanted to conclude an agreement and avoid a strike with PATCO. Ultimately, he fired all 10,000 members of the union.[17]

The consequences of the PATCO strike reverberated across the United States and beyond its borders. Reagan's actions sent a message to American employers that the government thought it acceptable to take a tough line against unions. That message, along with what happened in Britain in 1984, represented a significant departure from how unions had generally been viewed in the industrialized West during the Cold War years. Canadian unions did not face a defining national strike of disastrous proportions like the miners' action in the United Kingdom or the PATCO confrontation, but they duly noted what had happened south of the border and across the ocean.

The federal Liberals had essentially run out of political steam by 1984. Pierre Trudeau retired that year and was succeeded by John Turner, who was only in office for three months before being soundly defeated by a reinvigorated Conservative Party led by Brian Mulroney. Mulroney became very close to Reagan and Thatcher, and while he did not turn as hard right as his friends in America and Britain, he took steps that affected work and labour in Canada. This was especially true of how his government viewed the role of the state in the nation's economy.

Mulroney talked about giving federal public servants "pink slips and running shoes" — an allusion to firing workers and giving them the means to run out the office door — when he was elected in 1984, and indeed there were federal job losses during the nine years he was in office. He was briefly succeeded by Kim Campbell, who had served in his Cabinet. The Conservative government altered employment insurance rules, then called unemployment insurance (UI), so that workers could only receive benefits if they were terminated from their jobs, whereas it was previously possible to also collect benefits after resigning from a job. That change put employers firmly in charge of who received UI benefits, which meant people could only get away from a difficult working situation by immediately finding another job. Mulroney also withdrew the government from key sectors of the economy. Companies such as Air Canada and Petro-Canada had been Crown corporations under the Liberal government, but the Conservatives privatized both of them.

The late 1980s were a period of comparatively low unemployment, so the UI policy modification did not cause widespread public outrage. The UI system was historically intended to act as emergency relief, and there were variations in its use across the country. The number of weeks per year that a person had to work to collect benefits varied depending on the province in which a person resided. People in Ontario and the western provinces met more rigorous UI requirements and had to work more weeks of a given year to qualify if they lost their jobs because their provinces had lower unemployment rates than other parts of the country. Conversely, someone living in Newfoundland and Labrador had to work fewer weeks before being eligible for UI.

The Mulroney government also dealt with major public sector strikes, including a 1987 work stoppage by Canadian National Railway workers. The government displayed keen willingness to employ back-to-work legislation in that strike. Mulroney liked to portray himself as a labour lawyer. He had been legal counsel to an inquiry into corruption in the Quebec construction industry called the Cliche Commission. He also declared that Canada was open for business when he was elected in 1984.[18]

Every election is arguably important, and the 1988 federal one ushered in a crucial turning point in Canada's economic trajectory. The Trudeau government appointed former Liberal Cabinet minister Donald Macdonald to lead a commission on economic union and development in 1982 and his 1984 report recommended that Canada pursue free trade with the United States. Brian Mulroney's government followed that recommendation and entered into free trade negotiations with America.

The 1988 federal election was largely waged over free trade, and the Conservatives were re-elected. The Canada-U.S. Free Trade Agreement was a seismic shift in public policy. It opened many sectors of Canada's economy to more direct U.S. competition, but it also gave Canada more access to the market south of the border. Canadian economic policy had long depended on tariffs to foster the growth of domestic industry, and the 1988 agreement began the dismantling of that paradigm. Labour groups decried the implementation of free trade with the United States over fears of eventual job loss. Free trade would prove to be a threat to well-paid industrial work, but there were other seemingly inescapable trends transforming work at the same time.

Further technological innovations impacted Canadian workers even more than new departures in trade policy. There were still push-button phones with cords attached to their handsets on Canadian office desks at the start of the 1980s as well as formidable IBM typewriters built with steel housings. Managers had secretaries — the term *administrative assistant* was starting to come into use — and routine clerical work was delegated to them. Fax machines and photocopiers were ubiquitous in Canadian offices, but most administrative work was still reliant on endless reams of paper. Typing pools were still common and overwhelmingly staffed by women.

New workplace technology was being integrated by the end of the decade. Computers evolved from enormous, loud behemoths to something that sat on top of a desk. IBM introduced its model 5150 personal computer in 1981. Its two-tone green screen revealed the workings of the Microsoft Disk Operating System or MS-DOS. That computer became a common sight in 1980s workplaces, and Microsoft soon dominated the software industry, developing into a bigger corporation than IBM.[19] In

1982, *Time* declared the computer its "Machine of the Year," such was the device's growing importance.[20] The first version of Microsoft's Word program was offered in 1983.[21]

The proliferation of new technology such as desktop computers and word-processing programs altered the everyday nature of work. Computers were right next to employees rather than in another room housing a huge mainframe machine. They made life easier in some respects — correcting a document in MS Word was far easier and quicker than trying to do it by typing successive drafts on a typewriter. On the other hand, a typewriter could not log a person's work productivity with the ease of a computer. Office automation served to extend the influence of the founder of scientific management, Frederick Winslow Taylor, over modern workplaces.

The media messages, popular and news, that Canadians received in the 1980s about work and labour were different from what they had experienced in the 1970s. Depictions of the working class in films, television, books, and music markedly changed in the 1980s compared to the 1970s. For instance, the blue-collar Bunkers from television's *All in the Family* were replaced by a show such as *Cheers*, which portrays characters from a range of occupational backgrounds. Working women continued to be shown in television in shows such as *Murphy Brown*, but seeing work in television programs often meant stylized views of working in law enforcement or medicine. The working class was apparently only interesting if employed as police officers or nurses.

Some films released in the 1980s touched directly on workplace issues, but in lighter terms than presented in the 1970s. The movie *9 to 5* stars Lily Tomlin, Jane Fonda, and Dolly Parton as women who foil a misogynist manager played by Dabney Coleman. Women were no longer just portrayed as clerical workers or doing unpaid work at home. *Silkwood*, starring Meryl Streep, is based on the story of nuclear plant worker Karen Silkwood. Spike Lee depicts class and racial conflict in *Do the Right Thing*, and Ron Howard's film *Gung Ho* focuses on a culture clash when a Japanese carmaker takes over an American auto assembly plant. The impact of creeping industrial job loss, the challenges facing organized labour, and the impact of corporate and government policy were not often found in popular films, but they were the subjects of documentaries produced in both Canada and the United States.

Canadians produced two films in the 1980s that revealed much about the nature of the workplace, with one receiving more attention than the other. In 1981, the National Film Board of Canada released a documentary by Sturla Gunnarsson entitled *After the Axe*, which follows the progress of a fictional corporate executive who loses his job. All of the other characters in the film are played by real people. The film portrays the cutthroat nature of corporate life and the mercenary attitudes executives are encouraged to adopt as a survival mechanism, which perhaps helps to explain why senior management became so punitive in the 1970s and into the 1980s.[22]

After the Axe unfortunately did not receive a lot of public attention, but another film about 1984 negotiations between General Motors and the Canadian Region of the United Auto Workers became the most widely known labour documentary ever made in Canada. *Final Offer* was also directed by Sturla Gunnarsson and follows UAW Canadian region director Bob White as he leads his members through a process that ultimately results in the union separating from its American parent to form the Canadian Auto Workers (CAW) in 1985. The film displays the tensions of collective bargaining, corporate strategy, and the decidedly nationalist response from the autoworkers union. The creation of the CAW helped initiate a wider trend of Canadian union members choosing to be part of national rather than international unions.[23]

Released in 1985, *Final Offer* provides a contrast with what was happening with industrial work in the United States in the 1980s. Michael Moore's *Roger and Me*, released in 1989, describes the economic decline of Flint, Michigan, and the role of General Motors in that city's economy. Whereas *Final Offer* appears to show a moment of Canadian labour triumph, *Roger and Me* is about decay and survival. There seemed to still be hope for Canadian industrial employment, while such work was rapidly disappearing in the United States.

Music took somewhat of a turn away from work and labour issues in the 1980s. Bruce Springsteen became more popular than ever, but the messages of his songs were often lost on listeners. This is especially true of "Born in the USA," a lament for a working-class Vietnam War veteran unable to find work when he returns home. Ironically, its message of loss and desperation has been misconstrued as a patriotic anthem. Canadian Daniel Lanois included songs that link to working life on his album *Acadie*. Punk rock spoke to young working-class alienation, but that genre burned brightly in the late 1970s and early 1980s before being displaced by resurgent pop and rock. British bands were again at the forefront of creating narratives about working life. One of them, UB40, took its name from an attendance card completed by people claiming unemployment benefits. Country music did talk about economic challenges, but it had yet to be widely accepted by mainstream audiences across North America. The workplace continued to be the crucible in which issues emerged before they entered popular consciousness.

Major trends emerged in the 1980s that dealt with equity and fairness. The International Labour Organization, a United Nations agency, adopted a convention on equal pay in 1981, saying that it was a human right. In 1977, the Canadian Human Rights Code was passed, which included pay equity provisions. The issue of equal pay for work of equal value, commonly referred to as pay equity, became a leading employment issue in the 1980s, with women in the public sector at the forefront of the struggle to achieve equal wages. Pay equity compared jobs that were predominantly performed by men with those done by women and evaluated them based on four criteria — skill, effort, responsibility, and working conditions — to better determine the value of women's paid work. It was an ongoing effort, but the creation of pay equity tribunals and the development of expertise to address pay inequities were significant advances in how the value of women's work was viewed in Canada.[24]

Corporations did not welcome the arrival of pay equity. There was much more concern about maximizing profits than how to treat workers properly. Management theory in the 1980s often involved fleeting fads that added little value to workplaces while causing some havoc. For instance, a 1982 book by Thomas J. Peters and Robert H. Waterman, Jr., entitled *In Search of Excellence: Lessons from America's Best-Run Companies* was heralded for its alleged sage recommendations on how to improve organizations. As an example, they write approvingly about American computer firm Wang, which went out of business a few years after the book was published. Tom Peters was a faculty member at the Harvard Business School, and his career benefited enormously from the book's publication.[25]

There was just one problem: Peters later revealed that much of the content of *In Search of Excellence* was fabricated. That key fact did not prevent the work from staying in print, and Peters's reputation was not significantly diminished by his admission, which basically showed that much of the book was a work of fiction. The book's lessons, spurious though many of them were, did not stop it from becoming a management classic.[26]

24 ONE LAST BIG SHIFT
BEFORE THE 1990s

T he years from 1945 to 1989 were shaped by the grim reality of
the world divided into two competing Cold War blocs revolving
around the United States and the Soviet Union. Canadians lived
and worked in a world divided into capitalist- and communist-influenced
spheres. The Cold War was a contest of ideas as much as it was about economic and military might, and when civil unrest broke out in Eastern
Europe in 1989 and the Berlin Wall came down, it seemed that the United
States and its allies had prevailed. There was widespread belief at the end
of the 1980s that since the West had won the struggle, it also meant free
market capital was victorious. U.S. political scientist Francis Fukuyama actually argues in his 1992 book *The End of History and the Last Man* that
Western liberal democracy had decisively triumphed. The reality was far
more complicated for anyone working for wages in a country like Canada.[27]

The 1970s were full of contradictions and challenges for Canadian
workers of all types. A new wave of technology entered workplaces,

leading to new jobs requiring equally new education and training programs. New corporations such as Microsoft and Apple were created and eventually became dominant actors in free market capitalism. The downside to technology was that it could be used to rationalize work, meaning break it down into its different parts and sequences, and more insidiously monitor what people did on the job.

The end of post–Second World War economic expansion became evident in the 1970s. The 1973 OPEC embargo slowed growth and was followed by a recession in 1982. From the 1970s into the 1980s, Canada's working-age population swelled, and people were far more educated than they had been in preceding decades. Education was publicly subsidized, and governments clearly saw value in funding and extending it. On the other hand, the number of two-income households rose in the 1970s and 1980s. Having more skills and education did not necessarily lead to higher wages.

Government moved away from interventionist economic policies such as owning and operating Crown corporations and adopted more market-friendly approaches like implementing free trade, decisions that had major implications for workers. There was a substantial ideological shift in industrialized countries as neo-liberal economic policies became ascendant and Keynesianism was displaced. At the same time, the introduction of the Charter of Rights and Freedoms in Canada would have an influence on labour and employment that was not immediately evident. Governments began implementing policies such as pay equity that reflected concerns about human rights on the job. Changes in immigration policy, official bilingualism, the sovereignty movement in Quebec, and the adoption of official multiculturalism all shaped work in Canada. The workforce became more diverse, employment in the federal public sector could require proficiency in both official languages, and business looked warily at the Parti Québécois.

Canadian workplaces continued to be highly gendered from the 1970s into the 1980s, but women made progress. Pay equity was one example of the transformations that occurred, but so were changes in the jobs women performed. In 1971, just under 16 percent of managerial workers were women and that number grew to almost 25 percent by

1981. A large majority of managers were still male, but new trends were starting to take effect.

Baby boomers entered workplaces in huge numbers in the 1970s, and Generation X joined them by the end of the 1980s as Second World War citizens finished retiring. Canadians, regardless of their generation, lived in a country bedevilled by regional economic differences. Atlantic Canada still lagged behind the rest of the country economically, Quebec had more interventionist policies than other provinces, Ontario's industrial economy seemed to be holding on, and Alberta was poised for even greater economic growth as were the other Prairie provinces and British Columbia. However, Indigenous communities did not receive a commensurate share of the country's economic wealth.

PART V The Anxious 1990s and 2000s

DAY	TIME IN	TIME OUT
1	7 48	16 17
2	7 45	16 15
	7 42	

25 THE 1990s: THE END OF THE POST–SECOND WORLD WAR ERA

C anadian workers moved into the 1990s with both hope and trepidation. The Cold War world that most people had known was gone, which meant the previously ever-present threat of nuclear war was also presumably lessened. The brief stock market scare that happened in October 1987 did not lead to a major economic downturn, and the 1980s ended on a generally good economic note. There was every reason to believe the 1990s would bring prosperity to Canadians regardless of their occupations. The end of the century, indeed the millennium, was drawing closer as 2000 approached. There were reasons to feel optimistic about the coming of a new era in human history.

However, the reality proved harsher than expected. The early 1990s brought a short but sharp economic decline, and federal and provincial governments imposed austerity measures on public sector workers that changed labour laws and weakened unions. Technological change further accelerated as the internet and new forms of communication and media entered the workplace and wider society. Unfortunately, the end of the Cold War did not lead to global peace. The prospect of the 20th century winding down brought anticipation and dread as some people feared the end of the world was nigh, while others looked forward to a clean break with the past. The 1990s and 2000s were decades of enormous change for Canadian workers that marked a departure from what they had previously known while simultaneously reinforcing trends and practices workers had often opposed.

The 1990s dawned with another economic setback. The 1990 recession abated within two years but led to yet another reordering of the labour market in Canada. It was the first recession that caused widespread layoffs among managerial workers. The one in 1982 had led to unemployment in Canada spiking to 13 percent before dropping to just over 7 percent by the end of the decade. It shot back up again to just over 12 percent by 1992. Those numbers were hard enough for Canadian workers, but they did not tell the whole story of the job market at the start of the 1990s.[1]

The methods used by major industrialized countries to measure unemployment led to different numbers depending on the survey utilized. Media often talk at length about the unemployment rate without ever really saying what is being taken into account. Statistics Canada, a well-respected Canadian government agency, measures employment levels across Canada along with a wide range of other labour market indicators. Unemployment is calculated through a labour force survey and a survey of business employment, payrolls, and working hours. In the 1990s, respondents were asked among other questions — as they still are — if they were working in the last month or looking for work if they were unemployed.

The information the Canadian public receives does not usually provide an accurate measurement of the true unemployment rate. People who are underemployed or unemployed for one or more years do not ordinarily show up in the officially posted unemployment rate, nor do people on social assistance. The underemployment rate for young workers is also usually much higher than the rate reported across all age groups. Social scientists were well aware prior to 1990 of the problems associated with how underemployment, structural unemployment, and social assistance were determined, and more discussion of those social issues emerged as the 1990s progressed. Underemployment means having a job but not working as many hours as a person wants, such as working part-time and being unable to find full-time work.

There are also different forms of unemployment, with some being more prevalent in certain parts of the country than others. Seasonal unemployment involves working for a certain period during a given year in something like agriculture or natural resources, then being out of work until the seasons change and work is again available. Working in fisheries, farming, or even construction are examples of seasonal work and subsequent unemployment. The expectation is that people in those industries will be recalled to work once the weather improves, crops are ready for harvesting, or fish are available to be caught.

Frictional unemployment refers to the process of people leaving existing jobs and finding new ones. It was not unusual in the 1990s or later years for an organization to see 10 percent of its workers come and go in a given year. Frictional unemployment is more common when overall employment levels are strong in an economy. Some organizations, such as retail and food services, experience far higher turnover rates. Frictional unemployment is not considered a sign of good or bad economic conditions and is instead a constant feature of the labour market.

Structural unemployment was the most difficult form to address through public policy, since it meant trying to find work for people who had been out of a job for months, even years. No Canadian government in the 1990s and beyond talked about pursuing policies that would lead to full employment. Indeed, an unemployment rate of around 5 percent was considered full employment, and economists became concerned if it fell below that point. That was because the labour market is still essentially predicated on being a buyer's rather than a seller's market, regardless of how workers think it should function. The last thing any employer wants is to receive one application for a job vacancy; the preference is to have as many as possible to provide lots of hiring options. Unemployment in Canada, regardless of its type, did not fall below 5 percent during the 1990s.

Being on social assistance meant, and still means, collecting low monthly benefits from government. Although the term *welfare bums* was generally part of popular discourse well before the 1990s — one-time NDP leader David Lewis commented on "corporate welfare bums" in the 1970s — nobody lived extravagantly on social assistance. The same was true of other government income supplements such as the Canada Pension Plan, Old Age Security, and Guaranteed Income Supplement. Canadians who found themselves on social assistance ended up in the low end of the job market if they were unable to find work and often became part of the long-term structurally unemployed.

Economic austerity had a profound impact on labour and employment in Canada in the 1990s. The end of the 1990 recession helped usher a new Liberal government led by Jean Chrétien into power in Ottawa in 1993. Canadians, especially those working for the federal government, might have thought the election of a new government would result in a resumption of public spending after the adoption of budget cuts by the Conservatives. They would soon be disabused of that hope. A persistent narrative about public debt in Canada developed in the 1990s. There was a widespread view that the country's finances were dangerously out of control, public debt was too high, and government spending had to be reined in. The economy seemed unstable. For example, the prime rate, which is the interest rate that ultimately governs what people pay on mortgages and loans and earn on investments, hit 14 percent in 1990. It declined to just under 5 percent in 1993 upon the return of the Liberals to power in Ottawa. A lower prime means investors are unable to earn a lot of interest on their money, but it makes debt cheaper. For instance, being able to borrow money at low rates allows governments to run deficits — annual budget shortfalls — more easily.[2]

The Chrétien government came under pressure to cut public spending from the business community and also from much of Canada's news media. The *Globe and Mail*, one of the country's main daily newspapers, was a consistent if not shrill advocate of spending restraint. The government responded with thousands of public service job cuts, reduced spending, and some tax increases. The narrative that government debt was bad and that public finances had to be balanced became accepted orthodoxy by the end of the 1990s.

This shift in opinion about how government should source and spend money marked a major departure from the economic theories that had shaped policy since the late 1930s. Keynesian economic policy, which argued for governments to run deficits during downturns and pay down debt when the economy expanded, was in many ways abandoned. This had major implications for workers across Canada, most of whom understandably did not know a deficit was the amount of money a government borrowed in a fiscal year to cover expenses, while national debt was the amount accumulated over time.

Government policy regarding job creation also changed in the 1990s, as seen by what happened with the Atlantic cod fishery in the early years of the decade. Workers in the Maritime provinces were required to work fewer hours per year to qualify for unemployment benefits than their peers elsewhere in the country. This was because of the highly seasonal nature of a lot of work in the fishery, especially in Newfoundland and Labrador. The pattern of working for a short number of weeks, then collecting UI, as it was commonly called, was viable as long as there were fish in the ocean to catch.

By the early 1990s, scientists produced evidence that the Atlantic cod fishery was in jeopardy and that a fishing moratorium had to be put in place to allow stocks to replenish. The federal Conservative government responded by implementing the recommended pause on fishing, and the largest single industrial layoff in Canadian history ensued as 20,000 fisheries workers lost their jobs. Workers were offered compensation by the government beyond usual unemployment insurance benefits, but a combination of ecological change and government policy brought a pause to a way of working life that had existed since Europeans first sailed to the Atlantic coast of North America. The federal Conservative Cabinet minister sent to give the bad news to fisheries workers, Newfoundland's John Crosbie, was met by an angry group of workers, and his initial response was to tell them that he "didn't take the fish from the goddamn water."[3]

Governments at provincial and federal levels introduced policies in the 1990s that harmed workers, such as layoffs and revisions to unemployment insurance eligibility, while conversely providing incentives to encourage business to expand and establish operations in Canada. Incentives of various types, from minimal-interest loans to generous tax writeoffs, were particularly popular in the automotive industry, although they were also found in other sectors. Canada was actually an enthusiastic pioneer when it came to providing money to business.

In the mid-1970s, the Ford Motor Company decided to build a new engine factory, with Ontario and Ohio becoming the finalists for the new plant. Ford of Canada executives lobbied hard for the facility to be situated in Canada, and their efforts were successful. The factory, called the Essex Engine Plant, was built in Windsor with the help of provincial government subsidies. The UAW, the union representing the workers, opposed the payment of subsidies to business, but the Essex plant helped to establish a precedent that could not be reversed. The UAW wanted more jobs, but it was also concerned about the possible impact of states and provinces essentially paying companies to secure them. In time, organized labour also came to expect firms to receive public subsidies in order to preserve jobs.[4]

Corporate subsidies were political insurance for governments in the 1990s. Canada had companies that sold goods and services globally but also attracted foreign businesses to set up operations in the country, such as the Japanese automakers Honda and Toyota, demonstrating that subsidies did attract foreign investment and jobs. The Detroit automakers also continued to maintain robust employment and vehicle production levels in Canada during the 1990s. All of this showed that Canada was still able to secure automotive industry investment based on subsidies, infrastructure, an educated workforce, and, above all, a competitive currency value. The Canadian dollar's lower worth compared to the American dollar made Canada a reasonably appealing place to invest.

Bombardier, Canada's leading aerospace firm in the 1990s, was another recipient of federal financial assistance. The Liberal government, mindful of Bombardier aerospace jobs in Toronto and Montreal, was in turn glad to provide help to the firm. Other companies such as Nortel, formerly known first as Northern Electric and then Northern Telecom, additionally benefited from government support. The problem was that provincial and federal governments were essentially buying jobs, and there was no guarantee how long such employment would last. Government aid to corporations generally did not extend to the service sector, and that was where most job growth occurred in the 1990s.

Corporations were as dependent on government as they had ever been, but that dependence did not stop management from being even tougher on workers in the 1990s. More management theories appeared as total quality management became especially popular. Canadian corporations and workers were part of vast global supply chains in the 1990s. The passage of the North American Free Trade Agreement (NAFTA) in 1993 closely integrated the Canadian, American, and Mexican economies. Manufactured goods crossed the borders of all three countries before they became finished products.

Whereas manufacturing firms in prior decades operated large warehousing operations to maintain inventories, firms now adopted just-in-time manufacturing. For example, automotive companies no longer stockpiled parts in assembly plants. Instead, they relied on complex, integrated supply chains that brought parts from supplier plants at the exact time when the parts were needed for the production process. The Canadian trucking industry was fond of saying that every product travelled on a truck at some point, an assertion that was probably correct.

There were also a new set of business operating standards that accompanied modified manufacturing and logistics processes. The idea of product and service quality became so prominent in the 1990s that methods of evaluating quality were developed. For instance, Canadians might have passed by office buildings or factories and seen them adorned with banners or flags emblazoned with a code beginning with ISO and wondered what it meant. In that case, ISO stood for the International Organization for Standardization, which was founded in London, England, in 1947 by an association of civil engineers.[5]

ISO is part of a vast array of international treaties and standards that govern everything from the frequencies electronics operate in, treaties on the global movement of mail, the type of electrical plugs attached to electronics and appliances, and more seemingly mundane details such as the size and classification of fasteners used to bolt items together. As far back as 1906, Canada participated in international standards setting, including involvement in the International Electrical Congress that year.[6]

Intended to help establish and regulate continually evolving international standards for technology and manufacturing, including quality and productivity, ISO has multiple committees overseeing different aspects of those activities, standards that businesses embrace to hold and gain market share. The issue with such measures is that organizations and their workers have become highly dependent on them. However, individual companies also set their own quality standards. For example, the Ford Motor Company has a more specific measurement called Q1 — meaning quality is the main job at Ford — that is meant to exceed ISO, and a supplier firm that loses the designation can find itself no longer sending parts to Ford assembly plants.

The concern with quality extended beyond manufacturing, and managers were encouraged to believe that quality measures could be used in any organization. The Six Sigma method was a leading 1990s example of attempts to bring quality processes to industries such as finance. It was developed at Motorola, the U.S. telecommunications company, in 1980 and became very popular with senior managers such as General Electric chairman and CEO Jack Welch. As with most organizational theories, Six Sigma came with effects that reverberated outside the workplace.[7]

The application of measures and methods such as ISO, Q1, and Six Sigma meant workers had to be trained how to use them. The continuing education departments at Canadian community colleges duly swung into action and began offering programs of varying duration that focused on them. Private training firms also rolled out seminars on quality methods, and companies paid large fees for their employees to attend them. Worrying about service and product quality became a new job field and brought work intensification.

The 1980s North American fixation on Japanese production methods continued into the 1990s. The Detroit automakers were still losing market share to Japanese manufacturers as companies such as Honda, Toyota, and Nissan expanded their manufacturing operations in Canada and the United States. The Japanese brought their management practices with them, which were not always well received by workers. The so-called transplants built in the United States by Japanese and German car companies were concentrated in right-to-work states in the South. Right-to-work, which is designed to harm unions, was a misnomer that meant workers could be members of unions but were not required to pay union membership dues, while still receiving union protection and representation. The U.S. Southern states consequently had low union density compared with the northeastern and West Coast states. Japanese and German companies had unionized factories in their home countries, although the Japanese enterprise union model was very different from what predominated in Canada and the United States. Those companies assiduously avoided unionization in their respective Canadian and American operations. For example, Honda and Toyota paid hourly wages that were close, if not equal, to what Detroit automakers paid. However, the benefit and retirement plans were not equal to those earned by GM, Ford, and Chrysler workers.

Canada was successful in attracting Japanese automakers in the 1980s and had extensive Honda manufacturing facilities in Alliston, Ontario, by the end of the 1990s, with Toyota also operating a large plant in Cambridge, Ontario. Manufacturing firms were widely known in industrial relations circles to prefer smaller cities, towns, and rural areas as locations for factories. The Canadian labour movement believed that foreign firms chose to situate new plants in such places because it was believed they were more religious, conservatively minded, and less inclined toward unionization. Moreover, Cambridge and Alliston were not known as hotbeds of support for the labour-friendly NDP. Honda and Toyota did not unionize in the 1990s, even though the Canadian Auto Workers made efforts to organize workers at both companies. There was one exception to this pattern, which illustrated what could happen when Japanese management techniques met Canadian trade unionism.[8]

There were two notable joint ventures between American and Japanese automakers in the 1980s and 1990s. One was a General Motors/Toyota facility in Fremont, California, called New United Motor Manufacturing Incorporated (NUMMI); the other was a General Motors/Suzuki factory known as CAMI Automotive, located in Ingersoll, Ontario. The NUMMI plant is now owned by electric carmaker Tesla. Fremont was in a comparatively densely populated part of California, while Ingersoll was yet another small town chosen to host a large auto assembly plant. The

CAMI facility started off building small four-wheel drive vehicles aimed at entry-level car buyers.

CAMI, while ostensibly a joint venture, was run in accordance with Japanese management practices. The *kaizen* management system introduced at CAMI was ostensibly about continuous improvement, but workers saw something different. It was usual in Japanese companies for everyone in a factory to wear the same colour and type of work coveralls to encourage people to see themselves as part of a team. Gathering workers together for calisthenics prior to the start of a shift was also customary. CAMI's Canadian workers initially did not know how to react when they saw factory management standing before them swinging their arms and otherwise warming up for the workday. Something similar happened when Walmart opened its first Canadian store and visiting American managers began singing "O Canada" in front of assembled workers — the U.S. anthem, "The Star-Spangled Banner," was belted out prior to store openings in the United States — and the workers stood there watching them sing.

From the workers' perspective, *kaizen* meant lean production. Lean also ostensibly referred to continuous improvement and making the most efficient use of resources, but it also entailed doing more with fewer workers, a fast assembly line speed, and a high rate of worker burnout. CAMI opened with great fanfare in 1989 and was unionized, but workers were covered by a collective-bargaining agreement distinct from the master contract signed with General Motors of Canada. There was supposed to be co-operation in the workplace, a focus on quality, and a new direction for labour-management relations. The ultimate result was a five-week strike at CAMI by CAW members in 1992.[9]

The CAMI strike was important, since it showed that workers with access to a workplace voice through unionization would oppose lean production practices. The strike surely made Toyota and Honda even more determined to keep unions out of their Canadian factories. It was also a wider commentary on management practices implemented across Canadian business in the 1990s. The idea of an organization being lean became fashionable with companies, but it invariably meant doing more with fewer workers. The term *sweat the assets* really signified sweat the workers.

The challenges of management methods such as Six Sigma and lean production were exacerbated by the growing disconnect between people who worked in the entry- and mid-level ranks of companies and those who occupied executive suites. Senior executives were hired equipped with newly minted M.B.A. degrees from places such as the Richard Ivey School of Business at the University of Western Ontario (formerly Western Business School) without having much lower- and middle-level management experience. University business education programs were highly focused on teaching quantitative analysis skills, and graduates from top programs sought careers in fields such as consulting and finance. Industries like manufacturing, retail, or other services were less attractive; a job on Bay Street brought money and glamour.

It should not have been a surprise that workers became numbers on spreadsheets. Organizations were highly computerized by the end of the 1990s, and the emergence of the internet as a communications and monitoring tool most clearly demonstrated that trend. The internet, like a lot of other technology innovations, began as a project funded by the U.S. Department of Defense called the Advanced Research Projects Agency Network (ARPANET). The system was designed to allow computers to communicate with one another, which formed the basis for what came next. By 1990, engineer and computer scientist Tim Berners-Lee had invented what he called the World Wide Web and was musing about webpages and hyperlinks. Soon after, the public internet quickly came into being.[10]

Whereas the telephone had previously been the main method of workplace communication prior to the 1990s, the computer transformed how workers talked to one another. The first email is thought to have been sent by Ray Tomlinson in 1971 — he had been involved with ARPANET — and the use of email exploded by the end of the 1990s. Messages of varying lengths could be sent along with attached files. Photography had also long been part of work processes, and the invention of digital photography meant that limitless numbers of photos could be taken and shared through email.[11]

Organizations and workers of all types benefited from access to the internet but it also ushered in new concerns. For instance, viruses were formerly thought to be something humans and animals suffered. People rapidly learned that electronic viruses spread through computers and online networks. The internet could also be misused to track what people did on the job and what they viewed on their computer screens. This opened up new issues in work and employment law as employers wrote policies to regulate internet use on the job and unions pushed back when their members were unfairly monitored at work.

Other forms of technology also had a profound impact on workplaces, even though they did not get the same public attention as the internet. For example, global positioning system (GPS) technology, made possible by satellites, had a major influence on many jobs. It was often used on corporate and public sector fleet vehicles such as police cars, delivery vans, and utility vehicles of different types.

GPS was another invention of the U.S. military and did some things that made work easier for the average person. Most notably, people did not have to keep a stash of paper road maps in their vehicles to find their driving destinations. Instead, they were able to rely on GPS systems that guided them to where they wanted to go. GPS was also good for business, since it could ostensibly improve the efficiency of vehicle use. The best route to drive could be predetermined, the time that a vehicle was idling could be monitored, and vehicle maintenance could even be scheduled based on GPS data. The chief problem with GPS was that it closely monitored what workers were doing and produced data to use in disciplinary cases. There is an argument that a worker did not have anything to worry about if she or he was in the right work location, but GPS still represented a form of constant workplace monitoring.

Technology did not help to alleviate other long-standing occupational discrepancies. Women were still paid less than men in the 1990s. Immigrants to Canada often only found work in low-wage jobs. The Canadian population was more educated in the 1990s than in the 1980s, but there was also growing bifurcation in the workforce. An increasing percentage of Canadian workers were falling behind in terms of wages, while a smaller, more educated group of professional employees thrived, a pattern found across countries in North America and Europe.

In his landmark 1991 book, *The Work of Nations: Preparing Ourselves for 21st Century Capitalism,* American economist Robert Reich writes about the new jobs that were appearing. Reich was a long-time friend of U.S. president Bill Clinton and eventually became U.S. secretary of labor in Clinton's Cabinet when the latter was elected president. Reich particularly focused on the rise of employees that he called symbolic analysts. They were people in jobs that required post-secondary education, they usually lived in cities, and their work was more mental than physical. Reich also raised concerns about the long-term impact of this class of workers as their working lives became decoupled from those of people in more traditional jobs.[12]

Reich's book was enormously influential — few economics works about labour and employment trends climb bestseller lists — and a key problem that he identified would indeed grow worse over time. He argued there was no longer one American economy and instead suggested that groups of workers inhabited distinct economic spheres. People with better education and skills who were part of networks of their peers thrived. Everyone else saw their standards of living decline. Canadians and Americans were accustomed to think of social mobility as an upward process, but it was becoming worryingly evident by the end of the 1990s that people could slide down as readily as they climbed up.

There were certainly aspects of the new knowledge-based economy that benefited some Canadian workers. Computer systems needed a lot of support to keep them operating, and they included two distinct components: hardware and software. The former comprised an actual physical machine and the latter was the system that made it work. This key aspect of computers — hardware and software — made them different from machines that had come before them. The ubiquitous nature of computerization led to a slew of new occupational certifications, which were unsurprisingly developed and pushed by companies that made hardware and software. As Table 7 shows, Canadians were working in service sector occupations and managerial and administrative roles in considerable numbers.

TABLE 7: SELECTED OCCUPATIONAL GROUPS IN CANADA AND
TOTAL EXPERIENCED WORKFORCE, 1991

Occupation	Total Employment
Managerial, Administrative, and Related Occupations	1,739,165
Occupations in Natural Sciences, Engineering, and Mathematics	572,510
Occupations in Social Sciences and Related Fields	316,360
Teaching and Related Occupations	626,520
Occupations in Medicine and Health	727,340
Artistic, Literary, Recreational, and Related Occupations	245,505
Clerical and Related Occupations	2,573,065
Sales Occupations	1,308,705
Service Occupations	1,818,375
Total Service Sector	9,927,545
Total Experienced Workforce	14,220,230
Percentage of Experienced Workforce in the Service Sector	70

Source: Statistics Canada, *1991 Census of Canada*.

Whereas people once looked at General Motors as the symbol of industrial capitalism in North America, people now felt that about service industry companies. This new fixation was especially true of Microsoft. A firm founded by Bill Gates and Paul Allen in Washington State, it became the dominant maker of computer operating systems. The point-and-click Windows system was by far the most common one in use worldwide, and people who trained as Microsoft certified systems engineers had access to good jobs. The service industry also included low-wage employers such as McDonald's. That company had such a profound impact on the U.S. labour market that it claimed to have employed up to one-eighth of Americans at different points in their working lives.

Growth in computer systems employment of various types in the 1990s was also driven by the prospect of a looming global technological disaster called Y2K. That was an acronym for the year 2000, and widespread fear enveloped governments and business over what would happen when computer systems designed to measure time up to the end of

1999 had to deal with a change in the first digit of a year. Y2K became a millenarian phenomenon. As the year 2000 dawned, people pondered the prospect of planes falling from the air because their on-board computers failed. In the end, the many thousands of systems support people trained and hired to computer-code helped ensure there were few system failures on midnight of January 1, 2000. Planes did not fall from the sky, and the world did not regress to the Dark Ages.

The messages people received about work in popular 1990s media were different than what they had even seen in the 1980s. The working class became diminished in public media during the 1990s, and when it was portrayed, it was often in clownish terms in American television shows such as *Roseanne* and *Married ... with Children. Roseanne* focuses on the domestic travails of the blue-collar Conner family living in Illinois, *Married ... with Children* is about the equally working-class Bundy family residing in a suburb of Chicago. Members of both families feel betrayed by the American dream of upward social mobility and the loss of well-paid industrial work. The animated family in *The Simpsons* is another showcase of working-class dysfunction. Family patriarch Homer Simpson lives in the fictional Middle America town of Springfield, works as an operator at a power plant, and often sleeps while on shift.

The newspaper comic strip *Dilbert* first appeared in 1989 and became a staple of popular culture. Its creator, Scott Adams, adroitly drew and wrote wry commentary that was quickly recognizable to millions of readers. Aside from the main Dilbert character, the comic was populated by others such as Dogbert, the megalomaniac dog, and Catbert, the evil human resources director. Many people saw part of their own office workplaces in *Dilbert*.

People employed in service sector jobs were portrayed in television programs but not always in especially realistic terms. Al Bundy from *Married ... with Children* is a shoe salesman, and the life he lives correlates with his family's income, but the characters in *Friends* live in New York City apartments they could not possibly afford in real life. Working-class characters were also largely absent from Canadian popular media, with professional and managerial workers instead being featured more prominently. For example, Global TV's *Traders* depicts the drama of working in a boutique investment bank on Toronto's Bay Street.

Popular music in the 1990s did talk about work and labour, and in a variety of forms that reflected the working-class experience. Rap and hip hop often addressed themes of African-American life, country frequently spoke about the mishaps of blue-collar life, heavy metal was the soundtrack of young white male alienation, and rock artists continued to chronicle the challenges faced by working people. The emergence of rap, hip hop, and country in the 1990s was especially important as they became mainstream forms of music. Country, in particular, was no longer regional, while rap and hip hop came out of the African-American urban experience and earned popularity with white suburban youth.

Canadian musicians continued to sing about working life in the 1990s. Spirit of the West's "Home for a Rest" is a rollicking tale of the band's tour of England. Going on tour may seem like a vacation from a music listener's vantage point, but it is gruelling work for the musicians doing it. Great Big Sea sings about residing next to the ocean and making a living on it in songs such as "A Boat Like Gideon Brown." Music carried on as an escape from the drudgery of work while also being one of the best ways to comment on it.

Writers in Canada in the 1990s created fiction that often includes at least some observations of work. Michael Ondaatje's 1987 novel *In the Skin of a Lion* describes the immigrant work experience in 1930s Toronto. Douglas Coupland's 1991 *Generation X: Tales for an Accelerated Culture* is a commentary on youth culture, including working life, for the generation wedged between baby boomers and millennials. The trepidation people felt as the 20th century ended was manifested in literature.

News media covered changes in the workplace, usually doing so in terms that celebrated the introduction of new technology and forms of employment. Precarious work, meaning occupations that were part-time or short-term, had always been a portion of the job market, but it was now a larger percentage of overall employment in post–Cold War Canada and a feature of a wider trend.

Globalization, a term ordinarily associated with trade liberalization and the freer movement of capital among countries, proliferated in the 1990s. Canadian workers started hearing about the World Trade Organization (WTO) and wondered how its secretive tribunals could overrule policy decisions made by elected governments. There was push-back as the labour movement and social advocacy groups tried to promote a countervailing policy agenda. Unions disliked free trade because they felt it would lead to a loss of their members' jobs to lower-wage countries. Additionally, they believed free trade would empower corporations at the expense of workers and governments. Organizations such as the Council of Canadians and the Canadian Centre for Policy Alternatives published policy papers decrying trade liberalization and the effect it would have on Canadian society. The labour movement in Canada and the United States was not able to mobilize enough workers to stop globalization, but unions did articulate an opposing commentary in the popular media, which was particularly true of an unlikely demonstration in Seattle, Washington, in 1999.

The WTO met in Seattle for a routine meeting, with delegates from member countries discussing trade integration such as the lowering of tariff barriers. Unions and progressive groups from across North America also convened in the city, and the Battle in Seattle ensued. The term *battle* was employed, but the event in Seattle began as a huge street demonstration. The WTO and the City of Seattle did not see the protests coming. There were confrontations between protestors and police, but the main effect of the Seattle protests was to draw public attention to the problems of globalization. Thereafter, economic summits were held with more extensive security and in places less accessible to protestors.

The WTO meeting ground to a halt in the face of boisterous public protest, and the world witnessed tangible efforts to fight back against an economic system helping a few people while harming many others. The concentration of national incomes in the hands of a small group of people at the top of the income ladder increased after 1980, often as the result of deliberate policy decisions to cut taxes on high-income earners, a trend that has been insightfully described by French economist Thomas Piketty in his book *Capital in the Twenty-First Century*.[13] By 1999, it was no surprise that people were ready to take to the streets of Seattle.

The 1990s were a decade in which Canadian unions were under assault by federal and provincial governments. Austerity measures brought in by the federal Liberal government were compounded by attacks from governments in Ontario and Alberta. Labour experienced a chill in other provincial legislatures, but Toronto and Edmonton were the most challenging in the 1990s. The Progressive Conservative Party had governed Alberta since the early 1970s, enjoying robust government revenues due to the province's enormously successful oil and gas sector. Ontario was Canada's industrial heartland and the home of numerous domestic and international manufacturing firms. They both took a right turn politically under Alberta premier Ralph Klein and Ontario premier Mike Harris.

The Klein government was able to spend profusely while cutting taxes, thanks to the flow of oil and gas royalties. Ralph Klein was a Prairie populist who famously issued $400 cheques to every "man, woman, and child" in the province to help share the province's wealth and no doubt ensure a favourable outcome in the subsequent election. He routinely battled with Alberta's labour movement, and his policies were a change in course for the province but within the context of a political party that seemed to be in perpetual power.[14]

Alberta became a magnet for workers from across Canada and beyond. The long-standing internal migration from the Maritime provinces westward continued into the 1990s. Workers from Atlantic Canada held lobster boils in Fort McMurray, and employees slinging coffee at Tim Hortons outlets in the tar sands area were reported to earn close to $20 per hour. In such circumstances, opposing Klein's right-wing populism proved difficult.

The situation in Ontario was similar to Alberta's, yet crucially different. Natural resource extraction was important to Ontario's economy in the 1990s, but services and manufacturing employed more people. The Ontario labour movement was much stronger than Alberta's, and there were three viable political parties sitting in the Ontario legislature, whereas Ralph Klein faced weaker opposition. Ontario also voted different parties in and out of power.

The 1990s began in Ontario with the unlikely election of an NDP government led by Bob Rae. The victory was so surprising that not even Rae expected his party to win. The Canadian business community had been able to handle the election of past and present social democratic governments in Manitoba and Saskatchewan but went into hysterics over the election of the NDP in Ontario. It was a repeat of the corporate media's response to the 1972 election of British Columbia's first NDP government led by Dave Barrett. Rae's election unfortunately coincided with the 1990 recession, and the province's deficit ballooned.

Bob Rae's government made it easier for unions to certify, brought in employment equity legislation to address historical workplace inequities, and implemented other progressive policy measures. Employment equity involved creating policies to increase the workforce participation of four designated groups: women, people with disabilities, Indigenous people, and visible minorities. It mandated targets rather than hard quotas and was different than affirmative action policies in the United States.

The great irony of the Rae years was that unions turned out to be his government's most vociferous opponent. The NDP applied a series of public sector wage control measures called the Social Contract. The wage restraint measures included unpaid days off, commonly termed Rae Days. The Ontario labour movement was divided in its response, but public sector unions were steadfast in their opposition to wage freezes and cuts. Some writers and commentators on the left argued that opposing Rae was the correct choice, even if doing so hastened the NDP's defeat in the 1995 election. They did not have a clear appreciation of what would come next.

The 1995 Ontario election brought the Progressive Conservative Party under Mike Harris from third place in the provincial legislature to a majority government. Harris promptly revoked employment equity legislation, calling it a job-killing quota law; rolled back Rae's labour law reforms; cut social assistance payments; and quickly went to war with the province's public sector unions. Labour responded with Days of Action held across the province, with the largest one happening in Hamilton on June 8, 1995. The Days of Action were city-wide protests in which workers were encouraged to leave their jobs to participate. They were the closest events to general strikes that Canada experienced since the National Day of Protest on October 14, 1976.

Mike Harris was from North Bay, Ontario, and much of his party's Common Sense Revolution manifesto was populist. It was also anti-worker, even though lots of working-class voters supported the new premier. The labour leaders and activists who opposed Rae would not publicly say that doing so was in retrospect a poor strategic choice, but there is little question that a second-term NDP government would never have implemented policies like the Harris government's.

The 1990s were a period of reduced spending, deficit reduction, and overall austerity. A Liberal government led by Jean Chrétien was elected in 1993, and he appointed Paul Martin as finance minister. Chrétien dealt with Quebec's second sovereignty referendum and proved to be an ardent free trader. He also showed a willingness to legislate striking public sector employees back to work, and during his tenure, Canada experienced greater globalization.

For Canadian workers, the 1990s were an important period, and the first decade of the 21st century was anticipated with a mix of hope and anxiety. The trends that defined the 1990s, like the integration of technology into jobs and social life, seemed as if they would continue to accelerate. Moving from the 1990s to the 2000s would be far more of a jolt to working life than progressing from the 1980s. It would mark yet another shift in the nature of working life that would be as profound as the end of the Cold War.

26 THE 2000s: A FEW WINNERS AND MORE LOSERS ON THE JOB

The 2000s ostensibly began on the morning of January 1, 2000, but the direction of the decade really started during the following year. The federal Liberals were still in power — they would win three successive majority governments under Jean Chrétien — but the real change happened south of the border. Eight years of Democratic control of the White House ended with the legally dubious election of Republican president George W. Bush. The validity of Bush's first election would forever be under a cloud because his opponent, Al Gore, won the popular vote and the outcome of the vote was ultimately decided through an ideologically partisan ruling by the U.S. Supreme Court.

Bush's first months in office were underwhelming. He was viewed as an intellectual lightweight whose public statements sometimes validated that suspicion. Bush was from a moderate Republican family but surrounded himself with foreign policy hawks, including Vice-President Dick Cheney. They were about to take their country, and much of the world, on a new and dangerous direction.

On September 11, 2001, four American airliners were hijacked by members of the al Qaeda terrorist group. They had enrolled in pilot training in the United States and were legally in the country. Nobody at the flight school that the hijackers attended thought to report to authorities that the men had no interest in learning how to land a plane, just how to manoeuvre it while in the air. One jet crashed in a field in Pennsylvania after passengers overpowered the terrorists. A second slammed into the Pentagon, the headquarters of the U.S. Department of Defense, and the other two flew into the twin towers of the World Trade Center in New York City.

The post–Cold War era, initiated when the Berlin Wall fell in 1989, effectively came to a close with what became known as 9/11. The United States started its longest war ever after it sent troops to Afghanistan and later invaded Iraq. Canada was not directly drawn into the latter conflict but became embroiled in the former. The events of 9/11 and the years that followed had a major impact on Canada and on work and labour in the country.

The most immediate impact was on the Canada-U.S. border. Canadians were long accustomed to driving across the border, or even walking and cycling over it, without showing much identification beyond a driver's licence. The two countries were well known to share the world's longest undefended border. Canadians living in cities such as Windsor, Niagara Falls, Vancouver, Montreal, and many others were accustomed to driving to the United States to buy gas and groceries or attend sporting events and concerts. Countless Canadian retirees spent their pension money wintering in Florida and Arizona.

The United States introduced formal controls after 9/11 so that crossing the border now meant Canadians needed passports or NEXUS cards to go south of the 49th parallel. Canada continued to be heavily dependent on trade with other countries, and the United States was its largest trading partner, which meant border delays of any kind drove up exporting costs. Increased security measures were also instituted at Canadian airports, further slowing business and personal travel.

Paul Martin replaced Jean Chrétien as federal Liberal leader in 2003. His government's decision to commit military resources to Afghanistan also propelled Canada into its longest war ever, which in turn had an enormous impact on what it meant to be a member of Canada's military. The post–Second World War Canadian military was small considering Canada's size and economic strength. It was unlike some countries in the North Atlantic Treaty Organization, since it did not have conscription and instead relied on volunteers. While Canada played a key role in creating United Nations peacekeeping and Canadian troops died while on such missions, especially in Cyprus, the Korean War was Canada's last major conflict prior to Afghanistan. The Canadian military promoted itself as a place where a young person could acquire marketable skills, earn some money for civilian life, serve his or her country, and enjoy some adventure.

Afghanistan changed the usual military enlistment bargain. The Canadian Army bore the brunt of the country's mission in Kandahar Province. Soldiers were paid a premium for deploying overseas, but it did not really compensate for the perils they faced. Canada lost 158 soldiers in Afghanistan and another 1,800 were wounded. They were young men and women like Private Andrew Knisley, who was born and raised in London, Ontario. Knisley stepped on an improvised explosive device while on patrol in 2009. He lived but lost a leg in the process. The army was initially able to find continued work for him, but he was eventually discharged. The legacy of Afghanistan remained with Knisley and other soldiers long after they returned home. The Canadian military would no longer be perceived as a place to learn a trade and see some of the world. Joining now meant the possibility of actually going to war.[15]

The wars in the Middle East and Central Asia coincided with further transformation in business processes and employment policies in Canada. One particular Canadian firm and its workforce were at the forefront of innovative technology used on the job and beyond. Research in Motion (RIM) was founded by Jim Balsillie and Mike Lazaridis in Waterloo, Ontario, in 1984. In 1999, RIM brought out a device that had a keyboard that could be used to write messages. It was called the BlackBerry and became a technology sensation. Its popularity was such that it was often called the "CrackBerry" because using it became addictive for some people.

The BlackBerry represented a new form of communication that helped people be more productive on the job, but it also tethered workers to their occupations basically around the clock. The device represented wider bifurcation in the Canadian labour market. Waterloo was known as a technology hub. The University of Waterloo enjoyed a global reputation for its computer science and engineering programs. Proximity to Toronto further helped enhance the city's attractiveness to companies other than RIM.

Canadian cities that were not homes to firms like RIM or universities focused on science and technology did not fare as well during the 2000s as Waterloo. U.S. academic Richard Florida wrote about the rise of what he termed the "creative class" and the impact that group had on the cities in which they congregated. The creative class had a definite effect on housing, since it contributed to the gentrification of neighbourhoods. Gentrification meant renovating older homes, increasing their value while putting them out of reach of modest income earners. Houses in areas such as False Creek in Vancouver and the Annex in Toronto that were previously reasonably affordable family homes were often bought by investors, completely gutted and renovated, then flipped on the housing market for huge profits.[16]

People in Florida's creative class were U.S. economist Robert Reich's symbolic analysts. The trends Florida identified were not universally welcomed. The influx of well-educated and equally well-compensated workers into major cities fundamentally altered urban dynamics. Canadian workers were indeed well educated by the start of the new millennium and the country was creating a domestic creative class. As Table 8 shows, there was enthusiasm in Canada for earning credentials of different types. Community colleges, universities, and private vocational colleges provided a wide array of course and program choices. Often community colleges offered as many courses on evenings and weekends as they did during the day. The development of online learning made post-secondary education even more accessible. In fact, the first dedicated online learning system, WebCT, was invented at the University of British Columbia by Murray Goldberg.[17]

TABLE 8: EDUCATIONAL ATTAINMENT IN CANADA, 2001

Total Population 15 to 65	23,901,360
No Credential	7,935,075
High School Diploma	5,499,885
Trade Diploma or Certificate	2,598,925
College Certificate or Diploma	3,578,400
University Certificate or Diploma	601,425
University Bachelor's Degree	2,411,470
Master's Degree	642,055

Source: Statistics Canada, Highest Degree, Certificate or Diploma (12), Age Groups (13B), and Sex (3) for Population 15 Years and Over, for Canada, Provinces, Territories, Census Divisions, Census Subdivisions and Dissemination Areas, 2001 Census — 20 Percent Sample Data, Catalogue No. 95F0419XCB2001001.

Increases in the cost of housing across the country outstripped overall rises in inflation. The Bank of Canada closely watched housing market conditions, and a 2015 report revealed that housing prices in Canada and other countries grew faster than incomes between 1995 and 2010. The cost of borrowing declined during that period because interest rates were low. Nonetheless, low mortgage rates did not matter for a person not earning enough money to buy a home regardless of its type, or for someone barely able to make mortgage payments.[18]

The rising cost of living in major urban centres aggravated other fundamental realities of working life. Commuting, often by personal vehicle, became a torturous daily ritual for many Canadians. Governments built more highways, but they quickly filled with vehicles. Ontario's Highway 407 was perhaps the only one in the Greater Toronto Area that did not turn into a slow-motion parking lot during rush hour because it was a toll road and people preferred to drive without having to pay.

Longer commutes in the 2000s compelled workers of all types to search farther afield for housing. Cities such as Chilliwack, British Columbia, and Barrie, Ontario, which had previously been viewed as somewhat distant from Vancouver and Toronto, became desired places from which to commute. Commuting automatically added time to the workday, and spending two hours or more per day in a car was not uncommon for thousands of Canadian workers. Commuting was also worsened by poor urban and mass transit decisions made by successive public policy-makers.

Canadian cities had once been linked by relatively efficient rail networks. There were streetcars in Winnipeg, Vancouver, Toronto, Montreal, and other cities. The post–Second World War dominance of the automobile lessened public policy interest in building rail networks. Streetcar tracks were torn up in many cities and replaced with smooth asphalt roads. Canada's largest urban centres had transit systems with either above- or below-ground trains. VIA Rail, the national rail carrier, ran trains between major cities. Greater Toronto Area citizens could use the GO commuter system to get to work. Those who had to take mass transit across the country were mainly dependent on bus systems that operated with varying frequency.

Changes in technology altered where and when some groups of people could work. A factory worker obviously had to show up at a production facility every day and the same was true of people employed in many service sector jobs such as nursing. Some workers, like those in Richard Florida's creative class, were able to use technology to remove themselves from the actual workplace if they wanted. The term *telework* was coined in 1973 by Jack Nilles, a former National Aeronautics and Space Administration engineer.[19] The internet made working from home possible and the number of Canadians doing so increased from 17 percent of the workforce in 2000 to 19 percent in 2008, with most of them self-employed.[20]

Teleworking and other new workplace conveniences could not mask wider trends. Income and wealth disparity that had been occurring in Canada and other Western countries for years worsened. Protests against globalization represented one form of opposition to economic inequality, but public protest had limits. By 2007, economic storm clouds were gathering that no amount of protest could stop, a fact particularly evident with the start of yet another financial crisis.

The political environment in Canada changed in 2006 when federal politics took a rightward turn following the election of Stephen Harper's Conservative government. Harper was arguably the most controlling prime minister in modern Canadian political history. He prioritized ideology over pragmatism and was hostile toward workers, especially those in unions. For instance, his government actively muzzled public sector scientists who tried to comment on environmental and other issues in academic and popular media outlets. Harper was nonetheless forced to curb his ideological enthusiasm when confronting the economic crisis of 2008.

The Great Recession of 2008 was the sharpest and hardest economic downturn since the Great Depression in the 1930s. Much of the cause of that catastrophe was attributed to deregulation of global banking practices and the use of sophisticated, if poorly understood, financial tools such as derivatives (essentially, a form of legal betting) and subprime mortgages. Canada was able to weather the 2008 crisis better than the United States, but unemployment still reached double digits in a number of Canadian cities. For many workers, the crisis brought pain unlike anything they had previously experienced. The Conservative government engaged in Keynesian stimulus spending, which ran contrary to Stephen Harper's aversion to government intervention in the economy.

The recession began with the collapse of the American investment bank Lehman Brothers and quickly spread throughout the global financial system. Companies laid off workers across North America, with Canada's unemployment rate rising from 5.3 percent in 2008 to 8.7 percent in 2009. Unemployment began to fall in Canada by the end of 2009 but continued to worsen for Americans. Those national unemployment numbers were difficult to accept and also obscured much broader shifts happening to the nature of work and employment.[21]

Some communities and regions of Canada were hit much harder economically than others following 2008. Alberta and Saskatchewan continued to fare well as a result of the oil and gas industry. British Columbia was historically susceptible to major fluctuations in commodity prices. Atlantic Canada still suffered from declines in fisheries. Quebec and Ontario, especially Southern Ontario, experienced major challenges due to the loss of manufacturing jobs. Indeed, the entire meaning of industrial manufacturing work in Canada fundamentally altered after 2008.

The decline in factory work in Canada and the United States was most clearly exemplified by the 2008 bankruptcies of General Motors and

Chrysler. GM was once the world's largest and most powerful manufacturing corporation, but a combination of poor product design and quality, feckless senior management, relentless competition, and changing consumer tastes brought GM to bankruptcy protection. The investment decisions that GM, Ford, and Chrysler made reflected poor management. They all owned multiple brands — GM even had Sweden's Saab — which served to dilute the resources they could devote to profitable core operations.

North American automakers marketed cars using incentives such as steep discounts to get people into showrooms rather than striving to match better-quality Japanese vehicles. The common trope that the decline of GM, Ford, and Chrysler was caused by unions could not have been farther from the truth. Neither the United Auto Workers in the United States or the Canadian Auto Workers in Canada designed, marketed, engineered, or priced any of the products built by Detroit's automakers. In fact, nobody wanted those companies to build better, high-quality cars than the workers who assembled them.

GM emerged quickly from bankruptcy protection and used the process to extract concessions from its workers. It was not alone in adopting that management approach. Other firms viewed the economic downturn as a convenient pretext to reorder their business practices. Two of the more revealing examples of post-recession corporate behaviour occurred in London and St. Thomas, urban centres in the heart of Southern Ontario.

The first case involved the 2011 closure of a Ford vehicle assembly plant in Talbotville, a hamlet between London and St. Thomas. The plant opened in 1967 and represented the benefits the 1965 Auto Pact brought to Canada. Talbotville workers assembled a variety of cars between 1967 and 2001, from the Ford Pinto to the Lincoln Town Car. It was especially known for building Crown Victoria cars used by police services in Canada and the United States.

The Crown Vic, as it was popularly known, and the Mercury Grand Marquis and the Town Car were the three models assembled at Talbotville when the plant's closure was announced over a year in advance of the event actually occurring. The company's closure rationale seemed valid as there was little consumer demand for large rear-wheel drive cars powered by

V8 engines. Police services and limousine companies were not big enough markets to sustain the plant.

The closure was a major blow to London and St. Thomas. Ford worker Dennis McGee told the *Toronto Star* that he had been at the plant since 1978 and felt a sense of numbness over it closing. St. Thomas's mayor noted that the city had a population of 35,000 and had lost 3,000 manufacturing jobs in the three years preceding the Ford shutdown. Workers received training on how to search for jobs and adjust to the cold realities of the contemporary labour market.[22]

The Ford closure was bad enough, since it had secondary effects on the auto parts sector and other businesses surrounding the plant. What happened in London was even worse because of the circumstances that came into play. London was the home of a large facility owned by the Diesel Division of General Motors. It opened in 1950 and eventually assembled two large products: rail locomotives and light armoured vehicles (LAVs). While it might seem odd from a 21st-century perspective, corporations were once conglomerates and owned lines of business that were often completely unrelated to their core operations. For instance, GM also once owned appliance maker Frigidaire.

The idea of selling the Diesel Division seemed to make business sense, but it unnerved the plant's workers and their union. They had good reason to be concerned. In 2005, GM sold the Diesel Division facility in two pieces. The LAV side of the facility was purchased by American defence industry behemoth General Dynamics. Sales of military equipment were lucrative while the wars in Afghanistan and Iraq were in progress, and the LAV was a popular product with Western and Middle Eastern militaries. The locomotive part of the operation was sold to an investment firm called Greenbriar, which was known for buying and selling companies, not for making long-term investments in manufacturing plants.

Greenbriar then sold what became Electromotive Diesel to Caterpillar Corporation in 2010. Caterpillar was a large manufacturing firm with a locomotive division called Progress Rail, although it was more commonly known as a maker of heavy construction machinery such as bulldozers. The company was also regarded as an anti-union employer, so the table was consequently set for a showdown with the London plant's workers and their union.

The Canadian Auto Workers Local 27 entered into tough bargaining with Caterpillar in 2011, which eventually led to the unionized workers in the plant being locked out at the end of that year. The company demanded huge wage concessions, which the workers refused to accept. Caterpillar responded by closing the plant and shifting all production to a facility in Muncie, Indiana. The Caterpillar shutdown attracted worldwide media attention because of the punitive nature of the firm's actions and what the event represented. The London plant had been the recipient of government subsidies and had been in operation for 61 years, so many people in Canada viewed it as a domestic employer. As the *Guardian* newspaper in the United Kingdom noted, the Caterpillar closure in London raised important questions about the nature of foreign investment.[23]

Both the Ford Talbotville and Electromotive terminations spoke volumes about the 21st-century labour market and business environment. Workers at Ford had a lot more advance warning that they were going to lose their jobs and were also provided with decent severance packages if they were not eligible to retire. Ford seemed to be a much more humane employer than Caterpillar and was worried about harming its brand reputation. As a seller of major consumer products, Ford did not want Canadians to boycott its dealerships.

Caterpillar sold products to other businesses — a bulldozer is not something an individual consumer buys and parks in his or her driveway. Its management was thus far less concerned about public perceptions of how it negotiated with CAW. A boycott of Caterpillar-branded clothing was encouraged by the union, but it was not effective. The union won a moral argument in its struggle with the company, but its members still lost their jobs.

Unfortunately, job losses and plant closures are often forgotten. The Ford Talbotville factory was eventually demolished. While it will be remembered by the people who worked there and perhaps by their families, it is now a vacant tract of land to anyone driving past it. The factory was dismantled and literally ground into dust. The Electromotive plant was purchased by another company and put to different uses. The workers who lost their jobs inevitably live with consequences of varying duration; some deal with it for the rest of their lives.

The *Globe and Mail* devoted considerable coverage to the Electromotive workers who lost their jobs and followed a group of them as they tried to find new work. The newspaper reported that 485 former unionized workers had found work eight months after the closure, but only 68 had full-time jobs. The rest were working part-time, in contract employment, or were self-employed. United Way of London chief executive Andrew Lockie commented on the growing rates of addiction, mental health challenges, and marriage breakdowns among unemployed workers in the city. Parents were telling their children that they could no longer afford to pay for extracurricular activities, and food bank usage was up. There was terrible irony in a situation in which unionized factory workers had contributed half of the United Way's donations, and now many were unemployed and reliant on agencies funded by the United Way.[24]

The experience of former industrial workers in London mirrored what was happening across Ontario in the years following the recession. Other plant closures included Navistar in Chatham, Sterling Truck in St. Thomas, John Deere in Welland, and Heinz in Leamington. Hamilton's two notable steel manufacturers, Stelco and Dofasco, came under foreign ownership and barely stayed in business. The key aspect of all the various industrial job losses was that they signalled that Canada was finally showing the pattern of deindustrialization that had already occurred across the so-called Rust Belt towns and cities in the United States.

The job market into which displaced workers entered was much different than what many of them had known when they first entered the workforce. The process of looking for a manufacturing job in the 1970s and 1980s often involved going and "putting your name in" at a factory. A person may have had a family member or friend who could provide some inside information on job openings. A basic paper application was completed and submitted, some aptitude testing might be administered, and a hiring decision was made thereafter. There were organizations that employed psychological testing to screen applicants, but it was nothing compared to what was happening by the 2000s.

Finding a job in the new millennium could still involve completing a paper application, but it more often meant using an online tool through which a résumé could be submitted. Computer literacy skills were consequently required of former factory workers. Major employers often did not screen their own applicants and instead used third parties to do such work. Word-of-mouth job leads were still common, and people were encouraged to utilize their personal networks to find work. There was a great irony in telling laid-off factory workers to use their networks when everyone they knew was also unemployed.

There was also a large intermediate segment between potential workers and employers: employment agencies. Such companies had been around since Kelly Services was founded in 1946 to provide short-term clerical help. A company paid a fee to Kelly or one of the other agencies that came after it, and the agency hired and provided a worker for a period of varying duration. The key was that the agency was the employer, not the organization where the worker was actually situated. The early temp agencies were also highly gendered — the term *Kelly girl* became common — since they first focused on supplying clerical workers.[25]

The meaning of temporary employment significantly changed by 2008. Temp agencies could supply workers from all manner of backgrounds: technical, production, clerical, professional. The scale of the temporary employment industry was also remarkable in the years following the recession. Statistics Canada reported that the number of permanent jobs declined by 3.8 percent between 2008 and 2009, while temporary work increased by 0.7 percent. In 2011, there were 700,000 workers in Ontario alone working for 1,300 temporary employment agencies.[26]

Employment agencies came in different sizes and some aspired to hire people for all industries while others focused on specific areas. The large firms were multinational, with Swiss-based Adecco being the largest in the world. The staffing industry was a huge business globally. In 2010, it generated close to $9.4 billion in revenues in Canada. The profit margins were low — just 3.1 percent that year — but money was still made.[27]

The fact that huge revenues could be generated providing workers to other organizations led to another important fact of the early 21st-century job market: temporary staffing agencies were not going away, since they were a fundamental part of the Canadian labour market. Staffing agencies were not generally found at college and university job fairs in the 1980s, but they were in attendance by 2010. It was through agencies that new college and university graduates often found their first jobs and how unemployed workers made their way back into the job market.

However, there were major problems with the temporary staffing industry. The standard employment relationship that was the ideal work arrangement following the Second World War was under even greater assault after 2008. Temporary work was marketed by staffing firms as being rewarding, if not liberating. People could move among different work environments, perhaps learn new skills, and there was supposed to be the prospect of maybe securing a full-time job. Often, though, little notification of a possible job was given, and the organization that contracted the staffing agency to supply a worker could send him or her back with similar short notice. All workers in a given province are covered by employment standards legislation, if not covered by federal regulations, but temporary agencies were poorly regulated in the 2000s. Temporary workers were also almost impossible to unionize, since they were usually not around long enough to sign membership cards and participate in a certification vote.

Temporary work was precarious, meaning it brought little job security, but it was also misunderstood by people in full-time jobs. Precarious work was everywhere if people looked closely enough to recognize it. Media work was often done by freelancers, including reporters appearing on television. A dearth of full-time teaching jobs meant young teachers' college graduates often subsisted on a combination of short-notice substitute teaching assignments and other work such as tutoring.

The other unsettling aspect of precarious work after 2008 was who was doing it. Immigration was as central to Canada's economy as it had ever been, but immigrants often found themselves working in low-paid, insecure jobs. New Canadians were employed in everything from farm work to housekeeping in big-city hotels. Language and culture barriers often prevented them from understanding their rights on the job, and there was consequently a problem with worker exploitation.

There was also research that white male industrial workers were hardest hit by the 2008 recession. There is certainly a valid argument that white men occupy a privileged place in society regardless of their social class, but the loss of industrial work has profound social, economic, and political consequences. On a basic level, 218,000 manufacturing jobs were lost just between 2008 and 2009. Those jobs represented payrolls that were not coming back.[28]

Wages barely increased in Canada between 1990 and 2010. Average men's wages increased by only 8.5 percent when adjusted for inflation. Women's wages rose somewhat more by 22 percent during the same period. Women still made less than men, and a gendered wage gap remained a persistent labour market feature.[29] At the same time, the average number of hours worked per year in Canada decreased from 1,787 in 2000 to 1,715 in 2010.[30] The decline in working hours can be attributed to rising job casualization, which is the process of making jobs less secure by relying more on part-time, contract, and casual work arrangements. It is a deliberate shift away from full-time employment.

There was also the issue of who laid-off workers would blame for job loss. Nativism, which can be viewed as focusing on the interests of a dominant majority at the expense of non-white minorities and immigrants, has long existed in Canada, although not always as overtly as in the United States. The so-called Tea Party movement in the United States, which was ostensibly about economics and fiscal conservatism, can be more correctly viewed as a racist backlash to the election of Barack Obama as the first African-American president of the United States. Canada did not develop its own version of the Tea Party, but there was always a danger that the wrong groups in society would be blamed for the recession.

The 2008 recession also accentuated another understandable trend when Canadians talked about the mechanics of job loss. Labour and employment law is one of many legal subfields and is not the purview of average citizens any more than any other area of law. Nonetheless, terms such as *severance* and *constructive dismissal* came up in daily conversation. Workers who were unionized had at least some voice at work, but non-unionized workers had to resort to the courts.

The media messages Canadians received about work in the 2000s increasingly reflected the angst people felt about their futures. A 2009 CBC *The Fifth Estate* episode entitled "The Education of Brian Nicholl" revealed to working Canadians what their laid-off fellow citizens were facing after 2008. The show exposed what happened when a medium-sized auto parts plant owned by Edscha Canada closed in Niagara Falls, Ontario. It depicted the enormous difficulties the Canadian Auto Workers faced when trying to stop plant shutdowns by foreign-owned companies. Edscha's parent was based in Germany.[31]

The workers in Niagara Falls did everything possible to oppose the closure but to no avail. Brian Nicholl was president of their local union. Anyone watching the program might have thought there were people just like Nicholl in their communities. Nobody wanted the Edscha plant to stay open more than Nicholl and his co-workers. In the end, some outstanding wages were collected but not nearly the full amount owed to workers.

Television dramas and feature films do not generally talk about the experience of unemployment, obviously because the topic is too depressing. The office environment, though, is lampooned in the U.S. television show *The Office*, starring Steve Carell. It is based on a 1990s British series of the same name featuring Ricky Gervais. A 2005 film entitled *North Country* starring Charlize Theron depicts horrific sexual harassment endured by women working in open-pit mining in Minnesota. It is a cinematic exception and is based on the actual experience of a woman named Lois Jenson who began working at a taconite mine in Minnesota in 1975.

The upheaval that occurred in workplaces in the 2000s was not often covered in television and movies, but workers themselves became the focus of a new form of entertainment — reality TV. A 1973 program called *An American Family* was broadcast on the U.S. Public Broadcasting System, but the genre really grew in the 2000s. *Survivor* premiered in 2000 and was based on a Swedish program called *Expedition Robinson*. Shows on decorating, home renovation, automotive customization, personal makeovers, weight loss and exercise, and working in restaurant kitchens soon followed. Canadians made notable contributions to reality television. Mike Holmes, a home builder and renovator, saves distraught homeowners from their renovation catastrophes, while designer Sarah Richardson shows them how to decorate their homes. Sawing, cutting, drilling, painting, and other manual tasks make for compelling viewing.

Reality programs based in restaurants and cooking were ubiquitous by the end of the 2000s. They may have been entertaining for a lot of viewers, but they also revealed that restaurants can be appalling workplaces. The chefs portrayed in some shows — Gordon Ramsay is a particularly egregious example — manage their kitchen staffs through shouting and intimidation. The work pace in hospitality is shown to be relentless and driven by retrograde management doctrine.

Canada also produced a mockumentary program that was supposed to be comedic but almost looked like a documentary, such was the nature of the characters portrayed in it. *Trailer Park Boys* debuted in 2001 and revolves around three main characters — Ricky, Julian, and Bubbles — who reside in the eponymous trailer park. They occasionally work while often engaging in shady activities to try to make money. Middle-class viewers may not realize there are lots of people like Ricky, Julian, and Bubbles living on the economic brink in Canada. They have become the collective face of part of Canada's working class.

The working class appeared less often in other forms of media. Covering specific cases of layoffs makes for good human interest stories, but media consumers want to move on to something uplifting or exciting. The job losses that occurred across Canada after 2008 did not often enter popular media discourse. A song by local London, Ontario, band Pete Denomme and the Cosmic Cowboys is an exception. "They Keep Rollin'" is a musical indictment that focuses on the Electromotive closure and is a commentary on job loss across Canada, the rising use of food banks, and corporate behaviour.[32]

The legal system that regulated Canada's workplaces still had not significantly evolved despite every indication that jobs and employment were in constant flux. One notable exception was the passage of Bill 168 in Ontario in 2009. That act updated the province's occupational health and safety to include harassment as a workplace hazard. The change was made because of high-profile cases of women being murdered by co-workers and due to overwhelming evidence that a problem with people suffering different forms of harassment at work existed and was causing physical and psychological harm.[33]

One of the cases concerned a woman named Theresa Vince, who lived in Chatham, Ontario. Vince worked as a human resources manager at a Sears Canada store and was subject to sexual harassment by the store manager. He shot her to death at work. Another case pertained to a second woman named Lori Dupont who was a nurse killed on the job at a hospital in Windsor, Ontario. Dupont's murderer was an anesthesiologist who had turned into a violent stalker. The wider tragedy was that far more women suffering daily workplace harassment were silent.[34]

Work became more stressful in the 1990s and 2000s, which was most evident in the huge percentage of people going on stress leave. The number of people taking such leave increased by 220 percent between 1990 and 1999.[35] This was not just a case of "mental health" days taken at random; it was people with medical documentation saying they needed time off from work. The number of prescriptions written for antidepressant medication in Canada increased from 3.2 million in 1981 to 14.5 million in 2000,[36] a rate far exceeding the growth of the country's population.

A 1998 book by James E. Loehr entitled *Stress for Success* became a bestseller, but its message was flawed. There were two types of stress: eustress and distress. The former is good and is the type experienced by doing routine daily activities such as getting up, showering, dressing, and eating. Distress is what happens when too much is going on and people feel overloaded. There was clearly too much of that happening at the turn of the millennium in Canada.[37]

The end of the first decade of the 21st century was full of contradictions for workers. They were better educated than ever before, the participation rate for women was greater, there was more diversity in a variety of aspects, and people had access to more technology and information than at any time in human history. The Cold War era, which was always fraught with dread over the prospect of nuclear war, receded into history. The 1990s and 2000s should have been better for Canadian workers.

People with better education and more marketable skills should supposedly earn decent wages and enjoy a modicum of job security, but having improved education did not necessarily mean getting a higher-quality job. Technology made jobs easier for some workers. For instance, it was much simpler to use Microsoft Word to write and edit a document than doing repeated drafts on an electric typewriter.

On the other hand, having every move tracked by a GPS locator brought a new and invasive level of workplace monitoring. Every document written on a computer and scanned on a photocopier could be monitored, as could every website that a person visited on a workplace computer and all emails sent and received. Surveillance had not yet become as insidious as George Orwell warns in *Nineteen Eighty-Four*, but it was showing potential to go that way by the end of the 2000s.[38]

Rates of stress leave, massive increases in antidepressant use, the passage of workplace harassment legislation, more precarious work, and stagnant wages all showed that working in Canada was difficult overall from the 1990s to the 2000s. Y2K did not bring widespread calamity to Canada, but other trends wreaked havoc on workers and their families. The public policy-making apparatus in Canada, mainly government, had yet to grapple with what was happening in the Canadian labour market other than to extoll the virtues of lifelong learning. Further change was on the way, and some of it helped workers while other aspects brought yet more unexpected problems. Canadian workers were firmly in the 21st century; there was no going backward.

NAME	PART VI **Working in the 21st Century**	
DAY	**TIME IN**	**TIME OUT**
1	7 48	16 17
2	7 45	16 15
	7 42	

27 WORK IN CANADA IN THE EARLY 2020s

One of the most remarkable aspects of the contemporary Canadian economy is that it enjoyed a period of sustained growth once the country emerged from the 2008 recession. Unemployment was historically low, just over 5 percent, and domestic stock markets seemed robust as Canada entered the third decade of the 21st century. The federal Liberal Party, which had won a majority under Justin Trudeau in 2015, still found itself in power after the 2019 election but with a minority. The country was also about to experience the worst public health crisis since the 1918–20 Spanish flu pandemic as well as the most pronounced economic downturn — well beyond 2008 — since the Great Depression.

Public economic policy in the 2020s has followed a well established but problematic trajectory. Canadian workers are now firmly entrenched in a global economic system, and raising protectionist trade barriers is enormously difficult. Canada's historical dependence on exports for economic growth continues in the third decade of the 21st century, a fact complicated by American trade policy. Former prime minister Pierre Trudeau once observed that living next door to the United States was like being in bed with an elephant. Canada has become quite adept at dealing with that elephant — perhaps better than any other country — but there are still difficult shoals to navigate.[1]

The Republican administration elected in the United States in 2016 and led by Donald Trump as president pursued protectionist trade policies, including issuing a demand to Canada and Mexico that the North American Free Trade Agreement (NAFTA) be renegotiated on terms more favourable to America. Canada's government had little recourse but to engage the Trump administration, and the same reality was true for Mexico. The new United States–Mexico–Canada Agreement (USMCA) fulfilled Trump's campaign pledge to redo NAFTA, but the new trade treaty was not significantly different than its predecessor. Mexico gave up more ground and had to acquiesce to American demands, largely brought forward by the Democratic Party in the U.S. Congress, that the new deal include stronger protections for workers. The NAFTA agreement had also contained a provision requiring Canada to meet American oil and natural gas supply needs even in times of domestic shortage, but that stipulation was not in USMCA. The new agreement also mandated that cars built in the USMCA area must include 70 percent North American parts content.

Canada also concluded a wide-ranging trade agreement with the European Union in 2017 called the Canada-Europe Trade Agreement (CETA). This was a much more logical acronym than USMCA and gave Canada access to the vast European market. The country was also part of the Comprehensive and Progressive Agreement for Trans-Pacific Partnership (CPTPP) that provided almost unimpeded access to markets across the Pacific, including Japan. By 2020, Canada was a signatory to a total of 15 trade agreements that were either bilateral or multilateral in scope.[2]

No major political party in Canada publicly suggested that the Liberal government should refuse to renegotiate NAFTA and let the agreement lapse in the face of aggressive American demands. The political battles waged in preceding decades about whether or not Canada should sign free trade agreements were over and the free traders had won. The first problem with the trade policies pursued by successive Conservative and Liberal governments was that Canada's exports still predominantly went to the United States and insufficient effort was made by Canadian business to expand into other countries. The United States remains Canada's key trading partner.

A second problem with Canada's trade policies involved the country's continued reliance on natural resource production and processing. The auto industry was a vital part of central Canada's economy, and there were some national manufacturing firms such as auto parts makers Magna and Linamar and industrial conglomerate Bombardier. Natural resources were still bigger parts of the Canadian economy. There were large Canadian-owned firms in the natural resource sector, such as Suncor in oil and gas production, but there were also numerous foreign-owned firms active in Canada's resource economy.

The country's manufacturing sector was still a branch-plant economy, a status that was problematic in many ways. As noted in the previous chapter, little recourse was available to workers when a foreign-owned factory closed and the company's remaining assets were carted away. There was also the problem of how branch plants were viewed by Canadian workers and their communities. That fact was clearly illustrated in Ontario. Canadians came to see companies like Ford of Canada and General Motors of Canada as domestic employers. The labour movement, especially the auto workers' union, described cars made by General Motors, Ford, and Chrysler as domestic, whereas Honda and Toyota products were "offshore" cars, even though both Japanese firms had operations in Ontario.

The fact was that by 2020 two of the three Detroit automakers each only had one assembly plant left in operation in Canada, while one had two of them. Honda and Toyota were meeting and exceeding the Detroit Three's Canadian production numbers, which obviously raised the question of what constituted a domestic automobile. Vehicles were commonly known to include parts from across North America and beyond, so the idea of a vehicle being domestic was really predicated on where final assembly happened.

Manufacturing in Canada has often been associated with the automotive industry, but it was also in other sectors. Canada, specifically Toronto, was once home to firms such as Irwin Toy and John Inglis (appliances). Toronto and Montreal had thriving garment and textile industries. Kitchener, Ontario, was once the home of Bauer hockey equipment. Canadians, for the most part, no longer work in factories making things, a situation that persists in the 2020s. There are some exceptions; for example, Stanfield's still produces socks and underwear in Truro, Nova Scotia. Molson and Labatt are part of international firms, especially Labatt, but manufacturing is still a diminished sector of the economy compared to past years.

Major national firms fell because of competition, and in the case of a company like Nortel, because of poor management. Research in Motion, the inventor of the BlackBerry, was a major player in the cellphone market for several years before losing market share to larger manufacturers. The company changed its corporate name to BlackBerry in 2013, but its sales declined in comparison with larger companies such as Apple and Samsung. The firm did not act fast enough to introduce a touch-screen phone, which impacted its market share even though its devices had always been well regarded for their security features and operating system. BlackBerry managed to turn around its operations by focusing more on software, but its employment levels in Waterloo and other communities were considerably reduced.

Free trade agreements did not necessarily help Canadian firms. Two of the major banks — TD Canada Trust and Bank of Montreal — expanded their operations in the United States. TD was particularly successful and now has more American than Canadian branches. In comparison, the Bombardier conglomerate has been weakened by foreign competition. Founded as a recreational products company first known for the Ski-Doo, Bombardier expanded into aviation and rail products. The Canadian and Quebec governments provided incentives to the company and promoted its products overseas. Those efforts were not sufficient to prevent Bombardier from having to partner with European firm Airbus to keep its C-Series jet alive when the Trump administration placed a tariff on the plane. Airbus operates a factory in Alabama, which qualified it as an American company, so partnering with the Europeans became the only viable way to keep the jet's production moving forward, resulting in the C-series becoming the Airbus A220. Eventually, Bombardier sold its recreational products division. The experience Bombardier had with Airbus showed the difficulties that could arise even when free trade agreements were in place. Deals such as the Bombardier-Airbus one also revealed the problem that the loss or reduction of Canadian companies had on workers.

The early 2020s Canadian economy seemed robust prior to the start of the Covid-19 pandemic, since unemployment was historically low at slightly over 5 percent in early 2020. Employers across the country complained of labour shortages in virtually all areas of the economy, from personal support workers to information technology. The reality is that the seemingly strong employment picture that existed before the pandemic masked serious problems with the nature of work and labour in Canada, which is particularly true of the percentage of people actually working.

The unemployment rate is one way of measuring the health of the labour market, but so, too, is the labour force participation rate, which is also measured by Statistics Canada. Whereas the unemployment rate calculates who is unemployed and looking for work, the labour force participation rate takes everyone in the overall labour market into consideration regardless if they are employed or unemployed. A significant percentage of the working-age population between 15 and 65 was not working or looking for work before the pandemic began. At least part of that group was undoubtedly made up of people who lost their jobs in 2008 and never fully recovered. There are reasons workers should have felt discouraged in the 2020s even without the pandemic's impact on employment.

The process of job loss described in the previous chapter in cases such as Electromotive remained in the popular consciousness but slipped from the public's attention once media attention shifted elsewhere. The general assumption is that a person finds something to do after he or she loses a job, then otherwise muddles through with some degree of success. However, the process of recovering from job loss has been different in the 21st century and goes beyond the important role of job placement agencies. Workers are frequently expected to "adjust" to the job market after being laid off.

Workforce adjustment is a process that would not be known to anyone who has not experienced it. It essentially means that a person has been eased from one job to another through education and retraining, although there are more specific descriptions. For instance, Alberta's workforce adjustment service is intended to do things such as help people understand job loss, assess their personal situations, write résumés, and improve their interviewing skills. The provincial government supposedly brings labour and employer groups together to find solutions to help people cope with job loss.[3]

The goals of workforce adjustment seem benign, but the process is really about getting people to adapt to free market realities such as the growth of non-standard work like contract and short-term employment, the elimination of defined benefit pensions, and persistently low minimum wages. Unions participate in adjustment programs, such as after the Electromotive closure in London, Ontario, but they are not supposed to engage in any political action at adjustment centres, and criticism of workers' former employers is forbidden. Workers are supposed to move on and adapt to the labour market. Being successfully adjusted can furthermore mean something as simple as taking some night school classes at a local community college. Workforce adjustment is not just for laid-off unionized factory workers; an adjustment centre was opened in Waterloo, Ontario, for displaced former BlackBerry employees.[4]

Canada continues to have a remarkably well-educated labour force; indeed, it has the highest rate of post-secondary education among members of the Organisation for Economic Co-operation and Development. Nevertheless, there is still an ongoing problem with what sociologist David Livingstone has called the education-jobs gap.[5] For several years Canada has had a disconnect between higher educational attainment and higher wages. Canadians would be surprised to know that most jobs do not require post-secondary education. A 2013 Georgetown University study of the American job market reveals that only 31 percent of jobs required people to have post-secondary education skills.[6] The same can be said for Canada.

Of course, this raises the question of why only a third of jobs demand more than high school education. The answer principally relates to the literacy, numeracy, and problem-solving skills that a person needs to perform a given job. Many occupations now incorporate automation that makes tasks easier to do even while workers are being more frequently monitored. For instance, people working as cashiers in a supermarket in the 1970s stood in front of a mechanical cash register, had to remember prices of individual items, take cash from customers, and count back the amount of change to be returned.

The situation in 2020 is far different than it was even three or four decades ago. A cashier may not even be necessary in many supermarkets, since leading chains like Loblaws have installed automated checkout kiosks. Customers scan barcodes, and if they do encounter trouble with the kiosk, an attendant comes and presses a few touch-screen buttons or perhaps enters a code to return things to normal. Similarly, an actual cashier scans barcodes and the computerized cash register automatically tallies the bill. Cash is used less as debit cards are ever more ubiquitous. Cashiers need not count back change or remember item prices, since systems do those tasks for them.

Yet another example of the impact of technology and job deskilling is seen with Amazon, the American firm started by Jeff Bezos in his garage to sell books online. The company now offers virtually anything anyone could possibly want to buy. Amazon fills its orders from its network of "fulfillment centres," more than 100 of which are found across North America. *Fulfillment centre* is a euphemism for *warehouse*. Amazon has much in common with Walmart. The latter company dominated retail 20 years ago and has now been eclipsed by Amazon. Walmart has been the topic of a lot of popular and scholarly scrutiny, and now Amazon is the subject of such attention. Amazon has a profound impact on employment in North America, and the nature of the work in its warehouses illustrates the reality of the level of education required for jobs.[7]

In 2020, Amazon said that it employed more than 125,000 North American workers and that it paid wages on average 30 percent higher than other retailers. The work in an Amazon warehouse involves going around with a scanner and picking items that have been ordered, then taking those products to be packaged and shipped. Amazon organizes its facilities by space availability rather than by item type, so a book could sit on a shelf next to a hammer.[8]

A 2020 Amazon job notice for a warehouse associate specified that applicants would receive and stow inventory, pick and pack orders, and load boxes onto trucks. Applicants had to be able to lift 22 kilograms and stand for 12 hours, among other prerequisites, including the operation of forklifts and hand trucks. A high school diploma was the only required educational requirement. Indeed, the ability to lift 22 kilograms was the first necessity listed on the job notice, which meant it was the most pressing one in the minds of Amazon management.[9]

That job at Amazon was a clear example of why a high school diploma was the only essential for most jobs. Amazon's warehouses are known as difficult working environments due to the fast pace of work, but at least its management does not exaggerate the level of education required to do a job. There were undoubtedly people with more than high school education who applied to that Amazon job, especially new Canadians who suffered the indignity of not having post-secondary credentials from their home countries recognized in Canada, but anyone in that circumstance would have been considered underemployed if she or he was hired by Amazon.

The messages relayed to Canadian workers about job skills are often completely at odds with the nature of the actual occupations available. For instance, the *Toronto Star* ran a series of articles in 2020 on the future of Toronto that included analysis of current and projected jobs in the city. The newspaper eagerly listed the so-called "top jobs" in the city, including registered nurses and information systems analysts and consultants. The fact that retail jobs were going to be the most abundant category in 2020 was mentioned, but the paper then blithely and inexplicably announced that those jobs were not being included in any account of what qualified as a top job in Toronto. This assertion was terribly misleading because if retail was the biggest source of jobs in the city, retail work was a top job even if it paid poorly.[10]

There are basic reasons behind the education-jobs gap. Canadian workers receive relentless messages that they need to continually upgrade their skills and acquire ever more marketable abilities. The idea of marketability is closely linked to vocational learning of different types. Pursuing a liberal arts education, which is intrinsically not vocational, is generally described as lacking merit. The term *worthless degree* entered the popular culture lexicon by the end of the 1990s, even though it was an affront to everything university education embodied. Universities exist to produce and teach knowledge and to hopefully help people become better human beings.

Instead, students were urged by business and government by 2020 to learn how to code and manipulate computer programs and otherwise focus on academic subjects in science, technology, engineering, and mathematics (STEM), a remarkably myopic and misguided public education policy objective. Canadians have been living around electricity for more than a century, yet nobody suggests that students at any level of the education system should take a basic electrical course. STEM subjects are undoubtedly useful, but no wars have ever been fought over mathematics and engineering. Those subjects have been employed to wage wars, but the humanities and social sciences explain the origins and consequences of human behaviour over time. The idea of "trusting the science" has entered the popular lexicon, but faith in anything must be carefully placed. Science can solve problems, but it can also give humanity crises such as global warming as much it will find solutions to dilemmas.

Universities have never existed to prepare vast numbers of graduates for the job market, but they are now expected to do so. The government of Alberta currently links post-secondary funding to the employability of graduates, including salaries earned after graduation, while the government of Ontario plans to move in the same direction. This is a situation that causes understandable angst among college and university administrators and faculty, but their protests will likely be to no avail. Colleges and universities can do their best to forecast the fields and degrees that will command high wages in coming years, but they cannot accurately predict when recessions will occur that drive up unemployment. They are also unable to guarantee what job choices graduates will make, whether or not they will succeed or fail in interviews, or if they will have unexpected life events that throw their careers off course.

There is another broad issue: Why do governments and business push for a more educated workforce if post-secondary credentials are not always germane to available jobs? The simple answer is because they can do so. Education is principally a provincial function in Canada, while spending for it is usually right behind health care as a budget item. There is a vast education apparatus across Canada that is well established to move students through to apprenticeship, college, or university after high school. Students are now required to attend school until age 16 or 18, depending on the province or territory, and school boards have adult education functions to ultimately get everyone through even if some fall behind in their studies.

Canada now actively recruits international students to come and study at Canadian colleges and universities. There is considerable national self-interest behind that effort. International students pay up to three times the amount of fees paid by domestic students, so they are beneficial to the financial bottom lines of the institutions they attend. Such students are also on an expedited path to landed immigrant status, which means they can join the workforce after graduation. Indeed, they can work part-time while studying. Policy toward international students is yet another example of the labour market shaping government decision-making.

Canadian students now also expect their post-secondary credentials will prepare them for the job market. A 2013 CBC documentary called *Generation Jobless* profiles young underemployed Canadians and contrasts them with their peers in Switzerland, which has low youth unemployment and a comprehensive apprenticeship program. Young Canadians, such as urban geography student Azaria Botta, are profiled in the documentary. They lament being sold out by a society that promised good careers to people who go to university. A system like Switzerland's enables someone like Botta to move more easily between apprenticeship and university education. The challenge with the Swiss system is that it streams people into learning paths at a relatively young age. They can switch paths later on, but streaming is fraught with issues of class, race, gender, and ethnicity.[11]

Students in Canada have internalized a vocational view of post-secondary learning and expect colleges and universities to prepare them for careers. A 2020 *Toronto Star* article profiled students at Southern Ontario universities to learn what they wanted to do with their degrees. Jazz Dev and Shawn Cruz told the paper they were happy completing humanities and social science subjects but wanted more links to things like experiential learning, meaning learning by doing. Students have every right to such expectations, but it also places increased burdens on colleges and universities to be in continual adaption mode.[12]

The business community also has a keen interest in employing well-educated workers and generally promotes post-secondary learning. There are basic reasons for this position. Firstly, business prefers that people educate and train themselves rather than looking to corporations to handle that function. For example, Canadian employers are much less interested in participating in apprenticeship programs than their European counterparts. Driving policy narratives that encourage potential workers to educate themselves is viewed as more cost-effective for business in the short term.

The basic fact is that employers hire people who are over-educated because they can. To return to the job working for Amazon in the Bolton, Ontario, fulfillment centre: the company would have surely hired a person with at least some post-secondary education over an applicant who had just a high school diploma, because completing a college or university credential indicates that a person has some initiative and likely higher literacy and problem-solving skills. The fact that such a person can be paid the same as someone with lesser educational attainment is a bonus for an employer, although a problem for workers.

28 RETIREMENT IN CANADA

The stress of work continues in the 2020s. This is shown in the fact that Canadian workers are known to suffer from a lack of sleep. Health Canada guidelines stipulate that a person should sleep between seven and nine hours per night, but only around a third of people do so. The rest go to bed late, rise early, or spend part of the night awake fretting about a multitude of problems. Money and financial matters were reported as the most common reason for losing sleep. People ultimately work to live, not live to work, and the fact that so many people lack sleep surely indicates a need for greater work-life balance.[13]

The problem of fatigue and general life burnout seems particularly pronounced for working women. Ada Calhoun describes the competing pressures facing Generation X women in her 2020 book *Why We Can't Sleep: Women's New Midlife Crisis*. Her analysis was welcome because a generational divide exists between the baby boomers, who are not always sliding gracefully into retirement, and millennials, who were born between 1981 and 1996. Generation Xers were born between millennials and baby boomers from 1965 to 1980 and continue to be overlooked compared to the other two groups. That generational tension manifests itself in different and important ways. A large part of that friction relates to baby boomers and retirement, although it will soon pertain to the retirement prospects of all Canadians. Those prospects are shaped by the financial circumstances people face in retirement, and pension plans are central to the decisions people will make.[14]

There are two principal types of pension plan in Canada: defined benefit (DB) and defined contribution (DC). The Canada Pension Plan (CPP), Old Age Security (OAS), and Guaranteed Income Supplement (GIS) are meant to be supplements to DB and DC plans. A DB plan pays a fixed amount of monthly retirement income and is based on a formula that takes into account a person's years of service and pre-retirement income. Some plans, such as those of public employees, can be generous and pay up to 60 percent of a worker's pre-retirement income. DB plans can also provide partial or full indexing with the cost of living, and a person will receive lifetime payments from a DB plan. It is important to note that despite the periodic hysterics in the business press about the cost of public sector pensions, DB plan members like those in the public service have to make significant paycheque pension contributions and the cost of benefits are not solely born by taxpayers.[15]

DC plans are based on Registered Retirement Saving Plans (RRSPs). The RRSP was invented by the federal government in 1957 as an annuity plan. An annuity is a financial instrument that people can buy with their RRSPs and other retirement savings. It functions somewhat like a DB pension fund, since it pays out a fixed amount of money for the rest of a person's life. A worker in a DC plan receives a sum of money each year from his or her employer, often a percentage of income, and the funds are put into group RRSPs that comprise workers from the same organization. A person is also often required to contribute a percentage of his or her income, although not necessarily the same amount as his or her employer. An RRSP itself can be comprised of cash, company stocks, bonds, and other investment tools. The value of a person's workplace RRSP should theoretically increase in value as more money is contributed to it, especially because of compound interest. When a person decides to retire, he or she looks at the amount of money invested in his or her RRSP account and decides if there is enough there to last during retirement.[16]

Employers prefer to enroll workers in DC retirement plans because they help them to avoid the problem of DB pension plan liability. Pension plans are usually regulated by provincial legislation and are supposed to be solvent, which means they are expected to have enough assets to cover current and future liabilities. Unfortunately, many plans in Canada are underfunded. There is also the question of what happens when a company goes bankrupt and its DB plan was not solvent, which is what occurred at Nortel and Sears Canada. In those cases, retired workers had no resort but to go to court to try to hold on to at least some of their retirement incomes.

Thus, a DC plan seems like a better choice when considering the possibility of a DB plan being underfunded. In fact, DB plans suffer funding issues for two reasons: low returns on pension fund investments and employer contribution holidays. A contribution holiday means that an employer, but not workers, can stop making DB plan contributions if a plan appears solvent. Solvency is determined by actuarial calculations, and some actuarial analysis can determine that a plan is healthy but another examination may determine that the same plan is in financial trouble.

The key difference between DB and DC plans involves who holds liability in the event a person does not have the amount of money she or he anticipated when it comes time to retire. In a DB plan, a worker can be reasonably certain what she or he is going to receive as a monthly pension and the onus is on the employer to ensure the plan is solvent and can continue to pay benefits. In a DC plan, the amount of money a person has in retirement is entirely contingent on how well his or her investments performed and how much he or she saved. A DC plan places all of the liability on a worker.

This distinction between DB and DC may seem trivial, but it is enormously important for workers. A DB pension is a form of deferred compensation, meaning a person gets paid later rather than right now. A DC plan is portable — the invested money stays with the worker and money can be contributed into it by a future employer — but that is about the only strength it has. A DB plan does tie a worker to a specific employer, but the payoff and security of DB far outweighs the portability of a DC plan.

This discussion of the finer points of DB versus DC plans may make people wonder why it all matters as long as they are in some kind of retirement plan. The unfortunate fact is that precious few Canadians save enough money to afford even a modest retirement lifestyle. The number of men covered by DB plans declined from 52 percent in 1977 to 37 percent in 2011. The percentage of women covered by DB increased from 36 percent to 40 percent during the same period. Furthermore, DB plan coverage was much more common in larger organizations, public or private, than in those with fewer than a thousand workers.[17]

Private sector employers have assiduously eliminated DB plans when possible. As of 2018, only a quarter of Canadian private sector workers were members of such plans. By 2020, two-thirds of Canadians were worried that they would not have enough retirement money.[18] A 2015 survey by Ipsos found that only 48 percent of Canadians are saving for retirement.[19] An alternative view is that people are worried enough about retirement that at least half are doing something about it. The problem is that far too many people will not be able to end their working careers when they wish to do so.

There is no longer a mandatory retirement age in Canada. It was ruled a human rights violation except in certain occupations like firefighting and was phased out by the provinces and federal government by 2010. Canadians can now work until they die if they desire. Simple biology will get in the way for most people and retirement will occur at some point. A person's energy levels alter over time, interests change, and health issues will also cause personal priorities to be reordered. There is a serious danger that workers will not be able to stay in the labour market because their bodies will not let them, and they may well not have saved enough money to sustain themselves in retirement.

People receive highly contradictory messages about what they should do with their money. They are told to save for later, spend now, avoid buying what they do not need, finance things they want, and otherwise live for the moment with maybe an occasional eye on the future. Combine this with the facts that wages have been essentially flat for decades and personal debt loads are high and it is little wonder that less than half of Canadians save for retirement. Indeed, it is remarkable that even that percentage of people save anything for old age.

The federal government administers public pensions, with the exception of Quebec's provincial plan. The Canadian federal plans, including

CPP, are principally funded by current contributions. Workers often mistakenly believe they each have a CPP account in Ottawa with their names on them, but nothing could be farther from the truth. A percentage of the CPP fund is invested through the Canada Pension Plan Investment Board, which means in the stock market and other investment options, so CPP is supported by something beyond worker and employer contributions.

Public pensions are also means-tested. Everyone who has paid CPP premiums is eligible to apply for it starting at age 60, although benefits are reduced at that age. The OAS pension starts to be clawed back when someone earns more than $75,910 per year. GIS is paid to low-income retirees. A clawback means that a person is earning too much money through other retirement income to be eligible for OAS. The combined GIS and OAS in 2020 was $1,514 per month, while the maximum CPP someone could receive at age 65 was $13,855 per year. However, anyone earning more than $18,500 per year could not receive GIS, so a person could perhaps look forward to $13,855 per year in CPP plus $7,284 maximum in OAS for a total of $21,139. It is sobering to consider that amount of money within the context of the fact that the rent for a one-bedroom apartment in a comparatively less expensive city like Montreal was slightly over $1,400 per month in the spring of 2020 and close to $2,200 per month in Toronto. As the saying goes, nobody earning $21,139 per year will be living large. That monthly amount may seem reasonable until it is put into perspective. In 2018, the low-income cut-off (otherwise known as the poverty line) was $21,481 for a single person living in a city with a population of half a million or more. The line was lower in rural areas at $14,051.[20]

The public plans would keep someone at or slightly above the poverty line, especially if she or he was able to secure a scarce apartment in public housing or a co-op, but it meant that very little money would be left over at the end of the month. The level of public pensions links to intergenerational friction. Baby boomers are now retiring or have already done so, and the savings numbers described above show they did not always adequately anticipate what it would mean to retire. They grew up in households where their Second World War generation parents were usually members of DB pension plans.

Younger workers are already encountering huge difficulties paying down education debt, trying to secure full-time jobs that pay decent wages, and buying their first homes. It may well be inevitable they will resent having to pay public pension premiums for baby-boomer retirees who did not save enough money even though earning better wages than their millennial successors. Governments will be increasingly faced with the challenge of paying for social costs associated with baby boomers while having to pay for education for young families and also ensuring there is adequate housing and opportunities for everyone.

The problems with work in 2020s Canada are not being entirely ignored by public policy-makers and other stakeholders in society. Governments across the country have moved to increase their minimum wages, although some have done so with more enthusiasm than others. The minimum wage in 2020 ranged from $11.32 per hour in Saskatchewan to $15 per hour in Alberta. New Brunswick, Newfoundland and Labrador, Nova Scotia, Saskatchewan, and Yukon at least indexed their minimum wage rates so that they would rise with upticks in the consumer price index (cost of living). Benefits paid out by CPP have increased, since there was government recognition that a huge poverty problem will be part of the so-called retirement tsunami brought on by baby boomers, even if enhanced public pensions just pay enough to get by. There is still a severe lack of affordable housing in every major Canadian city. Housing, like jobs, is largely left to the mercies of the free market.

The 2020s Canadian workplace is thus a stressful place as people look to the future. There are reasons for hope and some dread depending on how different aspects of working life, social attitudes, public policy, and corporate behaviour unfold in the coming decades. It is consequently worthwhile speculating how work in Canada may develop. There are obvious perils in making predictions. On one hand, if studying the past is opaque, then trying to forecast the future is more art than science. On the other hand, an estimate that proves to be even a bit accurate is better than none at all. The idea of whether or not people will work in the future is a good place to start.

29 WILL WE STILL WORK?

M odern society periodically produces writers and theorists who postulate that the future will bring leisure and freedom from the bonds of paid labour. Speculative fiction is a good place to look for such ideas. The current ubiquity of science fiction and fantasy media, including films and television, may suggest that such forms of fiction have always been created. In fact, the idea of time travel — a favoured device in the science fiction and fantasy genres — was popularized by H.G. Wells in his 1895 novella *The Time Machine*. The future Wells describes is dystopian, with humanity split into two species called the Eloi and the Morlocks. The former live leisurely lives above ground, while the latter are savage subterranean cannibals.[21]

The aspiration of being relieved of the drudgery of work is also a key part of books that came out in the first decades of the 20th century. Yevgeny Zamyatin's novel *We* was published in English in 1924 and influenced George Orwell. Aldous Huxley's 1932 novel *Brave New World* depicts a dystopian future of carefully engineered humans organized hierarchically by intelligence. Sleep learning and a soothing drug called soma are key aspects of the book's plot. Huxley anticipates later trends in post–Second World War Western society, including the widespread use of therapeutic psychotropic medication and the utilization of social and psychological conditioning to mould people to avoid deviance and ensure compliance with authority. Huxley and Wells were also writing commentaries on social class in their books.[22]

The 1927 Fritz Lang film *Metropolis* explores themes of class difference, as well, with subterranean workers staging a revolution largely incited by a female robot who almost leads them to destruction.[23] The term *robot* was first used in Karel Čapek's 1920 play *R.U.R.* in which humanoid robots rebel.[24] Fans of science fiction novels may not always realize that it is a genre really about the present and not the future.

Futuristic fictional depictions of work assumed a different sheen after the Second World War. Utopian portrayals became more prevalent, although with some cautionary tales included for good measure. The original 1960s *Star Trek* series shows people working, but in a purposeful and personally fulfilling manner. There is virtually no reference to money in that show. Stanley Kubrick's 1968 film *2001: A Space Odyssey* portrays the wonders technology would bring by the end of the 20th century, although the HAL computer clearly represents the dangers automation could unleash on humans. *Star Wars* is unique because work and labour are woven throughout all of the films in that epic series. People continually do manual labour even though there are droids all around them.

Speculating about the future of work became popular in the early 1970s, particularly as a result of the publication of Alvin Toffler's 1970 book *Future Shock*. Toffler described himself as a "futurist" — a new and amorphous job classification — and his book soared up bestseller lists. Theorizing that too much change is happening too quickly, Toffler anticipates the fall and rise of industries, the impact of technological change, and the general inability of humans to handle what is happening to them. He also says that society has reached a point where permanence has ended. Toffler is generally considered a libertarian, but the views expressed in *Future Shock* at times substantiate Karl Marx's argument in *Das Capital* that under capitalism, everything solid melts into air and everything sacred is profaned.[25]

Toffler was the first self-described futurist able to present his ideas as something beyond science fiction. His success spurred others to follow him, including Jeremy Rifkin. Toffler does not suggest that work will disappear but that it will instead markedly change. Rifkin argues in his 1995 book *The End of Work* that jobs will disappear because of automation. He further champions the idea of paying people to do work that would otherwise be described as volunteer activity, which he defines as the "third sector." In Rifkin's view, a social wage will have to be paid in order for an economy to function, since vast numbers of people will no longer earn wages in exchange for providing labour.[26]

Rifkin's idea of technology bringing mass employment to an end is not new, but he seems authoritative in delivering his views. The idea of robots and other forms of automation displacing workers was later taken up in 2015 by Martin Ford in *Rise of the Robots*. Indeed, robots are being used in ways that were not possible when Toffler and Rifkin published their books. Increased computing power has vastly improved what robots can do. For instance, a company called Boston Dynamics has created a robot dog that moves in a graceful and unnervingly realistic manner.[27]

Much of the automation technology being implemented in workplaces is part of repetitive processes such as moving pallets around warehouses, welding automobile frames, and military and law enforcement applications such as bomb disposal. Cost is the main consideration when introducing automation. A robot is much less likely to be used in a factory where cheap labour can be readily found. India is an example, since car factories there have fewer assembly line robots than those in countries with higher labour costs.

The prospect of technology eliminating jobs has certainly been forcefully argued by Martin Ford and others, but there is a fundamental problem with the argument that work will disappear because it is a view that only really considers the threat to paid labour. Unpaid work, especially domestic labour, is as central to the 21st-century Canadian economy as it has ever been. While there are robot vacuum cleaners that will trundle around homes without stairs, a robot that will do even a significant minority of household tasks has yet to appear on the market, even though there would be great demand for it.

Manufacturing work will likely continue to be more automated. The development of autonomous vehicles also has the potential to displace many workers. Having automated paving equipment working around the clock on stretches of road such as Toronto's Gardiner Expressway or British Columbia's fearsome Coquihalla Highway is ultimately safer and more efficient than having crews of people working in dangerous conditions. It is easy to become sentimental about lost industrial jobs, but it is far better and safer to have robots doing things like descending into mines and deep into oceans instead of sending miners and divers. No human construction workers would give even passing thought to the idea that excavating equipment should be eliminated so that building foundations can again be dug by hand.

There are also many jobs that cannot be easily automated. No parent would willingly leave his or her child in the care of a robot daycare worker, and the prospect of an upright robot walking into a house to bathe and dress an elderly family member would be met with considerable skepticism. Having robot police forces instead of uniformed human officers, like those shown in the 1987 film *Robocop*, conjures visions of a violent dystopic future. Conversely, sending a firefighting robot into a burning building would surely be met with much approval as long as it was followed by a human firefighter who could rescue anyone trapped inside.

People will pay for a meal in a restaurant cooked and delivered to the table by a robot waiter but will prefer if the waiter looks and acts like a human. Sitting through a haircut done by a robot may be nerve-wracking for most people, never mind the prospect of having a tooth drilled and filled by one. Most services involving direct contact with people will still require at least some degree of human interaction because that is the experience consumers expect. Employers facing future labour shortages will, of course, want to make fuller use of workplace automation.

Legal liability plays a hugely important role in what jobs will continue to be performed by humans. Consider the use of remotely piloted aircraft. Militaries around the world are eagerly working to deploy weapon systems that do not require human operators. Remotely piloted drones are the most well-recognized examples of military automation, and remotely run surface ships, submarines, and fighter planes are in development. They will certainly be followed by remotely controlled tanks and artillery pieces, along with other types of military hardware.

Automation for military applications appears logical because the recruitment and training of soldiers, sailors, and pilots are expensive and there is always the possibility of suffering casualties. The employment of robotic weapons systems potentially mitigates possible casualties for the side using them, which means there may be more willingness to use them. A remote-controlled fighter plane represents less liability for the country using it, but a remotely piloted airliner is something entirely different. It is doubtful that anyone in contemporary society would be willing to fly on a plane not flown by a human pilot, even if one is only there for a backup, and even less likely that an insurance company would sell coverage to the airline operating it.

As previously argued, militaries are also workplaces, and virtually every Western military, including Canada's, has recruiting challenges. Young Canadians experiencing a tight job market in 2020 are aware of the possibility that joining the army means potentially going to war and often tend to look at the Canadian Armed Forces as an employer of last resort. Using automation helps militaries to skirt their recruiting problems, even if they do not always admit it. For example, the United Kingdom's Royal Navy recently launched two new Queen Elizabeth–class aircraft carriers comparable in size to the U.S. Navy's Nimitz-class supercarriers. The British ships will each have a crew complement of up to 1,600. In contrast, a Nimitz-class carrier is a floating city with more than 6,000 people on it. The Royal Navy made extensive use of automation on its new carriers ostensibly for the sake of efficiency but also because it will strain to crew even one carrier on deployment, never mind both of them. The Royal Canadian Navy has surely taken note of the Royal Navy's efforts.

30 SURVEILLANCE AND CONTROL

A curious practice began to appear in companies by 2017. Technology had developed to a point whereby a microchip could be inserted in a person's hand to permit him or her to unlock doors instead of using a hand-held swipe card. Companies started holding "chip parties" to get workers to enthusiastically submit to having monitoring devices implanted in their bodies. A person could be followed wherever she or he went in an office and conceivably anywhere beyond the workplace. As usual, sticking microchips into people's hands was presented as something that would immeasurably help them do their jobs, but George Orwell would have been aghast at the sight of a chipping session had he lived long enough to see one in progress.[28]

Employers now have a highly invasive ability to watch what their workers are doing on and off the job, and many show little reluctance to act on private employee behaviour they dislike. A lot of this relates to social media such as Facebook, Twitter, Instagram, and Snapchat. It is not currently common in Canada for prospective employers to request access to a job applicant's social media accounts, but it happens in the United States. Prospective employers in Canada will search for a job applicant or current employee on social media accounts like LinkedIn to see if anyone is saying or doing anything that could potentially have a negative impact on his or her past or current employers.

Making negative social media comments about an employer or engaging in behaviour that an employer does not like can get someone fired in 2020 Canada. For example, a Mr. Lube employee in Toronto was fired in 2013 after the company noted he had tried to buy marijuana through Twitter. A Canada Post clerk was terminated in 2009 for criticizing and mocking the company's management online. Workers can disguise themselves on the internet by doing such things as maintaining separate Facebook accounts for work and private lives, but the reality is that a person's social media presence can be of great interest to his or her employer.[29]

Technology has not reached the point where management can actually use it to read people's minds, but it does make it feasible to accurately predict what a person will do on a job, something possible because of the relentless application of algorithms to all aspects of daily life. An algorithm can be described as "a set of guidelines that describe how to perform a task." It is a mathematics tool that can also be predictive. For instance, Facebook Marketplace uses algorithms to show users items they may want to buy based on their prior use of the site. Algorithms are also employed in the workplace.[30]

Technology has also revolutionized how people find work and how organizations hire them. Websites like Monster and Workopolis have replaced job advertisements in newspapers. Computers and their systems play a prominent role in finding and evaluating job candidates. A recruitment tool called Wasabi Waiter shows what workers can expect in coming years when they search for work. The premise of that online game is that a job applicant plays the role of a waiter at a sushi restaurant. She or he has to make decisions as increasing numbers of customers enter the establishment. It only takes a few minutes for the program to measure applicants against a behavioural science formula — an algorithm — to determine if a person will be a good fit for the job vacancy in question.[31]

A program like Wasabi Waiter is supposed to be more effective and insightful than in-person interviewing. There are some obvious problems with using it or something similar. A computer program should not exhibit bias, but one could still be created that discriminates based on a variety of criteria. Algorithms can also be utilized to monitor and assess people once they are hired, with potentially problematic results. For example, the idea of being outwardly happy and positive is an expectation placed on many workers even if they suffer inwardly. Telling people how they should think and feel has long been a part of management practice, but algorithms make it worse.

Numbers are already available to assess employees' performances before they are hired for jobs and once they are employees. Statistical analysis to evaluate professional athletes entered popular consciousness as a result of Michael Lewis's book *Moneyball*. That work was later adapted into a film and shows how one professional baseball team, the Oakland Athletics, used new statistical analysis methods to choose good players underrated by conventional assessment methods. Algorithms can take things further than basic statistical analysis.[32]

Canadians are now living in what Shoshana Zuboff has termed "the age of surveillance capitalism," and a lot of that view is based on the use of algorithms. There is even something called "emotional analytics" that can determine and gauge people's responses to a range of events and stimuli. Zuboff is rightly concerned about the misuse of data large corporations can accumulate through advanced technology. Google looms large in her analysis with good reason. Its influence is so pervasive that its name has morphed into a verb. People google things with Google, and Google keeps track of where they went online and what they viewed. It is possible that the thought crime found in Orwell's *Nineteen Eighty-Four* may yet be identified by an algorithm.[33]

It would be incorrect to say technology will not bring workplace benefits despite its negative aspects. There are now many jobs that did not exist 20 or 30 years ago, such as web designer, and there will surely be jobs appearing in the next two decades that will be new and interesting. For example, more technology in workplaces requires greater numbers of workers who know how to operate and repair it. We may have android wait staff in restaurants, but there will still have to be at least some human workers on-site to ensure the machines are working properly. The principal problem with technological change and work is much more fundamental than focusing on a single theme such as how many robots are in a factory or the number of self-check kiosks in a drugstore.

31 COMING APART

The principal drawback with technology is that it contributes to an increased bifurcation of the labour market, a problem that will worsen in coming decades unless concrete policy changes are implemented by federal and provincial governments. The demand for in-person service workers, especially jobs like personal support worker, is growing. Canada has an aging population that needs assistance, yet there is a chronic shortage of personal support workers and that situation is unlikely to improve in the future.

The reason there are shortages of people who want to be personal support workers, bricklayers, crane operators, nurses, and other skilled occupations is that those jobs are physically demanding. Wages do not always compensate even if they result in middle-class standards of living. Being a personal support worker does not pay well and is also emotionally demanding. That job is not unlike being an early childhood educator, since it involves looking after the most vulnerable people in society while earning remuneration that does not reflect that responsibility.

Jobs such as personal support worker, nurse, production worker, and police and emergency services workers also involve shift work.

Approximately 30 percent of Canadians work at jobs that require irregular hours. Some shift work, especially in medical services, is unavoidable but can exact a heavy toll on people who do it. A 2002 Statistics Canada study shows that shift workers are more likely to suffer from lack of sleep, cardiovascular disease, hypertension, diabetes, and gastrointestinal disorders. Women working shifts, the study says, are more prone to reproductive problems and breast cancer. It should not be surprising that people are not flocking to jobs that bring such consequences.[34]

Low-paid service workers should not anticipate major pay hikes unless they decide to unionize in significant numbers. The relatively tight labour market of 2020 that was altered by the Covid-19 pandemic will likely return in the 2030s and 2040s as Canada's population ages, yet the minimum wage will not increase without opposition from business. Semi-skilled jobs that do not require the acquisition of professional designations or licensing have been eroding in North America as technology has displaced some jobs and simplified others. Canada, like other industrialized countries, will have a growing number of low-wage workers performing jobs that only really require high school level education and a smaller group of highly educated skilled workers who earn good wages and enjoy a modicum of job security.

The workplace training/job placement industry is now too large and entwined in the North American economy to disappear. It will instead persist into the coming decades as companies such as job placement firms like Adecco and Kelly expand their range of services. The public service will be at least a partial exemption to that trend due to the resistance of public sector unions to work casualization, but the practice of adjusting workers to their new circumstances will continue.

American public policy academic David Weil has written about the "fissured workplace," and the Canadian workplace reflects much of what he describes. Weil pays particular attention to corporate employment policy and the rising reliance on contracting out work to other firms rather than seeing big businesses directly employ large numbers of workers. Technology has made much of that practice possible. A person staying at a major hotel in any downtown core may assume the staff working at the facility are employees of the company with its name on the building.

In fact, hotels are full of staff supplied by other companies, most notably cleaners and housekeepers.[35]

The use of various levels of subcontracting companies can be readily seen in the airline industry. Airports themselves may not be directly owned by a government and instead might be operated under licence by a business. Baggage handling, aircraft maintenance, food services, security, and other functions are in turn handled by a range of third-party firms. For instance, Swissport handles baggage at airports and airport ground services. An airline may not even own its planes and might instead lease them from another business. Travellers walking into an airport in Canada would not have any idea of the commercial agreements that make their trips possible, and a lot of them would be indifferent to that news.

The labour market of the 2030s and beyond is going to follow trends already described by Weil but also by other commentators such as economist Guy Standing, who refers to the class of workers in temporary and tenuous employment as the "precariat." He convincingly argues that such a class of workers could become politically volatile and susceptible to messaging from populists and demagogues. Standing expressed that view in 2011, and within the contexts of the election of Donald Trump in the United States in 2016 and the Brexit vote in the United Kingdom the same year, his prediction now seems quite prescient. Populists have not stormed the gates of power in Canada as they have in America and Britain, but Canadian voters could prove as open to populism and demagoguery if inequality worsens and precarious work proliferates.[36]

If there is one organization that best exemplifies the precarious gig economy — so named because people move from one short-term job to another — it is Uber. That company was founded in San Francisco in 2009. It is a ride-hailing organization that has become a huge threat to existing taxi and limousine firms in 80 countries around the world. Anyone with a vehicle can download the Uber application and start driving, and there is usually much less regulation of Uber drivers than taxi and limousine ones.

All transactions with Uber are done electronically, with no cash being exchanged. People choosing to drive for the company can make their own hours, and being a driver is portrayed by Uber as providing flexibility with the chance to earn decent money. Uber has vastly increased the transportation options consumers can access, but there have been huge downsides and much of them relate to what the company has done to traditional employment relationships.

Uber promises a faster response time than traditional taxis, which requires having a lot of cars on the road at any given time. Thus, there are times when too many vehicles are chasing a limited pool of passengers. Uber may have thought people would drive for it as a supplemental source of income, but the job became a primary wage for many even though full-time Uber driving fails to provide sufficient funds. The company also describes its drivers as independent contractors, yet Uber unilaterally dictates and alters the terms of drivers' work. This led to unions and groups of drivers arguing before labour boards that driving for Uber makes people employees, not just contractors. An example of one such complaint was brought before the British Columbia Labour Relations Board and was still not resolved by the summer of 2020.

If Uber has transformed public mobility, Airbnb has done the same thing for how people find accommodation. Airbnb was founded in 2008, also in San Francisco, and is a site on which people can list their properties, even their family homes, for rental. It poses an enormous challenge to traditional hotels and is also highly unregulated. Airbnb is a threat to the hotel industry and the workers employed in it and additionally harms the housing market in which workers try to rent and buy homes. Rentals through Airbnb have been so prevalent in Toronto that it has led to an artificially low rental vacancy rate. The Toronto vacancy rate in spring 2020 would have been around 3 percent rather than 1 percent if apartments devoted to Airbnb rentals were instead listed as regular units that could be leased. A shortage of apartments drives up rent costs for the units that do become vacant, which in turn harms lower-wage workers who are often already facing income precarity.[37]

Gig work can be so thoroughly broken down that it can be completed in small time periods that may last an hour or much less in duration. Amazon has played a major role in making that trend possible with its Mechanical Turk site where organizations can post tasks of varying duration and complexity they want completed and people can take assignments of interest to them. Jobs can require doing something complex like computer programming or small tasks such as completing a consumer survey. Amazon describes each job as a "human intelligence task — HIT." The work is all done online and everything seems fairly benign until the potential consequences of Mechanical Turk are considered and how it relates to wider trends in precarious work. The main consequence of Mechanical Turk is that its piecework model could prove popular in other businesses and industries. Workers could find themselves paid for every step they take, computer key they tap, and barcode they scan.[38]

Skilled workers may also see their work diminished by technological change and precarious work arrangements. In their book *The Future of Professions: How Technology Will Transform the Work of Humans*, Richard and Daniel Susskind argue that all professions are open to diminishment by technology after 2020. Much of what the Susskinds and others have predicted is already happening. For instance, most Canadian university and college undergraduate students would be surprised to learn that on average 70 percent of the teaching done at their institutions is performed by part-time faculty of different types. Parents will also doubtlessly be surprised to hear that statistic, since they may have assumed they are paying high tuition and other fees for their children to be instructed by world-class full-time faculty.[39]

The creation of WebCT, discussed in chapter 26, helped lead to a situation whereby online learning is now a fundamental part of post-secondary education in Canada. Indeed, there are provincial governments that want to permanently introduce it in secondary school programs. Online learning has without question democratized higher education, since students working full-time or irregular hours, living in small or remote communities, or facing personal challenges that prevent them from going to a college or university campus now have access to a plethora of learning options. The problem is that the online courses being offered at colleges and universities are often taught by people with advanced degrees who are usually living on the brink of financial disaster because they are poorly paid and do not know if they will be working in the next academic term.

Technology will continue to impact workers in higher education and other professions in the coming decades, but something unexpected might happen as a result of demographic change. Public policy-makers are well aware of the fact that barely enough babies are born in Canada to equal the number of people who come to the end of their lives, something referred to as the rate of natural increase. This reality means that population growth in Canada is driven by immigration.

Canada will continue to employ its points-based immigration system to attract people from other countries in the future. The border to the south with the United States and oceans and seas to the east, north, and west mostly insulate Canada from having to deal with waves of unwanted migrants. The Canadian government can be much more selective when deciding who to let into the country than the United States and the European Union, both of which have long experienced waves of undocumented migrants from the global south and elsewhere.

Even the most liberal and open immigration policies may not ultimately prevent some population decline. Demographic change and the possibility of flat population growth or even decline are key issues facing labour and employment in Canada in the coming decades. Canada's low pre-pandemic unemployment and labour shortages in some occupations did not lead to massive increases in wages. Labour in 2020 continues to be the one commodity that defies classical economic theory, since scarcity persists in not affecting its cost. That is not because workers do not want to be paid more generously but rather because buyers of labour — employers — do not want to pay more wages.

There is regional variation in wage rates, but the way jobs are valued also needs to be seriously assessed. The people who do the most socially important work like child care workers, personal support workers, teachers, and protective service personnel are sometimes poorly paid or provide comfortable middle-class incomes. There are also a lot of jobs that anthropologist David Graeber has called "bullshit jobs." Such occupations make little societal contribution and may even be socially harmful but still bestow large salaries.[40]

Darrell Bricker and John Ibbitson write in dire terms about the looming prospect of population decline in their book *Empty Planet: The Shock of Global Population Decline.* While there is a major reason that some population decline is necessary, the idea of a national population shrinking rather than growing runs entirely contrary to conventional economic theory and practice. The reason that flat or declining population growth matters mainly involves what governments and businesses think about it. Parents and families show a range of emotions when a baby is born. They may simply and purely see a new person to love and adore, a son or daughter with whom to experience the world, a companion to a sibling who was born earlier, or a grandchild who restores some youth and hope to aging grandparents.[41]

Government sees little taxpayers when babies are born, and business imagines little workers and consumers. This is a clinical if not cynical view of population growth and decline, but it is important to appreciate how birth rates link to public policy. For example, public pension plans will inevitably run into trouble if there are fewer people paying into them than receiving benefits. This was a detail that was on the minds of the members of Prime Minister Lester Pearson's Liberal Cabinet when CPP was created in 1965.

Every major modern economic system that has been put into practice — capitalist, socialist, and communist — has been based on more growth of all types, including demographic and economic. Governments, most notably China's with its defunct one-child policy, have tried to artificially control population growth but often with unintended consequences. China now has an aging population, too many men due to an unfortunate cultural preference for male children over female offspring, and has difficulty enticing families to think about having two children after being told not to do so for years.

Today Canada has more people over the age of 65 than under 14. That means there will be fewer workers paying taxes to fund social programs like public pensions in the future. At the same time, there will be more demand for workers who perform tasks relating to the care of elderly people. There are unfortunately no guarantees younger workers will be willing to bear additional tax burdens to pay for elderly boomers and Generation Xers.[42]

The outlook for work and labour in Canada in many ways looks problematic if not depressing, as the country moves further into the third decade of the 21st century and beyond. The problem of precarious work, a shortage of housing in urban areas, population decline, and a highly educated workforce not earning enough money can seem overwhelming. The problem of occupational and income inequality is one of the most grievous facing Canadian policy-makers. A 2017 study found that 17 percent of Canadians are living below the poverty line, and there is reason to believe the poverty rate will increase in coming decades unless working- and middle-class wages rise.[43]

The foregoing work and labour issues, including poverty and the fractured workplace, are eclipsed by the challenge of global climate change. Human use of hydrocarbon fuels has been causing the planet to warm for decades. Ocean levels are rising, average temperatures increase, many countries face drought and water scarcity, enormous fires engulf forests, and crucial plant and animal species are lost every year. There are close connections between global climate change and work and labour.

Industrial work in Canada and elsewhere is fuelled by hydrocarbons. Power plants, trains, trucks, cars, and factory equipment are historically linked to natural gas, coal, or oil. Agriculture was once extremely labour-intensive and was transformed by the introduction of hydrocarbon-burning equipment that made work easier. The diets Canadian workers consume are closely tied to hydrocarbons, since an average food item in Canada travels 2,500 kilometres before it goes onto someone's plate, and lots of workers are involved in getting food from farms to homes and businesses. Most of the oil produced — 60 percent — is not made into gasoline and is instead found elsewhere in daily life, especially in the plastic products that fill modern societies.[44]

Global warming impacts work in Canada in several ways. The most important point is that people with lower incomes are the most affected by it. Rising ocean levels leading to coastal flooding means that workers will be displaced from communities that are inundated. People with money who live in coastal areas can escape to higher ground, but lower-income earners may be stuck in place. Hotter days are punishing on people who work outside for a living. Global climate change may have its most grievous effect on communities in Canada that have already been harmed for centuries.

First Nations, Métis, and Inuit communities are particularly impacted by climate change. The ongoing consequences of colonization have already ruined many aspects of the lives of Indigenous people. Traditional hunting, trapping, and fishing have been severely diminished due to the continuing implications of European colonization. Areas in the Far North such as Nunavut have seen the decline of local food chains, which is being caused by the loss of Arctic ice. Indigenous people do use hydrocarbons, but their contribution to climate change is infinitesimal compared to the impact non-Indigenous people have had on the natural landscape.

The scale of the problems facing workers of all types in Canada came into sharp focus in early 2020 when the country again dealt with a global pandemic. The Covid-19 virus first appeared in Wuhan, China. The exact way it made the jump from an animal to a human may never be definitively determined, but the key point is that it was a new virus. It quickly spread around the world, and countries have met it with differing levels of success.

The Canadian federal government and the various provincial and territorial administrations responded by closing workplaces and schools across the nation and communicated guidelines about the need to wear face masks when in public and to observe physical-distancing protocols. The closure of the overwhelming majority of the nation's workplaces soon led to unavoidable double-digit unemployment.

Many of the workplace trends already on the horizon in 2020 accelerated due to Covid-19. People were told to work from home and use video conferencing tools such as Zoom. Universities and colleges, which are some of Canada's most densely populated workplaces, made rapid plans to move their programs online. Elementary and secondary school students and their parents have also had to quickly adapt to online learning. Most importantly, the country became acutely reliant on workers who were undervalued and almost invisible in the economy prior to the Covid-19 pandemic. Grocery store workers and delivery drivers were hailed for their bravery.

People honked their car horns and applauded from their front porches and apartment balconies to show appreciation for medical and protective services staff. The federal government rediscovered Keynesian economics and provided considerable financial support to workers and businesses. The ultimate outcome of the pandemic will not be clear for several years, but it has claimed thousands of Canadian lives, especially among the elderly. Thinking about what comes after Covid-19 does afford an opportunity to contemplate the paths forward for work and labour in Canada.

32 COMING TOGETHER

I t may seem that work in the coming decades will be more precarious, wages will continue to stagnate, housing will be outrageously expensive, technology will dilute good jobs and eliminate others, and vast parts of the planet will become uninhabitable. Everyone will live in an Airbnb unit, ride around in autonomously driven Uber cars if they can afford the fare, subsist on week-long job contracts supplemented by minutes-long gigs on Mechanical Turk, and only have access to poverty-level public pensions because they could not afford to save for retirement. There are reasons to conclude that this is the only foreseeable future. The people and groups in Canadian society who work the levers of government and business often accept the casualization of work and the elimination of pension plans, and some even still wonder if global warming is, in fact, a left-wing conspiracy theory. To use a *Star Trek* analogy, trying to resist the myriad of forces shaping work and labour is presented as being like attempting to avoid being assimilated by the Borg. Resistance is considered at best futile and at worst delusional. But resistance is, in fact, possible, and so is a different future.

There is a fundamental reality underlying all the current and potential future challenges with work and labour in Canada: they are usually the result of conscious decisions made by government and business. Airbnb, Uber, and all the other new companies that have become prominent in the Canadian economy have devised novel business models made possible by social media and other forms of communication technology. A handful of new companies are now enormously powerful, especially the so-called FAANGs: Facebook, Apple, Amazon, Netflix, and Google (Alphabet). They are able to operate as they wish because governments permit them to do so. The business community invariably recoils at the prospect of government regulations of corporations, but provincial and federal governments in Canada have the power to pass laws that will improve the terms of employment for workers.

What it means to be an employee rather than a contractor can be determined through legal tests, including whether or not the employer sets working hours and assigns work, owns the equipment to perform the work, controls work processes, and if a worker is exclusively employed by the organization in question. There are other factors involved, but the main one concerns whether or not a worker is in a position of subordination to the employer and under rules of an employment contract. An independent contractor has much more discretion over his or her work than a regular employee. Courts and labour boards are now beginning to push back against misclassification of contractors.[45]

In a 2020 ruling, the Ontario Labour Relations Board permitted delivery couriers for a company called Foodora to join the Canadian Union of Postal Workers. The couriers had previously been classified as contractors but had no discretion over their work. The board rejected the company's assertions that the couriers were contractors. Foodora later responded by shutting down its operations in Canada. Nevertheless, more legal rulings such as *Canadian Union of Postal Workers v. Foodora* will help workers and unions to resist and hopefully reverse work casualization.[46]

There are other examples of service sector workers unionizing and their employers accepting collective bargaining. A successful organizing drive in 2016 at GoodLife Fitness is a particularly noteworthy example. In that case, 181 personal trainers at 42 locations voted to join Workers United in response to wage theft and other workplace issues. GoodLife Fitness is privately owned and is the fourth-largest fitness chain in the world and by far the biggest in Canada. Fitness industry work is often precarious, yet a successful organizing drive was mounted at GoodLife. It may well be a harbinger of future such initiatives. Foodora and GoodLife workers are people who continued a long tradition of workers fighting for rights on the job.[47]

Canadian society will eventually have to grapple with the legalization of an occupation that has always existed in the legal margin: prostitution. There is an ongoing, sharp debate in Canada over whether or not prostitution should be legalized to protect women engaged in it, or if it should be the subject of heavy penalties to stop men from buying sex and endangering women. The trend seems to be toward the former rather than the latter, and that trend started with a woman named Terri-Jean Bedford, who was a complainant and part of a lawsuit challenging the constitutionality of Canada's prostitution laws. She worked as a dominatrix — meaning someone who administered pain such as a spanking — for men who were inclined to such pleasures. The suit was initially filed in 2007 and finally made it to the Supreme Court of Canada in 2013. Bedford attended the court's hearing in Ottawa, all the while beaming at the media while clad in black leather and brandishing a riding crop. She was thrilled to win her case.[48]

The Conservative government led by Prime Minister Stephen Harper responded to the *Canada v. Bedford* case by criminalizing the purchase of sex and profiting from the avails of it, but not the sale of sex. This was intended to dissuade men from attempting to buy sexual services. However, in early 2020, a new case revolving around an escort service in London, Ontario, led a provincial court judge to strike down major parts of the Harper government's actions on constitutional grounds. The prospect of prostitution legalization raises thorny labour and employment issues. Brothels could well operate the same as any other legitimate businesses with sex worker employees who would in turn be covered by provincial labour and employment laws. They could even form unions, as has happened in other countries such as the Netherlands.[49]

Canadian courts were frequently hostile toward organized labour in the past, but the Supreme Court of Canada has in recent years expanded the right to unionization and collective bargaining. The court's 2015 *Mounted Police Association of Ontario v. Canada* ruling stated that the right to unionize and engage in collective bargaining is protected under the Charter of Rights and Freedoms. That decision has not yet led to waves of unionization among other previously excluded employee groups like managers, but it is a major change in labour law in Canada. One of the main reasons a majority of workers have never been unionized is because they were not legally permitted to do so. Organizing workers will require unions to use more sophisticated methods. For instance, if an algorithm can be employed to screen applicants, it can also be adjusted to identify workers who may be more prone to unionize. Unions need to consider adding algorithms of their own to their organizing techniques.[50]

The idea that unions could appear in unexpected occupations should not surprise Canadians. In fact, there are often unionized workers right in front of them even if they do not know it. National Hockey League players are members of the National Hockey League Players' Association, and athletes in other professional sports such as football and baseball are members of unions. There have even been efforts to unionize college and university athletes in the United States and junior hockey players in Canada. Television and movie actors belong to the Screen Actors Guild in the United States and the Alliance of Canadian Cinema, Television and Radio Artists in Canada.

The Canadian labour movement has often struggled to respond to globalization and technological change. There are several reasons for this problem, including having to operate in a labour law framework that has not markedly altered since the passage of the Public Service Staff Relations Act in 1967. The rules for organizing new workers are good when bringing in new members who work full-time and who are concentrated in one workplace but are not at all suited to organizing workers in precarious employment relationships and who are dispersed across many work locations. Private sector unions have also not devoted sufficient resources to organizing new members since the upsurge in membership from the late 1930s into the 1940s.

There is still reason to be hopeful about organized labour's future in Canada. Unions remain the best possible advocate for all workers, unionized or not, despite their occasional flaws. A union can bring better wages and benefits and a modicum of job security for workers, which means unionized workers can at least do some planning for themselves and their families. Union density in Canada has also remained fairly consistent over the past 40 years even as it declined across other industrialized countries, including the abysmal deterioration of the American labour movement. Unionized workers currently comprise just over 30 percent of the Canadian workforce.[51]

Improving labour law to make it easier for workers to join unions will help counter employment precarity. Canada and the United States have never adopted European works council models of worker representation, which do not necessarily involve formal unionization, but introduction of a Canadian form of works council would give people a voice at work. That is important because, despite business community rhetoric about unions lying to workers to con them into joining, people decide to sign up because they feel they lack a voice on the job and do not get respect from their employers.

As previously noted, efforts to raise minimum provincial wages across Canada have met with mixed success. The minimum wage in Canada at the end of 2019 ranged from $11.32 per hour in Saskatchewan to $15 per hour in Alberta. There is no mandated federal minimum wage, and it is time for Ottawa to introduce one. A $15 per hour minimum wage indexed to inflation and enforced in every province would raise many Canadian workers and their families out of poverty. A $15 per hour minimum wage has also yet to cause widespread layoffs anywhere that it has been implemented, regardless of the dark warnings issued by conservative-minded politicians and business groups.[52]

The country's long-term policy objective should be to move away from a hydrocarbon economy. Doing so is not going to be easy because of Canada's long history of reliance on natural resources for economic prosperity. Climate change is the main reason for moving away from hydrocarbons, and there are related reasons for making such a transition. The introduction of new green technologies like wind power, better solar panels, electric cars, and expanded plastic recycling means that less oil, gas, and coal will be used because they will not be needed. In

1956, a geologist named M. King Hubbert theorized that oil production would eventually peak and not be able to meet demand. Hubbert's theory looked valid for decades, but a surprise happened in early 2020: when the price of oil collapsed, disastrous results ensued for Canada's oil-producing provinces. The economic boom that began for Alberta at Leduc in 1947 is probably over.[53]

Moving from a hydrocarbon-based economy will bring challenges but more benefits. Oil and gas pipelines were once viewed as symbols of economic progress but now represent global warming. The fact that pipelines like the Trans Mountain expansion from Alberta to British Columbia will cross ancestral Indigenous land makes them an even greater affront to many Canadians. The obvious but challenging solution is to focus on renewable energy sources that are already leading to the creation of new jobs.

New technologies will not replace every job lost due to a shift to renewable energy, and there is considerable variation in so-called "green jobs." For instance, someone who installs solar panels and programs their control systems is in a green job, but so, too, is a worker sorting plastic containers in a recycling warehouse. Canada's education infrastructure is turning toward environmental sustainability and renewable energy by offering new programs focused on those areas. Solutions must still be found for people who cannot find work equal to their old hydrocarbon-dependent jobs.

There has been considerable discussion among policy-makers in recent years about paying a guaranteed basic wage to everyone in Canada, an issue that has captured everyone's attention even more because of Covid-19. Ontario's previous Liberal government began a pilot guaranteed basic wage program that was stopped by its Progressive Conservative successor, but the utility of a basic wage is shown to be valid. It can be a supplement to other income supports like public pensions, or it can take the place of a range of different income programs.[54]

The federal government guaranteed $2,000 per month to anyone who was laid off because of the pandemic and additionally subsidized corporate payrolls. Post-secondary students were provided with $1,250 per month for four months if they could not find summer jobs. Discussion of a universal basic income (UBI) quickly came up during the pandemic. A basic income provides dignity and also confers citizenship rights in a society in which being able to consume is valued.

There is a possibility that Covid-19 will lead to a sea change in how the public views the role of government in helping people, and the federal government is implementing policy modifications that reflect changing public sentiment. The federal government has already moved to replace the Canada Emergency Response Benefit (CERB) with enhanced unemployment benefits and is making it possible for workers to take paid sick days, though that provision will require agreement with provincial governments. The Canadian government is also continuing the Canada Emergency Wage Subsidy (CEWS) to help employers with payroll costs. Expanding employment insurance is crucial because of precarious work and also because 15 percent of Canada's workforce is self-employed and has not been eligible for employment insurance coverage. It is also important to note that the federal Liberal government implemented CERB and other income support provisions because it needed support from the NDP to stay in power, which is the same situation that gave Canadians universal public health care and public pensions.[55]

The 2015 election of the federal Liberal government led by Justin Trudeau was remarkable for a few key reasons. The Liberals were the third-place party in Parliament, and the NDP was the Official Opposition. The simple fact that Trudeau brought his party to a majority government from being in third place counted as the greatest political comeback in modern Canadian political history. The Liberals have an established habit of poaching policy positions from the NDP, such as universal health care, and in 2015 they actually ran to the left of the NDP when it came to deficit spending. Canada's federal public sector unions could understandably not abide Stephen Harper, and they were quite pleased to see Trudeau enter the prime minister's office.

The Liberal government has shown interest in reforming the federal labour and employment law framework. It commissioned a 2019 report that examined issues such as a federal minimum wage, a collective voice for non-union workers, and labour protections for non-standard work. The panel that wrote the report solicited input from a wide range of groups, including representatives from business and labour. While it is unrealistic to expect that even some of the report's recommendations will be implemented, such as a federal minimum wage indexed to the cost of living, it nonetheless represents a tangible effort to at least consider policy options to address the realities of the 21st-century workplace.[56]

There is a pressing need to reform labour and employment law at the provincial level. British Columbia's NDP government updated that province's Labour Relations Code and Employment Standards Act in 2019 and brought in progressive policy adjustments such as changes to union certification requirements to make it easier to unionize and regulate temporary agencies. Quebec has long been recognized as having the most pro-worker labour and employment law framework in Canada. Other provinces, such as Ontario, have either stood still on labour and employment law reform or stepped backward. As political scientist Leah Vosko and her colleagues have noted, Ontario's Employment Standards Act was founded on three principles: establishing social minimums, universality, and fairness. The act did create minimum standards, but they are not universally implemented nor is the law fairly applied.[57]

There are also ongoing problems with workplace health and safety across Canada. Health and safety systems such as the Workplace Hazardous Materials Information System are there to mitigate dangers at work, but some workplaces are still quite perilous. Approximately 1,000 Canadians die on the job every year. Labour groups around the world advocated for an annual day to remember workers who died at work, and April 28 was designated in 1990 in Canada as a day of mourning for workers killed or injured on the job and those who suffered from illnesses acquired on the job. A day of mourning for workers is now observed in 100 countries to remember those people who have lost their lives while earning a living.

Immigration will continue to be central to labour and employment policy in Canada, largely because of the nation's flat birth rate. The Trudeau Liberals had to deal with a refugee crisis shortly after being elected in 2015 when the civil war in Syria led to a mass exodus of people from that country. Canada has a long history of welcoming refugees, and by the end of 2016, the country had accepted 25,000

Syrians. Canadians can be certain they will be receiving more refugees who have left their home countries because of war, persecution, global climate change, and other factors.

The problem of high housing costs can be met through more rent controls and occupancy regulation, as well as through construction of more social housing and assistance to co-operative housing projects. One of the great curiosities of modern Canadian housing policy is that governments no longer display much interest in helping co-ops to get up and running even though a co-op rental apartment is often a better and more affordable option than basic renting. Public transit should be expanded and made more accessible through cheaper fares. Workers making average wages can then afford to find decent housing and be able to travel around their communities without financial hardship.

Canadians, like all people, have many complex identities. They are male, female, nonbinary, gay, straight, partners, spouses, parents, colleagues, neighbours, descended from European settlers, Indigenous, immigrant, workers, and combinations thereof, among other things. The worker identity usually does not seem to loom large in people's minds, but Covid-19 has changed that equation.

LOOKING BACK, LOOKING FORWARD

This overview of the history and meaning of work and labour has endeavoured to cover a lot of ground in a reasonable amount of space. There are some key themes in the history of work in Canada that recurred, and it is important to reflect on them after seeing them sequentially appear in the country's past. This book started by speaking about the land and the relationship that Indigenous Peoples and European settlers had with it. The vastness and physical diversity of Canada set the basic parameters of how work and labour would develop in subsequent centuries.

As noted earlier, the National Film Board documentary *High Steel* reveals the lives of Indigenous high-steel workers in the 1960s. The community that Kanien'keha:ka ironworkers created in Manhattan is the focus of a 2008 documentary called *Little Caughnawaga: To Brooklyn and Back*. That film pays particular attention to the role of women in ironworker families. Remembering the work done by all Canadians from past centuries until the present day is important along with thinking about fundamental aspects of what it has meant to work in Canada. That means not just looking in the usual places such as factories and offices but also at the work experience of people who have not received enough attention, such as the Indigenous workers who travelled from Canada to build Manhattan's skyline.[1]

The Canadian experience of work is rooted in European concepts of it, and everyone is expected to adapt to it. This process began when North America was colonized. At its core, the employment relationship means selling your labour to an employer for a specific or indeterminate period of time. That relationship generally favours employers more than workers. Indigenous Peoples lived in social arrangements markedly different from those inhabited by Europeans. They also often died from European illnesses before they even saw a colonist. The people who led and encouraged European settlement of the Americas intended to reproduce the social hierarchies and practices of their home countries, and they did so successfully. Colonial authorities used established legal frameworks to regulate labour, and European workers who thought they could escape the power of the state by crossing the ocean were disappointed when they arrived in their new colonial homes.

Securing a steady supply of labour has been a key aspect of the Canadian economy, and the state has implemented policies to ensure employers would have access to enough workers. The conditions that immigrants found when they arrived in Canada were often not auspicious. Working life was short and hard in pre-Confederation Canada. Labour organizations were illegal, and mounting opposition to the colonial authorities was fraught with risk. Indentured servitude was a common feature in pre-Confederation Canada. The journey across the Atlantic Ocean was long and treacherous and arriving in Canada meant hard toil. There were certainly Europeans who came to Canada viewing themselves as adventurers with a sense of mission, but the reality was that leaving a country like the United Kingdom was an escape from crushing poverty and an impossibly rigid class system. Indentured servitude terribly disadvantaged workers bound to masters as part of their terms of indenture, but it was not equal to the horrors of bonded slavery.

A continual supply of labour was needed by Canadian capital and the state to colonize the country and develop material wealth from its resources. Harold Adams Innis's work on his "staples theory" of Canadian economic development may look dated to 21st-century readers, but Canadian economic prosperity is still very much tied to resource extraction and production. There have been notable exceptions to that trend, such as technological advances like the BlackBerry, but drawing resources like oil and potash from the ground and exporting them overseas remains a key economic activity.

Canadians often prefer to think that African slavery was found in the United States and not in their country, but it did play a role in early colonial Canada. It did not happen on the scale seen in the United States and did not lead to a civil war, but it was part of the colonial imperative to ensure a steady supply of labour. Using enslaved Black workers also helped establish a racial hierarchy in Canada that influenced attitudes about what kind of work people could do based on their skin colour. Slavery may have been more widespread and enduring in Canada had the climate made it a viable prospect. It is instructive to note that the captains of slave ships did not sail to the Bight of Benin off the west coast of Africa in the 18th century and start offering generous wages and a comfortable sea voyage to anyone who expressed interest in working in one of the colonies in America or the Caribbean. Slave masters instead utilized coercion to obtain workers and send them into bondage.

The ongoing problem of ensuring a sufficient supply of labour in Canada was met with measures that frequently defied the laws of economics. A shortage of workers did not always cause wages to go up in value, or even for compensation to be paid, which is what classical economics argues should have happened. Scarcity did not drive up prices. Instead, workers often found themselves earning subsistence wages while prices rose around them. Canadians live in a country with a capitalist, free market economy, and 85 percent of them sell their labour for wages. The only other option is to be self-employed.

Canadian workers have always been influenced by developments south of the border. The American War of Independence brought Canada into existence as much as it did the United States. Canadians fought one war against the United States and other wars alongside it. They joined labour organizations based in America and were employed by companies headquartered there.

Confederation eventually led to better labour laws, but the weight of workplace power rested with employers rather than workers. Master-and-servant acts were replaced with other legislation, but Canada still developed a legal system that conferred more power on employers than workers. Canadian workers chafed under that legal system and occasionally pushed back against it. Masters were replaced by managers and bosses, while servants became employees and workers. The labour and employment law framework in Canada is designed to induce people to work.

American labour and employment law had a major influence on the development of equivalent 20th-century legislation in Canada. The practice employed to run large organizations in Canada, otherwise known as management, was substantially shaped by methods and theories fashioned in the United States. Canada moved from the United Kingdom's economic orbit into the magnetic pull of the United States and was firmly linked economically to America by the end of the Second World War.

The imperative of who Canadians think about when they consider the meaning and experience of work involves how work is valued. This monetary differentiation between how jobs are ranked is another fundamental aspect of working in Canada. The term *work* is often associated with paid activities, but unpaid work has been as central to Canadian life as paid labour. This has been the case since people first earned wages in North America. Unpaid work is still pivotal to the lives of many Canadians, particularly women and children. Cleaning, sewing, cooking, and child-rearing by women are not paid forms of work, but the labour of those who do them underpins family economies. There have been some changes in how gender shapes work roles in the home, especially with same-sex couples, but the Covid-19 pandemic has shown that gender is often a key determinant of who performs certain jobs at home. It has also had a disproportionate impact on women in paid employment and has led to the 2020 economic crisis being called a "shecession" rather than a recession.

The work done by women is as crucial in the 21st century as it has ever been in Canada's history. Women still bear the brunt of domestic tasks, are usually the main parent involved with child-rearing, and also have careers. Canadians will often look at the United States and conclude that their public services make it easier for women to be in the paid workforce, but glancing south of the border is in many ways a poor comparator. Canadians would be better served gazing across the Atlantic Ocean to the social safety networks in Scandinavian countries such as Norway and Sweden. Those countries have actually made it easier for both parents in a family to work due to policies like subsidized daycare and meaningful minimum paid vacation.

Technological change has been a constant influence on work in Canada. Wooden sailing ships gave way to vessels powered by steam and later oil. Navigation became an exact science. Canals were built, rivers dammed, and Canada's interior gradually colonized. Railways were laid across the country, and airplanes eventually made it possible to cross the nation in a few hours. Workers watched movies that progressed from black-and-white format with no sound to colour film with rich sound-tracks, then television, and now can access a plethora of social media outlets. New technologies and industries brought wonderful transform-ations to Canadian life but often brought equal numbers of challenges.

The internal combustion engine made mechanized travel possible, but it also eventually led to communities being built around their trans-port systems rather than the people who lived in them. Economic pro-gress also came with a significant environmental toll. Canada became a country built on hydrocarbon fuels, and Canadians eventually had to reckon with the environmental consequences of their dependence on oil and its many associated products, from gasoline to the synthetic fibres in clothing.

Canadians became increasingly well educated, particularly during the 20th century. Education was often linked to the labour market. This trend was especially evident in the rapid founding of community col-leges during the late 1960s. The standards associated with different jobs changed beginning in the late 19th and early 20th centuries. There were valid reasons for requiring people in skilled trade and professional oc-cupations to demonstrate proficiency in their jobs. Technology created new jobs while also making it possible for people such as electricians, engineers, mechanics, physicians, scientists, and teachers to in turn spur technological change across the country.

The Canadian labour market became more complex and stratified. Rising standards of living brought post–Second World War prosperity to Canadian workers, and the working class had a chance to enjoy a middle-class standard of living. Workers made tangible economic gains and those improvements were often achieved through collective action.

Forming a workers' organization to advance mutual aims was enough to get England's 19th-century Tolpuddle Martyrs sentenced to transportation to penal colonies, but workers were still determined to obtain better economic rewards. Unions were first organized to represent craft workers in the 19th century. Factories were built as Canada went through waves of industrialization. The years immediately following the First World War brought ferocious attacks against labour from the state and business, with the 1919 Winnipeg General Strike forever etched into history as the country's most famous labour struggle. Industrial unions linked to American labour federations — the AFL and the CIO — surged starting in the late 1930s.

Public sector workers began to organize unions in large numbers in the late 1960s, which has led the Canadian organized labour movement to essentially be a public sector movement. That reality does pose challenges for organizations such as the Canadian Labour Congress as efforts are made to recruit private sector workers, especially in the enormous service sector. Workers engaging in collective action, whether through unions or professional associations, is a long-standing aspect of labour and employment in Canada, and while private sector unions face difficulties as we enter the third decade of the 21st century, it would be entirely erroneous to think organized labour's day has passed.

The Supreme Court of Canada affirmed a right to collective bargaining, and courts have overall shown themselves to be more friendly toward workers than in past decades. So the legal imperative is to now revise the various labour and employment laws in place across the country. Legislatures often pass laws in response to events and trends that have already happened, but the labour and employment legal framework in Canada is rooted in laws passed many decades ago.

Canadians have created and consumed a lot of media messages about work and labour. Films, television, visual art, literature, and music have all been forums in which the prospects and perils of work have been deliberated. Work has been lampooned, memorialized, and pastoralized. Many of the messages Canadians received about work have emanated from the United States, but Canada has also produced insightful films, especially documentaries, that strive to reveal the nature of working life in the country in its varied forms. Canadians can be sure that commentary on work and labour will continue to the end of the 21st century and beyond. Print media may be eventually supplanted by digital forms of communication, but people will still want to use media to critique the meaning of work.

Social class has always been a fundamental aspect of Canadian society. Canadians cannot easily differentiate one another based on an accent associated with a given social class, as their British cousins can do, but the common question "What do you do?" is always taken as a query about your occupation and its social status. Hearing that question can make a person burst with pride and confidence or recoil in awkward shame. The reality that personal identity is inextricably woven into a person's occupation has existed since jobs were first divided by the skill and education required to perform them. Job titles acquired great significance and could bring social prestige or obscurity depending on the occupation.

Having identity so closely bound to jobs has been both beneficial and detrimental for workers. There is definite pride in earning a decent wage, performing meaningful work, and especially in being able to provide for dependents. Such motivations are universal for workers. Many Canadians now toil in conditions that have been purposely designed to make it impossible to fulfill those common aspirations. Precarious work makes it far harder for a person to know with confidence if she or he will be able to earn a reasonable income, take care of his or her family, and feel a sense of pride and place at the end of a workday.

Corporations of different sizes and types provide most of the jobs in Canada. They are not democracies, and workers have to unionize if they want to have any influence over how their workplaces are run. There is now a lot of talk in all organizations — public and private — about the need for policies that foster diversity and inclusion. This is a laudable and necessary objective, yet it can often appear superficial in practice.

Diversity in a corporate setting can seem to mean that instead of everyone wearing blue golf shirts half of the staff can instead wear red ones. Real diversity means employing people with different beliefs, opinions, and life experiences, and those who speak their minds are not deviant and dissent at work should not be pathologized.

People may well decide that it is wise to unmoor themselves from all but the most necessary bonds of the workplace, and such a trend would have profound implications for employers. Workers who do not feel their employers bear any sense of loyalty to them will in return not demonstrate any lasting commitment to those who have hired them. The gig economy can make people into workplace mercenaries who always have a necessary eye on their next short-term contract.

The gig economy is tied to the wider globalization phenomenon that accelerated following the end of the Cold War. Canadian workers find themselves competing with workers in other countries just to hold on to the jobs they already have. Governments at all levels are obliged to provide incentives to corporations in order to attract new facilities and the jobs that hopefully come with them. Globalization began to fall out of favour after the 2008 financial crisis, but sending a job to another country is a lot easier than bringing it back to Canada. Cities previously prosperous because of well-paid industrial employment now have lower standards of living and are dependent on the service industries they can attract and retain.

Public policy-makers face colossal challenges in 21st-century Canada. The country has long been a home for immigrants but will soon face population declines without the arrival of new people from other countries. There are no guarantees that immigration will carry on as before, since global population declines will likely continue and countries will want to keep their best and brightest at home and not lose them to emigration. It is also unlikely that Canadians will suddenly decide to start having large families, since the cost of raising children while trying to stay afloat financially is simply too onerous.

Race, gender, class, and ethnicity still have a profound impact on employment. Women, workers of colour, and immigrants are more likely to perform precarious work than white men, the role of Indigenous workers in Canadian society remains undervalued, and a small percentage of

Canada's population still controls a much larger share of the country's material wealth. Canadians live in a capitalistic economy, and even if measures are in place to mitigate the impact of job loss, the overwhelming majority of people have to make a living by selling their labour to someone else, and the basic employment relationship is not likely to change. Work is not, however, all about money, since it does have intrinsic value that is tied to self-worth.

Canadians found themselves again facing a major public policy challenge in 2020 with the arrival of Covid-19. Unemployment rose to levels not seen since the 1930s, companies teetered on the brink of insolvency, and governments responded by trying to stimulate recovery. It is important to recall that Canadian workers have dealt with worse conditions and have the ability to demand public policy changes that will help them hold on to their jobs and improve their standards of living. The problems currently experienced by Canadian workers will still have to be addressed long after everyone has received a Covid-19 vaccination.

This book shows there are a few aspects of the history of work and labour in Canada that were accidental. Pandemics are one such unknown variable. The truth is that most policies shaping work and labour have been deliberate and were made with the expectation of specific results. For example, the post–Second World War labour relations system was devised to regulate workplace conflict and largely fulfilled that objective. Workplaces began to be automated to make them more productive and efficient, and technological change quite often led to that result. Workers were deliberately chosen for jobs based on race, gender, and ethnicity. Students continued to be streamed into occupations based on social class.

Policy changes can also be pursued that will make working life better, just as they were in the past. Bonded and indentured labour were banished long ago. The right to unionize was legally guaranteed, and workers can engage in collective bargaining. Canada has health and safety laws to protect people on the job — and minimum wage rates. Women can no longer be fired for marrying or becoming pregnant. LGBTQ2 workers cannot be legally discriminated against in the workplace. A universal basic income can be achieved in the same way that public pensions and universal public health care were implemented. The wage gap between men and women can be closed, and young workers can be hired for meaningful first jobs on which they can build their careers. Workplaces can be organized so that they can provide purposeful jobs for people living with physical challenges. Environmentally sustainable economic models can be successfully implemented that will improve the working lives of Canadians. More appropriate definitions of what constitutes essential work can be applied to jobs.

Working in Canada has indeed often been a struggle that unfortunately left many people behind, but it has also brought victories and advances that can be an inspiration for the future. Workers of all sorts and from across the land made it into the nation it is today. It is important to bear in mind that while there is much about which Canadians can feel proud, there were times when the good old days were not necessarily that good. Canada can be a rewarding place for all people to live and work, otherwise successive waves of people would not have come from around the world to become Canadians. It is ultimately up to workers of all types to decide the paths they wish to take and the country in which they want to live and work.

ACKNOWLEDGEMENTS

Canada, A Working History is an effort to try to bring analysis of the development of work and labour in Canada out of the university and into popular discourse. I thank many colleagues and students who have helped me hone my thinking about the meaning of work in Canada over the years. The actual researching and writing of this book began following a discussion with Dundurn publisher Scott Fraser, and I thank him for agreeing to take on this project. I also want to recognize the contributions Russell Smith, Michael Carroll, Elena Radic, Kendra Martin, Melissa Kawaguchi, and everyone else at Dundurn have made to this book.

Many of the events and themes described in *Canada, A Working History* were experienced by people in my family back to the time when they arrived in Canada, and they were often on my mind as I was writing. This book is being published at a time of crisis in Canada. Young people are leaving secondary school to enter college and university in altered learning circumstances, vast numbers of workers have lost their jobs, and organizations of all types and sizes are undergoing extensive change. Many young Canadians have already been in the workforce by the time they finish secondary school. I hope this book is read by young workers and that it helps them make sense of their working lives and those of the people around them. They have already contributed to the history of work in Canada and will continue do so into the future.

NOTES

PART I: EUROPEAN ARRIVAL TO CONFEDERATION

1. See Ronald Segal, *The Black Diaspora: Five Centuries of the Black Experience Outside Africa* (New York: Farrar, Straus & Giroux, 1995).
2. See Fred Glover and Celine Cooper, "Black Enslavement in Canada," *The Canadian Encyclopedia*, June 10, 2020, thecanadianencyclopedia.ca/en/article/black-enslavement-in-canada-plain-language-summary; Statistics Canada, "Upper Canada & Loyalists (1785 to 1797)," August 26, 2015, www150.statcan.gc.ca/n1/pub/98-187-x/4151286-eng.htm; and Public Broadcasting System, "Africans in America — Map: The Growing Nation," pbs.org/wgbh/aia/part3/map3.html.
3. H. Clare Pentland, *Labour and Capital in Canada, 1650–1860* (Toronto: James Lorimer, 1981), especially chapter 1, "Slavery in Canada"; and Nova Scotia Archives, *Nova Scotia Gazette and Weekly Chronicle*, September 1, 1772 (microfilm no. 8155), archives.novascotia.ca/africanns/archives/?ID=10.

4. On the East India Company, see William Dalrymple, *The Anarchy: The Relentless Rise of the East India Company* (London: Bloomsbury, 2019).

5. Ellen Meiksens Wood, *The Origin of Capitalism: A Longer View* (London: Verso, 2017), 98.

6. Christopher Tomlins, "Reconsidering Indentured Servitude: European Migration and the Early American Labor Force, 1600–1775," *Labor History* 42, no. 1 (2001): 5–43.

7. Edith Burley, *Servants of the Honourable Company: Work, Discipline, and Conflict in the Hudson's Bay Company, 1770 to 1879* (Toronto: Oxford University Press, 1997), 68.

8. Gustav Lanctôt, *Filles de joie ou filles du roi: étude sur l'émigration feminine en Nouvelle-France* (Montreal: Du Jour, 1964).

9. For an account of the evolution of modern personal hygiene, see Peter Ward, *The Clean Body: A Modern History* (Montreal and Kingston: McGill-Queen's University Press, 2019).

10. On the economic role of the British state in the early 19th century, see Michael Bliss, *Northern Enterprise: Five Centuries of Canadian Business* (Toronto: McClelland & Stewart, 1987).

11. On the spread of British influence, see James Belich, *Replenish the Earth: The Settler Revolution and the Rise of the Anglo World, 1783–1939* (Oxford: Oxford University Press, 2009).

12. Craig Heron, *The Canadian Labour Movement: A Short History*, 2nd ed. (Toronto: Lorimer, 1996), 12.

13. Jeremy Webber, "Labour and the Law," in ed. Paul Craven, *Labouring Lives: Work and Workers in Nineteenth-Century Ontario* (Toronto: Province of Ontario, 1995), 136.

14. Jacqueline Riding, *Peterloo: The Story of the Manchester Massacre* (London: Head of Zeus, 2018), 4.

15. Riding, *Peterloo*, 266–67.

16. John V. Orth, *Combination and Conspiracy: A Legal History of Trade Unionism, 1721–1906* (Oxford: Clarendon, 1991), chapter 5.

17. Ellen Castelow, "The Tolpuddle Martyrs," Historic UK, historic-uk .com/HistoryUK/HistoryofEngland/Tolpuddle-Martyrs.

18. Castelow, "The Tolpuddle Martyrs."
19. Heron, *The Canadian Labour Movement*, 12.
20. On the origins and development of Chartism, see Edward Royle, *Chartism*, 3rd ed. (London: Routledge, 1996).
21. Elizabeth Jane Errington, *Wives and Mothers, School Mistresses and Scullery Maids: Working Women in Upper Canada, 1790 to 1840* (Montreal: McGill-Queen's University Press, 1995), 18.
22. Errington, *Wives and Mothers*, 69.
23. Jeremy Webber, "Labour and the Law," 123.
24. See Peter Way, *Common Labour: Workers and the Digging of North American Canals, 1780 to 1860* (Cambridge: Cambridge University Press, 1993).
25. On the potato famine and Irish migration to Canada, see Mark McGowan, *Death or Canada: The Irish Famine Migration to Toronto, 1847* (Toronto: Novalis, 2009).
26. Bryan D. Palmer, "Discordant Music: Charivaris and Whitecapping in Nineteenth-Century North America," *Labour/Le Travail* 3 (1978): 5–62.
27. Saint Mary's University, University History Campuses, smu.ca/academics/archives/campuses.html.
28. For the University of Toronto's history, see Martin L. Friedland, *The University of Toronto: A History* (Toronto: University of Toronto Press, 2002).
29. Law Society of Ontario, "The Law Society of Ontario in Context: A Chronology," lso.ca/about-lso/osgoode-hall-and-ontario-legal-heritage/collections-and-research/chronology?lang=en-ca.
30. Harold Adams Innis, *The Fur Trade in Canada: An Introduction to Canadian Economic History* (New Haven, CT: Yale University Press, 1930).
31. Donald Creighton, *The Commercial Empire of the St. Lawrence, 1760–1850* (New Haven, CT: Yale University Press, 1937).

PART II: CONFEDERATION TO THE 1930s

1. Heron, *The Canadian Labour Movement*, 14.
2. On the Knights of Labor, see Bryan D. Palmer and Greg S. Kealey, *Dreaming of What Might Be: The Knights of Labor in Ontario, 1880–1900* (Cambridge: Cambridge University Press, 1982).
3. Library and Archives Canada, "Building the Canadian Pacific Railway," collectionscanada.gc.ca/settlement/kids/021013-2031.3-e.html.
4. Sandra Rollings-Magnusson, *Heavy Burdens on Small Shoulders: The Labour of Pioneer Children on the Canadian Prairies* (Edmonton: University of Alberta Press, 2009).
5. See Hugh J. Johnston, *The Voyage of the* Komagata Maru: *The Sikh Challenge to Canada's Colour Bar* (Vancouver: University of British Columbia Press, 2014).
6. Heron, *The Canadian Labour Movement*, 24.
7. Sally Gibson, "Distillery Historic District/Gooderham & Worts National Historic Site," *The Canadian Encyclopedia*, March 4, 2015, thecanadianencyclopedia.ca/en/article/distillery-historic-district -gooderham-worts-national-historic-site.
8. On the history of Labour Day in Canada, see Craig Heron and Steve Penfold, *The Workers' Festival: A History of Labour Day* (Toronto: University of Toronto Press, 2005).
9. Canadian Medical Association, "The Canadian Medical Association: Proud History, Strong Future," iPolitics, May 15, 2017, ipolitics.ca/2017/05/15/the-canadian-medical-association-proud -history-strong-future.
10. See Keith Walden, *Becoming Modern in Toronto: The Industrial Exhibition and the Shaping of a Late Victorian Culture* (Toronto: University of Toronto Press, 1997).
11. Mariana Valverde, *The Age of Light, Soap, and Water: Moral Reform in English Canada, 1885–1925* (Toronto: University of Toronto Press, 2008).
12. Geo. P. Wood and E.H. Ruddock, *Vitalogy or Encyclopedia of Health and Home* (Chicago: The Vitalogy Association, 1912).

13. Charles Darwin, *On the Origin of Species by Means of Natural Selection, or the Preservation of Favoured Races in the Struggle for Life* (London: John Murray, 1859); and Karl Marx, *Das Kapital: Kritik der politischen Oekonomie*, vol. 1 (Hamburg: Verlag von Otto Meissner, 1867).

14. See Ramsay Cook, *The Regenerators: Social Criticism in Late Victorian English Canada* (Toronto: University of Toronto Press, 1985).

15. William Lyon Mackenzie King, *Industry and Humanity: A Study in the Principles Underlying Industrial Reconstruction* (Toronto: Thomas Allen, 1918).

16. *They Shall Not Grow Old*, directed by Peter Jackson (Wellington, NZ: Wingnut Films, 2018), DVD.

17. University of Toronto, "The Discovery and Early Development of Insulin," insulin.library.utoronto.ca.

18. Christopher J. Rutty, "Origins: from the Connaught Fund & Back to Connaught Laboratories," University of Toronto, connaught.research .utoronto.ca/history/article1.

19. Toronto Public Library, "Ontario's Tuberculosis Sanatoriums, 1897– 1960," April 18, 2019, torontopubliclibrary.typepad.com/local-history -genealogy/2019/04/ontarios-tuberculosis-sanatoriums-1897 -1960.html.

20. On the rise of department stores in Canada, see Donica Belisle, *Retail Nation: Department Stores and the Making of Modern Canada* (Vancouver: University of British Columbia Press, 2011).

21. Professional Engineers Ontario, peo.on.ca/index.php?ci_id=1792 &la_id=1.

22. Eric Tucker, *Administering Danger in the Workplace: The Law and Politics of Occupational Health and Safety Regulation in Ontario, 1850–1914* (Toronto: University of Toronto Press, 1990), 193.

23. Kevin L. Borg, *Auto Mechanics: Technology and Expertise in Twentieth-Century America* (Baltimore: Johns Hopkins University Press, 2007).

24. Alfred Chandler, *Scale and Scope: The Dynamics of Industrial Capitalism* (Cambridge, MA: Belknap, 1990).

25. Frederick Winslow Taylor, *The Principles of Scientific Management* (New York: Harper and Brothers, 1911), 10.

26. On the impact of Mayo and Hawthorne, see Richard Gillespie, *Manufacturing Knowledge: A History of the Hawthorne Experiments* (Cambridge: Cambridge University Press, 1991).

27. Howard Markel, *The Kelloggs: The Battling Brothers of Battle Creek* (New York: Vintage Books, 2018).

28. National Peanut Board, "Who Invented Peanut Butter?," nationalpeanutboard.org/peanut-info/who-invented-peanut-butter .htm.

29. See Don Nerbas, *Dominion of Capital: The Politics of Big Business and the Crisis of the Canadian Bourgeoisie, 1914–1947* (Toronto: University of Toronto Press, 2013).

30. On the founding of the National Hockey League, see Andrew Ross, *Joining the Clubs: The Business of the National Hockey League to 1945* (Syracuse, NY: Syracuse University Press, 2015).

31. See David Farber, *Sloan Rules: Alfred P. Sloan and the Triumph of General Motors* (Chicago: University of Chicago Press, 2002).

32. Co-operative Commonwealth Federation Program, scaa.usask.ca /gallery/election/en/view_image.php?image=45.

33. See Eric Strikwerda, *The Wages of Relief: Cities and the Unemployed in Prairie Canada, 1929–39* (Edmonton: Athabasca University Press, 2012).

34. Heron, *The Canadian Labour Movement*, 61.

35. Jefferson Cowie, *The Great Exception: The New Deal and the Limits of American Politics* (Princeton, NJ: Princeton University Press, 2016).

36. John Maynard Keynes, *The General Theory of Employment, Interest and Money* (London: Macmillan, 1936).

37. Library and Archives Canada, William Lyon Mackenzie King Diary, September 8, 1933, bac-lac.gc.ca/eng/discover/politics-government /prime-ministers/william-lyon-mackenzie-king/Pages/item .aspx?IdNumber=14466&.

38. Arthur Degreve, "Challenge by the CIO," *Globe and Mail*, April 24, 1937.

39. Kathryn McPherson, *Bedside Matters: The Transformation of Canadian Nursing, 1900–1990* (Toronto: Oxford University Press, 1996).

40. David Goutor, *Guarding the Gates: The Canadian Labour Movement and Immigration, 1872–1934* (Vancouver: University of British Columbia Press, 2007).

PART III: THE SECOND WORLD WAR TO THE 1960s

1. Keith Grieves, *Sir Eric Geddes: Business and Government in War and Peace* (Manchester: Manchester University Press, 1989).

2. Dominion Bureau of Statistics, *Census of Canada 1941*, vol. 4 *Earnings and Employment*, Table 4.

3. R. MacGregor Dawson, *The Conscription Crisis of 1944* (Toronto: University of Toronto Press, 1961), 13.

4. Pamela Sugiman, *Labour's Dilemma: The Gender Politics of Auto Workers in Canada, 1937–1979* (Toronto: University of Toronto Press, 1997), 19.

5. Library and Archives Canada, "Service Files of the Second World War," bac-lac.gc.ca/eng/discover/military-heritage/second-world-war/second-world-war-dead-1939-1947/Pages/files-second-war-dead.aspx.

6. Matthew Bellamy, *Profiting the Crown: Canada's Polymer Corporation, 1942–1990* (Montreal: McGill-Queen's University Press, 2005).

7. Sugiman, *Labour's Dilemma*, 32.

8. Heron, *The Canadian Labour Movement*, 71.

9. Heron, *The Canadian Labour Movement*, 76.

10. Packard Motor Car Co. v. National Labor Relations Board, 330 U.S. 485.

11. Norman Albert, "Conacher Scored Six for North Toronto," *Toronto Star*, February 9, 1923, 12.

12. George Grant, *Lament for a Nation: The Defeat of Canadian Nationalism* (Toronto: McClelland & Stewart, 1965).

13. Graham D. Taylor and Peter A. Baskerville, *A Concise History of Business in Canada* (Toronto: Oxford University Press, 1994), 413.

14. Veterans Affairs Canada, "Canadian War Brides," veterans.gc.ca /eng/remembrance/history/second-world-war/canadian-war-brides.

15. Franca Iacovetta, *Such Hardworking People: Italian Immigrants in Postwar Canada* (Montreal: McGill-Queen's University Press, 1992), 66.

16. "31 Latvians, Fleeing from Communism, Safe," *Halifax Mail-Star*, August 23, 1949.

17. Dominion Bureau of Statistics, *Census of Canada 1951*, vol. 4, *Labour Force — Occupations and Industries*, Table 5.

18. Dominion Bureau of Statistics, "Social Implications of the 1951 Census," Table 24.

19. Barry Broadfoot, *The Veterans' Years: Coming Home from the War* (Toronto: Douglas & McIntyre, 1985).

20. Doug Owram, *Born at the Right Time: A History of the Baby Boom Generation* (Toronto: University of Toronto Press, 1996), 54–55.

21. Lizabeth Cohen, *A Consumer's Republic: The Politics of Mass Consumption in Postwar America* (New York: Knopf, 2003).

22. Harold Kalman, "Shopping Centre," *The Canadian Encyclopedia*, thecanadianencyclopedia.ca/en/article/shopping-centre.

23. Pamela Klaffke, *Spree: A Cultural History of Shopping* (Vancouver: Arsenal Pulp Press, 2003), 22–24.

24. Eileen Sufrin, *The Eaton Drive: The Campaign to Organize Canada's Largest Department Store, 1948 to 1952* (Toronto: Fitzhenry & Whiteside, 1982).

25. David E. Nye, *America's Assembly Line* (Cambridge, MA: MIT Press, 2013).

26. Jeremy Milloy, *Blood, Sweat, and Fear: Violence and Work in the North American Auto Industry, 1960–1980* (Vancouver: University of British Columbia Press, 2017).

27. Peter Drucker, *Concept of the Corporation* (New York: The Joy Day Company, 1946).

28. Statistics Canada, "A Note on Canadian Unemployment Since 1921," www150.statcan.gc.ca/n1/en/pub/75-001-x/1992003/87-eng .pdf?st=AHvJPDsm.

29. David Sterritt, *The Honeymooners* (Detroit: Wayne State University Press, 2009).

30. Stephanie Coontz, *The Way We Never Were: American Families and the Nostalgia Trap* (New York: Basic Books, 2000).

31. Jason Russell, *Our Union: UAW/CAW Local 27 from 1950 to 1990* (Edmonton: Athabasca University Press, 2011), 40.

32. Janet Frank, "Daddies," in *Tibor Gergely's Great Big Book of Bedtime Stories* (New York: Golden Press, 1970), 257.

33. Office of Naval Research, "Digital Computer Newsletter," September 1, 1949, 4.

34. Columbia University, "Columbia University Computing History," columbia.edu/cu/computinghistory/hollerith.html.

35. Vicki Porter Adams, "Captain Grace M. Harper, the Mother of COBOL," *InfoWorld* 3, no. 20 (October 1981): 33.

36. IBM, "IBM Typewriter Milestones," ibm.com/ibm/history/exhibits /modelb/modelb_milestone.html.

37. Dorothy Sue Cobble, *Dishing It Out: Waitresses and Their Unions in the Twentieth Century* (Urbana: University of Illinois Press, 1991).

38. Dominion Bureau of Statistics, *Census of Canada 1961*, vol. 3.1, Table 6.

39. Dominion Bureau of Statistics, *Census of Canada 1961*, "Advance Report AL-1," Table 3.

40. Taylor and Baskerville, *A Concise History of Business in Canada*, 408.

41. Dimitry Anastakis, *Auto Pact: Creating a Borderless North American Auto Industry, 1960–1971* (Toronto: University of Toronto Press, 2005).

42. Jason Russell, *Leading Progress: The Professional Institute of the Public Service of Canada, 1920–2020* (Toronto: Between The Lines, 2020).

43. CBC Digital Archives, "Getting Divorced Becomes Easier in Canada," July 2, 1968, cbc.ca/archives/entry/getting-divorced -becomes-easier-in-canada.

44. Arlie Russell Hochschild, *The Managed Heart: Commercialization of Human Feeling* (Berkeley: University of California Press, 1983).

45. William H. Whyte, *The Organization Man* (New York: Simon & Schuster, 1956).

46. Sloan Wilson, *The Man in the Grey Flannel Suit* (New York: Simon & Schuster, 1955).

47. Julie Berebitsky, *Sex and the Office: A History of Gender, Power, and Desire* (New Haven, CT: Yale University Press, 2012).

48. Betty Friedan, *The Feminine Mystique* (New York: W.W. Norton, 1963).

49. Gloria Steinem, "A Bunny's Tale," *Show*, May 1963, 90–116.

50. *High Steel*, directed by Don Owen (1965; Ottawa: National Film Board of Canada), nfb.ca/film/high_steel.

51. John Porter, *The Vertical Mosaic: An Analysis of Social Class and Power in Canada* (Toronto: University of Toronto Press, 1965).

52. James Lorimer and Myfanwy Phillips, *Working People: Life in a Downtown City Neighbourhood* (Toronto: James Lewis and Samuel, 1971).

53. *The Things I Cannot Change*, directed by Tanya Ballantyne (1967; Ottawa: National Film Board of Canada), nfb.ca/film/things_i _cannot_change.

PART IV: THE TUMULTUOUS 1970s AND 1980s

1. MexicoNow, "Volkswagen Plant in Puebla Builds Its 12 Millionth Vehicle," August 20, 2018, mexico-now.com/index.php/article /4425-volkswagen-builds-its-12-millionth-car-at-the-puebla -assembly-plant.

2. United States Department of Defense, Office of Secretary of Defense, Historical Office, "Charles E. Wilson: Dwight Eisenhower Administration," history.defense.gov/Multimedia/Biographies /Article-View/Article/571268/charles-e-wilson.

3. Statistics Canada, "Work Force by Industrial Category and Sex, Census Years, 1911 to 1971," www150.statcan.gc.ca/n1/pub/11 -516-x/sectiond/4057750-eng.htm#1.

4. Bibliothèque et archives nationales du Québec, Ahuntsic Prospectus, 1976.

5. Langara College Library, Box 1 of 2, 1976 to 1977 Prospectus.

6. George Brown College Archive, Box E-164, Extension PT Calendars, 1974–75.

7. Berebitsky, *Sex and the Office*, 3.

8. Harry Braverman, *Labor and Monopoly Capital: The Degradation of Work in the Twentieth Century* (New York: Monthly Review Press, 1974); James Rinehart, *The Tyranny of Work: Alienation and the Labour Process* (Don Mills, ON: Longman Canada, 1975); Michael Burawoy, *Manufacturing Consent: Changes in the Labor Process Under Monopoly Capitalism* (Chicago: University of Chicago Press, 1979); Irving Abella, *The Canadian Labour Movement, 1902–1960* (Ottawa: Canadian Historical Association, 1975); and Ian McKay, *Reds, Rebels, Radicals: Rethinking Canada's Left History* (Toronto: Between the Lines, 2005).

9. Larry Savage and Charles W. Smith, *Unions in Court: Organized Labour and the Charter of Rights and Freedoms* (Vancouver: University of British Columbia Press, 2017), 3.

10. Canadian Broadcasting Corporation, "The *Ocean Ranger* Disaster," cbc.ca/archives/topic/the-ocean-ranger-disaster.

11. Lee Iacocca and Sonny Kleinfeld, *Talking Straight* (New York: Bantam, 1988).

12. Peter C. Newman, *The Establishment Man: A Portrait in Power* (Toronto: McClelland & Stewart, 1982).

13. Statistics Canada, "1981 Census Highlights," 19.

14. George Brown College Archive, Box E-164, 1981 to Fall 1985, Winter 1985.

15. Statistics Canada, "1981 Census Highlights," 45–46.

16. Jacqueline Howard, "The Truth About 'Patient Zero' and HIV's Origins," CNN, October 29, 2016, cnn.com/2016/10/27/health /hiv-gaetan-dugas-patient-zero/index.html.

17. See Joseph McCartin, *Collision Course: Ronald Reagan, the Air Traffic Controllers, and the Strike That Changed America* (Oxford: Oxford University Press, 2011).

18. Canadian Broadcasting Corporation, "Brian Mulroney Takes on Organized Crime," December 9, 1974, cbc.ca/archives/entry /brian-mulroney-taking-on-organized-crime.

19. Computerhistory.org, computerhistory.org/timeline/1981.

20. Computerhistory.org, computerhistory.org/timeline/1982.

21. Computerhistory.org, computerhistory.org/timeline/1983.
22. *After the Axe*, directed by Sturla Gunnarsson (1981; Ottawa: National Film Board of Canada), nfb.ca/film/after_axe.
23. *Final Offer*, directed by Sturla Gunnarsson (1985; Ottawa: National Film Board of Canada), nfb.ca/film/final_offer.
24. Government of Canada, "Fact Sheet: Evolution of Pay Equity," canada.ca/en/treasury-board-secretariat/services/innovation /equitable-compensation/fact-sheet-evolution-pay-equity.html.
25. Thomas J. Peters and Robert H. Waterman, Jr., *In Search of Excellence: Lessons from America's Best-Run Companies* (New York: Warner Books, 1982).
26. Brian Milner, "Excellence Guru's Surprising Confession Is Bizarre," *Globe and Mail*, November 23, 2001.
27. Francis Fukuyama, *The End of History and the Last Man* (New York: Free Press, 1992).

PART V: THE ANXIOUS 1990s AND 2000s

1. CEIC Data, "Canada Unemployment Rate 1976–2019," ceicdata.com/en/indicator/canada/unemployment-rate.
2. Statistics Canada, "Interest Rates and Exchange Rates," www150 .statcan.gc.ca/n1/pub/11-210-x/2010000/t098-eng.htm.
3. Canadian Broadcasting Corporation, "Newfoundlanders Protest Cod Moratorium on Canada Day," cbc.ca/player/play/2651777968.
4. See Dimitry Anastakis, *Autonomous State: The Struggle for a Canadian Car Industry from OPEC to Free Trade* (Toronto: University of Toronto Press, 2013), 107–8.
5. International Organization for Standardization, iso.org/about-us.html.
6. See JoAnne Yates and Craig N. Murphy, *Engineering Rules: Global Standard Setting Since 1880* (Baltimore, MD: Johns Hopkins University Press, 2019).
7. Internet Archive, "About Motorola University: The Inventors of Six Sigma," web.archive.org/web/20051106025733/http://www.motorola .com/content/0,,3079,00.html.

8. For an account that explains why employers often favoured rural communities as factory locations, see Doug Smith, *Stickin' to the Union: Local 2223 Versus John Buhler* (Winnipeg: Fernwood, 2004).

9. For a full account of what occurred at CAMI, see James W. Rinehart, Christopher Huxley, and David Robertson, *Just Another Car Factory?: Lean Production and Its Discontents* (Ithaca, NY: Cornell ILR Press, 1997).

10. Centre for Computing History, "Tim Berners-Lee Toyed with the Idea of Web Pages and Hyperlinks," computinghistory.org.uk/det/5936 /Tim-Berners-Lee-toyed-with-the-idea-of-web-pages-and-hyperlinks.

11. Centre for Computing History, "First Email Sent by Ray Tomlinson," computinghistory.org.uk/det/6116/First-e-mail-sent -by-Ray-Tomlinson.

12. Robert Reich, *The Work of Nations: Preparing Ourselves for 21st-Century Capitalism* (New York: Knopf, 1991).

13. Thomas Piketty, *Capital in the Twenty-First Century* (Cambridge, MA: Belknap, 2014).

14. Canadian Broadcasting Corporation, "$400 Rebate Cheque Coming in January," cbc.ca/news/canada/calgary/400-rebate -cheque-coming-in-january-1.521453.

15. CTV News, "Canadian Soldiers Won't Let Amputations Slow Them Down," ctvnews.ca/canadian-soldiers-won-t-let-amputations-slow -them-down-1.573465.

16. Richard Florida, *The Rise of the Creative Class and How It's Transforming Work, Leisure, Community, and Everyday Life* (New York: Basic Books, 2002).

17. "Goldberg Pioneers On-Line Education," *UBC Science Synergy* 2, no. 1 (October 1996): 5, science.ubc.ca/sites/science.ubc.ca/files /synergy/2-1.pdf.

18. Bank of Canada, "Remarks by Lawrence Schembri, Deputy Governor of the Bank of Canada," August 25, 2015, bankofcanada .ca/wp-content/uploads/2015/08/remarks-250815.pdf#chart2.

19. Jack M. Nilles et al., *The Telecommunications-Transportation Tradeoff: Options for Tomorrow* (New York: John Wiley & Sons, 1976).

20. Statistics Canada, "Working from Home: An Update," June 25, 2020, www150.statcan.gc.ca/n1/pub/11-402-x/2012000/chap /information/information02-eng.htm.
21. Statistics Canada, "Unemployment Rates in Canada and the United States, 1976 to 2016," June 25, 2020, www150.statcan.gc.ca/n1 /daily-quotidien/170707/cg-a003-eng.htm.
22. Canadian Broadcasting Corporation, "Ford Plant Closure Mourned by St. Thomas, Ontario," cbc.ca/news/canada/ford-plant-closure -mourned-by-st-thomas-ontario-1.1048415.
23. Sian Griffiths, "Caterpillar Feels Force of Canada's Anger as It Closes Country's Last Train Plant," *The Guardian*, February 15, 2012, theguardian.com/business/2012/feb/15/caterpillar -canada-anger-emd-rail-factory.
24. Tavia Grant, "For Laid-Off Caterpillar Workers, the Fall Continues," *Globe and Mail*, October 5, 2012, theglobeandmail.com/report-on -business/economy/manufacturing/for-laid-off-caterpillar -employees-the-fall-continues/article4593258.
25. On the founding and expansion of the temporary employment agency, see Erin Hatton, *The Temp Economy: From Kelly Girls to Permatemps in Postwar America* (Philadelphia: Temple University Press, 2010).
26. Institute for Work and Health, "Investigating Temporary Employment in Canada," iwh.on.ca/newsletters/at-work/62 /investigating-temporary-employment-in-canada.
27. Statistics Canada, "Employment Services, Summary Statistics, by North American Industry Classification System (NAICS)," doi.org/10.25318/2110011801-eng (inactive).
28. Sébastien LaRochelle-Côté and Jason Gilmore, "Canada's Employment Downturn," Statistics Canada, www150.statcan.gc.ca /n1/pub/75-001-x/2009112/article/11048-eng.htm.
29. Statistics Canada, "Average Real Hourly Wages of Men and Women Employed Full-Time, 1981 to 2011," www150.statcan.gc.ca/n1 /pub/11f0019m/2013347/ct002-eng.htm.
30. Organisation for Economic Co-operation and Development,

"Average Annual Hours Actually Worked Per Worker," stats.oecd .org/Index.aspx?DataSetCode=ANHRS.

31. Canadian Broadcasting Corporation, "The Education of Brian Nicholl," October 2, 2009, cbc.ca/fifth/episodes/2009-2010/the -education-of-brian-nicholl.

32. Pete Denomme and the Cosmic Cowboys, "They Keep Rollin'," thecosmiccowboys.bandcamp.com/track/they-keep-rollin.

33. Legislative Assembly of Ontario, *Bill 168: An Act to Amend the Occupational Health and Safety Act with Respect to Violence and Harassment in the Workplace and Other Matters* (Toronto: Queen's Printer, 2009).

34. Canadian Broadcasting Corporation, "Women Killed at Work Memorialized in New Law," cbc.ca/news/canada/windsor /woman-killed-at-work-memorialized-in-new-law-1.886499.

35. Gabrielle Bauer, "Stress Leave: Boon or Bust?", *Globe and Mail*, June 25, 2003, theglobeandmail.com/report-on-business/stress-leave -boon-or-bust/article1017921.

36. M.E. Hemels, G. Koren, and T.R. Einarson, "Increased Use of Antidepressants in Canada: 1981–2000," *Annals of Pharmacotherapy* 36, no. 10 (October 2002): 1652.

37. James E. Loehr, *Stress for Success* (New York: Crown, 1998).

38. George Orwell, *Nineteen Eighty-Four* (London: Secker & Warburg, 1949).

PART VI: WORKING IN THE 21ST CENTURY

1. Canadian Broadcasting Corporation, "Pierre Trudeau's Washington Press Club Speech," cbc.ca/player/play/1797537698.

2. Government of Canada, "Trade and Investment Agreements," international.gc.ca/trade-commerce/trade-agreements-accords -commerciaux/agr-acc/index.aspx?lang=eng.

3. Province of Alberta, "Workforce Adjustment Service," alberta.ca /workforce-adjustment-service.aspx.

4. *Waterloo Region Record*, "RIM Job Centre Helps 150 Former

Employees Move On," November 29, 2012, cambridgetimes.ca/news -story/2617190-rim-job-centre-helps-105-former-employees-move-on.

5. See David W. Livingstone, ed., *Education and Jobs: Exploring the Gaps* (Toronto: University of Toronto Press, 2009).

6. Anthony P. Carnevale, Nicole Smith, and Jeff Strohl, *Recovery: Job Growth and Education Requirements Through 2020* (Washington, DC: Georgetown University Public Policy Institute, Centre on Education and the Workforce, 2013), 6, cew.georgetown.edu /wp-content/uploads/2014/11/Recovery2020.FR_.Web_.pdf.

7. Amazon, "Our Fulfillment Centers," aboutamazon.com /amazon-fulfillment/our-fulfillment-centers.

8. Amazon, "Amazon's Fulfillment Network," aboutamazon.com /working-at-amazon/amazons-fulfillment-network.

9. Amazon, "Amazon Warehouse Associate (Full-Time) Bolton, Ontario," search.amazondelivers.jobs/job/bolton/amazon-warehouse -associate-full-time/3413/15354279.

10. Joseph Hall and Astrid Lange, "These Are the Best 25 Jobs in Toronto Right Now," *Toronto Star*, February 13, 2020, thestar.com/ business/2020/02/13/these-are-the-best-25-jobs-in-toronto-right -now.html.

11. Canadian Broadcasting Corporation, *Generation Jobless*, January 31, 2013, curio.ca/en/video/generation-jobless-2594.

12. Jacob Lorinc, "School Isn't Preparing Students for the Jobs of the Future," *Toronto Star*, February 21, 2020, thestar.com/business /2020/02/21/school-isnt-preparing-students-for-the-jobs-of-the -future-heres-what-these-gta-students-say-needs-to-change.html.

13. Mario Canseco, "Canadians Losing Sleep over Money, Finances and Employment," *Business in Vancouver*, January 13, 2020, biv.com/ article/2020/01/canadians-losing-sleep-over-money-finances -and-employment.

14. Ada Calhoun, *Why We Can't Sleep: Women's New Midlife Crisis* (New York: Grove Press, 2020).

15. For a typical example of an anti-pension media article, see Patrick Brethour, "How Government Pensions Are Blowing Up the Federal

Deficit," *Globe and Mail*, March 6, 2020, theglobeandmail.com
/business/article-how-lower-interest-rates-are-blowing-up
-the-federal-deficit.

16. Tom McFeat, "8 Things You Need to Know About RRSPs," February
29, 2012, cbc.ca/news/business/taxes/8-things-you-need-to-know
-about-rrsps-1.1104801.

17. Marie Drolet and René Morissette, "New Facts on Pension
Coverage in Canada," Statistics Canada, December 18, 2014,
www150.statcan.gc.ca/n1/en/pub/75-006-x/2014001/article
/14120-eng.pdf?st=KurCCE7d.

18. Gordon Pape, "Should You Be Worried About Retirement? If
You Don't Have a Pension, You Probably Should," *St. Catharines
Standard*, February 19, 2020.

19. Ipsos, "Only One Half (48%) of Canadians Are Saving for Their
Retirement," February 10, 2015, ipsos.com/en-ca/only-one-half
-48-canadians-are-saving-their-retirement.

20. For details on Canada's public pension plans, see Government of
Canada, Public Pensions, canada.ca/en/services/benefits
/publicpensions.html. See also rentals.ca/blog/rentals-ca-april-
2020-national-rent-report and www150.statcan.gc.ca/t1/tbl1/en/
tv.action?pid=1110024101.

21. H.G. Wells, *The Time Machine* (London: Henry Heinemann, 1895).

22. Aldous Huxley, *Brave New World* (London: Chatto & Windus, 1932);
and Yevgeny Zamyatin, *We* (New York: E.P. Dutton, 1924).

23. *The Complete Metropolis*, directed by Fritz Lang (1927; New York:
Kino, 2010).

24. Karel Čapek, *R.U.R. (Rossum's Universal Robots)*, trans. Claudia
Novack (London: Penguin, 2004).

25. Alvin Toffler, *Future Shock* (New York: Random House, 1970).

26. Jeremy Rifkin, *The End of Work: The Decline of the Global Labor
Force and the Dawn of the Post-Market Era* (New York: Putnam,
1995).

27. Martin Ford, *Rise of the Robots: Technology and the Threat of a
Jobless Future* (New York: Basic Books, 2015).

28. Jeff Baenen, "Wisconsin Company Holds 'Chip Party' to Microchip Workers," *Chicago Tribune*, August 2, 2017, chicagotribune.com /business/blue-sky/ct-wisconsin-company-microchips-workers -20170801-story.html.

29. Workopolis, "14 Canadians Who Were Fired for Social Media Posts," July 12, 2015, careers.workopolis.com/advice/14 -canadians-who-were-fired-for-social-media-posts.

30. Jacob Brogan, "What's the Deal with Algorithms?," *Slate*, February 2, 2016, slate.com/technology/2016/02/whats-the-deal-with -algorithms.html.

31. Tara Kimura, "How Games, Social Media Are Changing the Way People Get Hired," Canadian Broadcasting Corporation, September 14, 2015, cbc.ca/news/technology/how-games-social-media-are -changing-the-way-people-get-hired-1.3194664.

32. Michael Lewis, *Moneyball: The Art of Winning an Unfair Game* (New York: W.W. Norton, 2003).

33. Shoshana Zuboff, *The Age of Surveillance Capitalism: The Fight for a Human Future at the New Frontier of Power* (New York: Public Affairs, 2019).

34. Margot Shields, "Shift Work and Health," Statistics Canada, July 2002, www150.statcan.gc.ca/n1/en/pub/82-003-x/2001004 /article/6315-eng.pdf?st=OcTXrPwL.

35. David Weil, *The Fissured Workplace: Why Work Became So Bad for So Many and What Can Be Done to Improve It* (Cambridge, MA: Harvard University Press, 2014).

36. Guy Standing, *The Precariat: The New Dangerous Class* (London: Bloomsbury, 2011).

37. Samantha Edwards, "Airbnb Is Exacerbating Toronto's Low Vacancy Rate: Report," *Now*, February 21, 2020, nowtoronto.com/news /airbnb-exacerbates-toronto-vacancy-rate.

38. Amazon Mechanical Turk, "Pricing," mturk.com/pricing.

39. Richard Susskind and Daniel Susskind, *The Future of Professions: How Technology Will Transform the Work of Humans* (Oxford: Oxford University Press, 2015).

40. David Graeber, *Bullshit Jobs: A Theory* (New York: Simon & Schuster, 2018).

41. Darrell Bricker and John Ibbitson, *Empty Planet: The Shock of Global Population Decline* (Toronto: Signal, 2019).

42. Statistics Canada, "Section 2: Population by Age and Sex," www150 .statcan.gc.ca/n1/pub/91-215-x/2015000/part-partie2-eng.htm.

43. Citizens for Public Justice, "Poverty Trends 2017," cpj.ca/poverty -trends-2017.

44. Emily Hotton, "Eating Local: Why You Should Bother!," University of Toronto Food Services, ueat.utoronto.ca/eating-local-bother.

45. David Doorey, *The Law of Work: Industrial Relations and Collective Bargaining* (Toronto: Emond, 2017), 18–21.

46. Canadian Union of Postal Workers, Applicant v. Foodora Inc., Ontario Labour Relations Board, OLRB Case No: 1346-19-R, olrb .gov.on.ca/Decision/1346-19-R_Foodora-Inc-Feb-25-2020.pdf.

47. Larry Savage, "Building Union Muscle: The GoodLife Fitness Organizing and First-Contract Campaign," *Labour/LeTravail* 84 (Fall 2019): 167–97.

48. Heather Loney, "Who Is Terri-Jean Bedford, the Dominatrix Fighting Canada's Prostitution Laws?," *Global News*, December 20, 2013, globalnews.ca/news/1043102/who-is-terri-jean-bedford-the -dominatrix-fighting-canadas-prostitution-laws.

49. Justin Zadorsky, "Judge Rules Sections of Canada's Prostitution Laws Are Unconstitutional in Landmark Case," *CTV News*, February 21, 2020, london.ctvnews.ca/judge-rules-sections-of -canada-s-prostitution-laws-are-unconstitutional-in-landmark -case-1.4821544.

50. Mounted Police Association of Ontario v. Canada, 2015 SCC 1, scc-csc.lexum.com/scc-csc/scc-csc/en/item/14577/index.do.

51. Statistics Canada, "Union Status by Industry," www150.statcan .gc.ca/t1/tbl1/en/tv.action?pid=1410013201.

52. Retail Council of Canada, "Minimum Wage by Province," retailcouncil.org/resources/quick-facts/minimum-wage-by -province.

53. M. King Hubbert, "Nuclear Energy and the Fossil Fuels," March 1–9, 1956, web.archive.org/web/20080527233843/http://www.hubbertpeak.com/hubbert/1956/1956.pdf.

54. Government of Ontario, "Ontario Basic Income Pilot," ontario.ca/page/ontario-basic-income-pilot.

55. Lahouaria Yssaad and Vincent Ferrao, "Self-Employed Canadians: Who and Why?," Statistics Canada, May 28, 2019, www150.statcan.gc.ca/n1/pub/71-222-x/71-222-x2019002-eng.htm.

56. Employment and Social Development Canada, *Report of the Expert Panel on Modern Federal Labour Standards*, Ottawa, 2019.

57. Leah Vosko and the Closing the Enforcement Gap Research Group, *Closing the Enforcement Gap: Improving Employment Standards for People in Precarious Jobs* (Toronto: University of Toronto Press, 2020), 11.

LOOKING BACK, LOOKING FORWARD

1. *Little Caughnawaga: To Brooklyn and Back*, directed by Reaghan Tarbell (2008; Ottawa: National Film Board of Canada), nfb.ca/film/little_caughnawaga_to_brooklyn_and_back. For more on Kanien'keha:ka ironworkers in New York City, see a collection of images taken in 1970 and 1971 by David Grant Noble, which can be found online at the Smithsonian Institution site: sova.si.edu/details/NMAI.AC.113?s=0&n=10&t=C&q=#ref505.

INDEX

Page numbers in italics refer to tables.

ABOUT THE AUTHOR

Jason Russell received a Ph.D. in history from York University and is an associate professor at SUNY Empire State College in Buffalo, New York. Russell is the author of *Our Union: UAW/ CAW Local 27 from 1950 to 1990*; *Making Managers in Canada, 1945–1995: Companies, Community Colleges, and Universities*; and *Leading Progress: The Professional Institute of the Public Service of Canada, 1920–2020*. He lives in London, Ontario.